THE
FIXER

THE
FIXER

MOGULS, MOBSTERS, MOVIE STARS, *and* MARILYN

JOSH YOUNG *and* MANFRED WESTPHAL

GRAND
CENTRAL

NEW YORK   BOSTON

Grand Central Publishing
Hachette Book Group
1290 Avenue of the Americas, New York, NY 10104
grandcentralpublishing.com
@grandcentralpub

First Edition: April 2024

Grand Central Publishing is a division of Hachette Book Group, Inc.
The Grand Central Publishing name and logo is a registered trademark
of Hachette Book Group, Inc.

The publisher is not responsible for websites (or their content)
that are not owned by the publisher.

The Hachette Speakers Bureau provides a wide range of authors for
speaking events. To find out more, go to hachettespeakersbureau.com or
email HachetteSpeakers@hbgusa.com.

Grand Central Publishing books may be purchased in bulk for business,
educational, or promotional use. For information, please contact your local
bookseller or the Hachette Book Group Special Markets Department at
special.markets@hbgusa.com.

Interior book design by Timothy Shaner, NightandDayDesign.biz

Library of Congress Control Number 2023950737

ISBN: 9781538751428 (hardcover), 9781538751411 (ebook)

Printed in the United States of America

LSC

Printing 1, 2024

To Freddie O, Doris, Colleen, Orietta . . .

and the Truth

CONTENTS

THE
FIXER

FREDDIE O

The Hollywood dream machine is powered by stories.

On an early October day in 1990, I was an ambitious twenty-five-year-old development coordinator in Building One, the Spanish Revival home of Warner Bros. Television, my morning spent reading through all manner of scripts and books and unpublished galleys, magazine and newspaper articles, searching for something, *anything*, that might propel my nascent career to new heights, when my mother called to confirm I was coming for lunch. She wanted me there as soon as possible so we had time to talk about an extraordinary man who lived in her building.

"His name is Fred Otash," she eagerly noted. "We've known each other for a while and you need to hear his stories."

I didn't give it much thought as I braved my geriatric Jetta up and over the Hollywood Hills to the Park Wellington, a palm-festooned, resort-style condominium nestled on a cascading hillside just off Sunset Boulevard in an affluent enclave where most Angelenos only dream to live and die in LA. The

1

building was chock-full of colorful characters: Sharon Osbourne lived next door; my adopted grandfather and mentor Max Youngstein, who launched United Artists with Charlie Chaplin, owned one of the elite garden townhouses; a litany of nomadic actors, supermodels, and above-the-line talent that would come and go on a regular basis; a widowed "iron jaw" trapeze artist who once told my mother she used to swing from her teeth with Barnum & Bailey before marrying into money, and apparently a person of interest to my mother named Fred Otash, whom I had never heard of.

That changed the minute I walked in the door and was handed the just-released October issue of *GQ* magazine, turned to a provocative five-page spread titled "The Man Who Bugged Marilyn Monroe."

"You need to read this *now*," my mom instructed.

And so began my journey into the incredible life of the legendary private detective who lorded over LA's scandalous underbelly in the conservative, hush-hush, highly moral climate of the 1950s and '60s. From Hollywood's crème da la crème to the highest echelons of political power, the icons of an era, most of them dead, leapt to life across the magazine's pages telling the tale of an intrepid dark knight who would do "anything short of murder" for his A-list clients.

"Yep. I was number one in my profession. I don't care who it was about—a movie actress, a mobster, a studio head or a whore—if you wanted to get the lowdown on Hollywood, you came to see Fred Otash," declared an opening salvo depicting his Eisenhower-era "erstwhile career" as "a keyhole peeper, wire tapper, morals enforcer, dirt collector and all-purpose scandalmonger to the stars."

"This is the Holy Grail!" I declared as my mother set lunch on the table.

"He lives upstairs in Unit 302," she exclaimed. "Now come and get it."

Indeed, upstairs lived the real-life Zelig, the forerunner of modern-day private eyes who rose from the ashes of a postwar Los Angeles Police Department (LAPD) riddled with corruption to open the Fred Otash Detective Bureau, where he soon became known as the man who knew Hollywood's secrets, using then state-of-the-art high-tech surveillance techniques to listen in on the who's who of Tinseltown while its greatest movie stars, studio heads, and business leaders clamored for his favor, influence, and power to expose (or extinguish) the frailties and infidelities of their friends, foes, or cheating spouses. Mom was right. This was a *story* . . . and I wanted in.

Returning two days later for a highly anticipated introductory dinner, I found Otash in the kitchen playing sous chef to my mother, draining the pasta for her famous linguine and clams while she elucidated on the true meaning of *al dente*. He seemed nothing like the notorious sleuth depicted in *GQ*—my only point of reference, as there was no Google to troll in 1990, not even a photo in the magazine, just an artist's black-and-white rendering of the back of his head as he affixed a wiretap microphone to an alluringly inquisitive Marilyn Monroe. Notwithstanding the colander of steaming pasta in his grip, he exuded the polished, well-mannered presence of an old movie star, as if groomed and refined by the same

studio system that had manufactured the majority of his former clients and targets.

My fascination would dominate the lion's share of our
dinner conversation, and when he grew weary of slaying us
with salacious snippets from his private eye past, my mother
chimed in with her tales of Rome's Cinecittà Studios in the
early 1950s, singing "Volare" with Domenico Modugno and
working up close and personal with Italian cinema legends
Michelangelo Antonioni, Gabriele Ferzetti, and Valentina
Cortese, "back when Sophia Loren was still an extra." They
had that in common, a nostalgic personal connection to an
all-but-oxidized Hollywood era so far and foreign from my
own. Otash also enjoyed a healthy dose of political discourse,
a passion he shared, along with his first name, with my civi-
cally minded, armchair-historian father.

When my work at Warners was broached in more detail,
Otash disclosed a recent meeting with Joel Silver, the prolific
uber-producer behind *Lethal Weapon* and *Die Hard* whose
rich overall deal at the studio was legend. He said Silver's *people* were interested, in what exactly neither he nor they seemed
to know for certain.

"Not the first time Hollywood kicked my tires," he
quipped, before riffing on an industry that had purloined his
persona for decades, from the dashing investigator played by
Efrem Zimbalist Jr. in the classic TV series *77 Sunset Strip*, to
Jack Nicholson's star turn as the ex–police officer turned private eye protagonist in director Roman Polanski's neo-noir
masterpiece, *Chinatown*. Even his best friend Mickey Spillane
gleaned portions of his character for the best-selling author's
Mike Hammer detective novels adapted for TV first in 1958,
then again in 1984.

And while he wore these variations on a Hollywood theme like bittersweet badges of honor, it was clear the sixty-seven-year-old Otash felt his own stranger-than-fiction story blew them all out of the water. He was making notes for his second book, which, unlike the more sanitized *Investigation Hollywood* he had penned and published in 1976, would tell "the whole truth and nothing but" regarding his relationship with Marilyn Monroe, his surveillance of her love affairs with President John F. Kennedy and his brother Robert F. Kennedy, and his knowledge of events leading to her tragic death in 1962, revelations he broadly described as being "way too hot to handle" in bicentennial America.

The more I heard, the more I was captivated by his controversial and commercial nature. Obviously I couldn't compete with the likes of Joel Silver, but my work at the studio had afforded me firsthand knowledge of how biopic formats of this nature were nurtured from concept to creation by the best in the business—or in less fortunate scenarios, picked to death by "creative" executives who wouldn't know a good story if it bit them in the ass. I offered to be his wingman on the inside to help navigate the minefield of magic and make-believe that was the modern-day Hollywood ecosystem. Otash appreciated my passion, and I was further encouraged when he invited me to his condo that weekend to check out his "scrapbooks."

When I arrived for our meeting at his contemporary, Kreiss-filled one-bedroom condo, he laid two king-size folios bound in black silk, the likes of which I had never seen, across a table in his kitchen, their pages stuffed with newspaper and magazine clippings chronicling his illustrious life from the late 1940s to present day. It was a writer's dream, a Hollywood private eye's Library of Alexandria just waiting to be mined. Adjacent to this jaw-dropping display, I made note of a vintage steel filing cabinet painted fire engine red that could be locked by inserting a key into a cylinder on the top drawer and pushing it inward.

"Those are my hot files," he said in his deep-resonating voice. "Nobody goes in there but me."

"So that's everything?" I timidly inquired.

He laughed. "Are you kidding? That's the tip of the iceberg, man. I have boxes and boxes, all locked away in a vault in Bank of America."

———————

Time passed, and "Freddie" became a valued member of our extended family and a frequent guest at my mother's many dinner parties and informal gatherings. He even gave my parents a set of keys to his unit, to use should one or both of my out-of-town older brothers need a place to sleep if he was traveling when they happened to visit. He and I would continue our conversation over lunches at his favorite haunts, Nate 'n' Al's on Beverly Drive; his best friend Nicky Blair's eponymous hotspot on Sunset Boulevard; and the Cock 'n' Bull tavern at the end of the Strip, where he recalled classic movie stars like John Barrymore, Bette Davis, and Richard Burton holding court "when Hollywood was still Hollywood." Our excursions invariably began with a featured guided tour of his fabled city from the front seat of his classic Cadillac Eldorado Biarritz with its personalized OTASH license plate and "Freddie O" etched into its polished brass frame, reminiscent of his glory days when, as one *Los Angeles Times* story wrote, he "prowled Hollywood by night in a chauffeured Cadillac full of women he called 'little sweeties,' and much like a fictional private eye conjured up by Raymond Chandler, drank a quart of Scotch and smoked four packs of cigarettes a day."

We soon started working on a multimedia pitch that could shapeshift as needed since the content was adaptable for any format available at the time: a network or cable series, movie for television, miniseries, or feature film. I wrote treatments for everything, and a friend at one of the edit bays in town helped me produce a VHS sizzle reel utilizing his recent appearances on *Hard Copy*, *A Current Affair*, two BBC documentaries, and a stand-alone segment on *Yesterday, Today and Tomorrow*, a short-lived docuseries hosted by a then thirty-four-year-old news media darling named Maria Shriver, the niece of John and Robert Kennedy. I simply followed the same recipe we used at the studio, crafting a concise and immersive presentation that properly articulated the content and its potential. Only then would I finally muster the courage to propose that Freddie and I sign a formal agreement to make our partnership legal.

"A contract?" he gently scoffed. "Listen, kid. You don't need a contract with me. My word is worth more than any bullshit piece of paper."

This, I had by now learned, was classic Otash, but I believed him. And even if I didn't, I had little to no leverage to negotiate. But after all the time we had spent together, I knew in my heart I could trust him.

———————

I t was spring 1991, one of those gorgeous late afternoons in Beverly Hills when the air is infused with the signature scent of night-blooming jasmine. Freddie and I were having an early farewell dinner on the empty street-side patio at Tse Yang, a small upscale Chinese restaurant on Doheny Drive next to the Writers Guild Theater. He would depart the following night for seasonal sojourns at his pieds-à-terre in Miami Beach and the South of France, and I wouldn't see him again for months. But despite his imminent journey, he seemed oddly preoccupied with the past.

"Something about this stretch of Doheny . . . how many times . . ." he said pensively without finishing his sentence before pointing out our proximity to Marilyn Monroe's last apartment, about a mile north at 882 North Doheny Drive. He told me she had twice leased the same small one-bedroom above the garage, first in 1953 before her marriage to Joe DiMaggio, then again in 1961 when she was dating Frank Sinatra and "entertaining" the Kennedys before she purchased her final home in Brentwood.

"It was their love nest," he disclosed.

"What really happened to her?" I asked for the umpteenth time.

Freddie smiled back, a hint of resignation in his eyes. Then he took a deep, labored breath and exhaled slowly as if his emphysema was flaring up again, but it wasn't. He had always evaded giving me a straight answer before, conjuring the accidental-overdose scenario without committing to it or providing any clarity. But now, perhaps because we had established a certain level of trust, he brought up an incident in 1985 when he was interviewed by ABC's *20/20*. The popular prime-time newsmagazine had produced a special two-part episode on Monroe's life that sought to shed light on her

alleged affairs with the Kennedy brothers and the events leading up to her untimely death.

"They killed it," he said. "Ripped from the schedule by
ABC brass just hours before it was supposed to air."

As he began sharing some of what he told the ABC producers during his two on-camera interviews, Freddie became
restless, apprehensive, rubbing the palm of his right hand
back and forth across his jawline, as if what he said or was
about to say made him increasingly anxious. Then he caught
himself and shut it down.

"Aw, fuck it," he said, exasperated. "That's all I can tell
you, kid. I don't want to . . . I don't want to get into it . . . not
right now. Let's just leave it at that, okay?"

I had never seen him so unnerved and melancholic. It
confirmed my suspicion there was likely much more to the
story than the official, whitewashed talking points that had
kept the world guessing for the past twenty-eight years. Something perhaps rooted in all the conspiracy theories bandied
about since her death. Something buried deep in his psyche
that still shook him to the core whenever it happened to rear
its ugly head. My question clearly put him off this time, so I
pivoted to what I thought might elevate his mood: his upcoming book and possible collaboration with James Ellroy.

I knew from day one he had befriended Ellroy. The celebrated author had published *L.A. Confidential* three months
before sitting in on Freddie's interview with *GQ* magazine.
Freddie often mentioned their frequent phone conversations
or occasional get-togethers when Ellroy was in town, always
hinting they might work together since their discussions
invariably centered on the taste and texture of Freddie's

real-life exploits. It gave him such pride that Ellroy had what
he described as an almost sycophantic obsession with his
story, sending him handwritten notes of praise and apprecia-
tion following their encounters and claiming he was going to
"take my brain out of retirement."

It wasn't until after Freddie's death that I became privy to
their origin story, when I came into possession of his archives
and found four handwritten notes from 1989 to 1990 in a
manila folder simply marked "Ellroy." In the first, dated January 1, 1989, a young James Ellroy, just shy of his forty-first
birthday, thanks Freddie for the previous weekend, writing
that his revelations were brilliant, that he was certain they
would infuse *White Jazz* with a color and authenticity it
wouldn't have had otherwise, that meeting him was a pleasure
and an honor, and that he looked forward to developing a
long and profitable relationship with him.

That afternoon, however, mentioning Ellroy's name triggered Freddie for the worst.

"That cocksucker can kiss my ass!" he exclaimed in a sudden burst of anger. "He sent me a check for twenty-five hundred dollars! Can you believe that?! What the fuck do I need
his money for?!"

When I asked him what had happened, he begrudgingly
revealed how wrong he'd been to trust Ellroy, that it was "all
just a shill" to feign friendship, to pump him for details and
plunder his life for Ellroy's personal agenda. When Freddie
finally caught on to the grift, he cut Ellroy out cold from all
communication.

"I'll write my own goddamn book," he snorted.

We never spoke of Ellroy again.

A few days later, after Freddie had repaired to his seaside residence in the Grand Hotel on the Boulevard de la Croissette in Cannes, I arrived at work to find the May issue of *Vanity Fair* sitting in my inbox. A resplendent photo of Audrey Hepburn graced the cover with a banner draped across her forehead teasing "The Man Who Kept Marilyn's Secrets," exclusive excerpts from James Spada's upcoming biography on Peter Lawford. I sat there dumbfounded as I read the opening paragraphs that echoed some of what Freddie had disclosed during our dinner, how Lawford begged him to help clean Marilyn's Brentwood home of any evidence of the Kennedys the night she died. I rifled through my Filofax, found Freddie's number in Cannes, and dialed it from my studio private line, reaching him nine hours ahead just as he was sitting down for dinner with friends.

"Freddie, can you hear me?" I asked, not waiting for an answer. "It's urgent. Can you talk?"

He put me on hold and took the call in his bedroom, where I proceeded to spend the next thirty minutes reading him the entire article that focused on myriad claims, speculations, and theories from numerous sources that may or may not have taken place the night Marilyn Monroe died—with Freddie sprinkled throughout like a ground zero star witness.

I was incredulous. "Can you believe this? What's going on? How did this happen?"

Freddie started laughing.

"Great story!" he chortled. "Glad I'm out of the country!"

He said he had granted Spada the interview but only shared enough to build buzz for his own upcoming book. Then he asked me to keep an eye out for another imminent

salvo, the May issue of *Los Angeles* magazine, which arrived
on my desk two days later with a stellar six-page feature story
on Freddie, comically titled "The Dick." Our project was getting hotter by the day, and with all this renewed ink, his place
in the cultural zeitgeist was rising like the summer sun.

Freddie had been a card-carrying member of the Friars Club
of Beverly Hills for decades. Housed in a windowless building at 9900 Santa Monica Boulevard designed by Sidney Eisen-
shtat (the celebrated Jewish architect of Temple Emanuel of
Beverly Hills and the landmark Temple Sinai on Wilshire Boulevard), the renowned private showbiz club founded by Milton
Berle in 1947 touted a star-studded membership that in its heyday included Hollywood's finest: Bing Crosby, Lucille Ball,
Sammy Davis Jr., Judy Garland, Bob Hope, Jerry Lewis, Dean
Martin, and Frank Sinatra, to name a few.

At around 9 p.m. on Sunday, October 4, 1992, Freddie
stopped by my parents' condo unannounced. He was all giddy
and dapper. His frame, thirty pounds leaner courtesy of
recent hip surgery, looked like a million bucks in a dark blue
suit over a crisp white shirt, accented by a red silk pocket
square. We marveled at his appearance as he proudly proclaimed he was feeling and looking better than he had in
years. In fact, he had just been given a clean bill of health
from his longtime physician, Dr. Frank Mancini, one of his
closest and dearest friends, whom he trusted with his life,
both literally and literarily.

After forging a close bond as Boy Scouts, the two young
men lost track of each other in the chaos of World War II, but

reunited once more when the rookie LAPD cop and young medical student ran into each other on Hollywood Boulevard. Freddie had recently asked Frank's wife to type the latest draft of his manuscript, to ensure no one knew what he was writing. Hence the reason for his impromptu visit that night, to share in the afterglow of a dinner held in his honor at the Friars Club to celebrate the completion of his soon-to-be-published memoir. After a half hour of casual banter, Freddie retired to his condo, and I to my humble studio apartment near the La Brea Tar Pits. It had been almost two years to the day since we first met.

The next morning, I was jolted awake at 7:30 a.m. when both my phone and alarm clock went off simultaneously. My mother was on the line, anxious and distraught, weeping between her jumbled words as I heard her say, "Freddie died," then, "I found his body."

I thought she was referring to my father.

"No . . . Freddie," she corrected through tears. "Freddie Otash."

The Old North Church at Forest Lawn Memorial Park in the Hollywood Hills is an exact replica of its historical counterpart in Boston that ignited the Revolutionary War in 1755 when Paul Revere spotted two lanterns hanging from its steeple, signaling the British were coming by sea across the Charles River. It was there on Friday, October 9, 1992, that we would attend Freddie's funeral, a symbolic location to say farewell to a son of Massachusetts.

My parents and I sat in the rear pews and solemnly watched as Freddie's family and friends took their seats in

front of us, including his daughter, Colleen; his longtime lawyer and executor, Arthur Crowley; Dr. Frank Mancini and his
wife; as well as numerous business leaders and celebrities
including actor Robert Forster, who served as a pallbearer.
But of all the mourners, one stood out and apart from the
rest. She was a beautiful and elegant, mysterious woman with
platinum blonde hair styled in a dramatic cascading swoop
just as Marilyn Monroe had the night she sang "Happy Birthday" to President John F. Kennedy during his forty-fifth
birthday celebration at Madison Square Garden. Surreal
given Freddie's close ties to Marilyn, I thought.

I would not discover her identity until over a decade later,
on August 5, 2003, when I tuned in to a special episode of
Larry King Live devoted to the forty-first anniversary of
Marilyn Monroe's death. Larry introduced her as "Jeanne
Carmen, Marilyn's closest friend in Hollywood." During the
interview, which dealt primarily with the mysterious
circumstances of Monroe's death, Carmen told King in no
uncertain terms that Marilyn had affairs with both Kennedy
brothers; that she lived in the apartment next door to Marilyn
on Doheny Drive; and that their apartments were "attached,"
so she was always over there and had often seen Bobby
Kennedy—whom she insisted Marilyn loved. She then told
King that she believed the rumors that the Kennedy brothers
were somehow associated with her passing, at which point he
asked her to elaborate.

"Well, I really can't say what I think," Carmen replied,
"because Peter Lawford told me the story, and I believed him,
even though he was drunk as a skunk. Johnny Roselli told me
the same story. I had to leave town for eighteen years, you
know."

After the service, Freddie was laid to rest at Forest Lawn Memorial Park Cemetery among such Hollywood luminaries as Lucille Ball and Bette Davis (both of whom had hired him back in the day to spy on their estranged husbands), Buster Keaton, Andy Gibb, and Liberace. The wake was held at Nicky Blair's, his best friend's noisy and equally glitzy, high-end Italian and continental restaurant on the Sunset Strip, a place to see and be seen at a time when many legends of Hollywood's Golden Age were still alive and well and regarded as American royalty. The restaurant was located just a short walk from the Park Wellington next door to the Playboy building near Sunset Plaza, arguably the most beautiful and pristine quarter mile of real estate the Strip has to offer.

My parents decided not to attend so I went solo with the main intention of introducing myself and offering my condolences to Freddie's daughter, Colleen. Freddie had shown me pictures of her in the past. Much like her mother, the former Columbia Pictures starlet Doris Houck, Colleen was a beautiful and statuesque young woman, easy to spot among the crowd of Hollywood Alter Cockers. I didn't take too much of her time for obvious reasons, but we exchanged numbers and I promised to call her soon.

I was about to leave when I noticed Freddie's lawyer, the infamous Arthur Crowley, standing alone in front of a stone column that gave him a broad view of the restaurant and all who entered. He was an odd-looking older man, primarily due to an oversize toupee precariously perched atop his head. Regardless, I kindly approached and introduced myself, offering my condolences before highlighting my connection to Freddie and how we'd been working together for the past two years.

"I'm sure Freddie must have told you about me," I affirmed. "He certainly told me a lot about you."

Crowley didn't acknowledge what I had said. He just stood there steely-eyed, cold and expressionless. His only response was to slowly square me up and down with a disarming and dismissive gaze I could feel in my bones. And then he spoke.

"Will you excuse me for a moment?" he said, not waiting for an answer as he walked past me toward a group of guests a few yards away.

I stood there for what seemed like a long time, watching him speak to other guests, thinking he would return, until he finally looked back and shot me a maleficent glare before turning away again. It was a brutal cold shoulder. I left a moment later, uncertain of how exactly to process what had just happened.

———————————

A few weeks later, I was sitting at my desk at Warner Bros. when the studio's mailroom called to see if I was there. Why? Because they had a "ton of boxes" all marked "Bank of America" addressed to me in Building One. I told the caller to bring them right away.

A mailroom intern arrived with eleven taped and sealed boxes, Freddie's vaulted files, the same ones he had referred to the first time we visited in his condo two years earlier. As he began stacking them wherever possible in my small vestibule, I immediately became anxious. There was no way I could keep them in my office, so I helped him reload everything back onto his long flatbed golf cart, and we drove them to my car.

We were barely able to stuff them inside—four in the trunk, six stacked in the back seat, and one in the front passenger area. I left the studio immediately. It took me an hour and a half, three times my normal drive time, to reach my apartment due to limited visibility. I was exhausted by the time I carted them all up and into my apartment—but not enough to wait on exploring Freddie's glorious remains of the day.

Fred Otash kept meticulous files on everyone and everything he encountered throughout the course of his personal and professional life—a practice first implemented during his tenure on the LAPD that he no doubt refined as Hollywood's preeminent private detective. In his world, details were *every-thing*, and he surveilled his own life in much the same manner in which he scrutinized his famous clients and targets. While we will never know the contents of the "hot files" he kept inside the fire engine red filing cabinet at the Park Wellington disposed of by Arthur Crowley shortly after his death, his salvaged eleven boxes of investigative and personal files constitute the legacy of a remarkable and complicated man who kept Hollywood's secrets during one of the most iconic eras in entertainment history.

This vast archive of materials—a museum-worthy treasure trove of investigative case files, surveillance reports, published memoir and unpublished manuscript, personal correspondence, recordings, interview transcripts, photographs, taped television appearances, countless newspaper and magazine articles, calendars, daily diaries, historical ephemera, treatments and synopses we wrote together prior to his death, and numerous interviews with his daughter, Colleen, and the personal records she provided over the decades—constitute the primary source material of intellectual property utilized during the writing of this book.

Throughout this journey, our objective has been to present Otash's first-person perspective, his truth that has often been lost in the retelling of the events by others, particularly those mythmakers who were neither witnesses nor participants. To that end, we have taken great care to present the events, conversations, perceptions, and direct quotes herein as he said they happened, all of which are sourced from his aforementioned archives and related materials.

And yet, despite everything you are about to read, these stories represent just a fraction of what is contained in the files, for there are many more tales to be told when it comes to the private eye who never blinked, Freddie Otash.

—MANFRED WESTPHAL

ONE

THE CITY OF ANGELS

When Fred Otash arrived in Los Angeles in September 1945, he almost couldn't believe that what he had seen in magazines and on black-and-white newsreel footage was real. On his first walk down Hollywood Boulevard, the twenty-three-year-old was mesmerized by the green hills that sprung up in the distance and the grand sign etched across the landscape that read HOLLYWOODLAND. The famous locales on Hollywood Boulevard were even bigger and brighter than he imagined.

There was the Mocambo, with its signature marquee traced in neon green. Five doors down was Ciro's, with its luxe baroque interior cloaked behind an elegant yet unadorned façade. He knew from the magazines that they were both samples of a handful of hangouts, hotspots, and nightclubs reserved for the Hollywood royalty who dined and sipped martinis and Manhattans while talking shop and shit with their kindred power brokers *in the purple*. And, of course,

there was Schwab's Pharmacy, the legendary drugstore acces-
sible to anyone hoping to be discovered and launched into
stardom, like Lana Turner had been when spotted at the ice
cream counter at age fifteen—or so legend had it.

Towering above it all were giant billboards advertising
current and upcoming movies like Hitchcock's *Spellbound*,
starring Ingrid Bergman and Gregory Peck; Billy Wilder's
The Lost Weekend, with Ray Milland and Jane Wyman; and
the patriotic musical comedy *Anchors Aweigh*, starring Frank
Sinatra and Gene Kelly. Looking up at the boldface names
with gimlet eyes, he thought, *They all live here.* And now he
did as well, having rented a one-room apartment in the Selma
Hotel a block below Hollywood Boulevard.

But unlike the army of young, aspiring wannabes who
arrived daily in Hollywood from the small towns and big cit-
ies across America to pursue their dreams, Otash was a prag-
matist. He lived in the real world. Good looks and charm
notwithstanding, the street-smart son of poor Lebanese rug
merchants knew that without money and a job there was no
way he could afford to keep courting the former "Miss Tar-
zana," whom he had just started dating.

One afternoon in his first few weeks in town, Otash spotted a small billboard above a low-slung cement building that
read: THE LAPD NEEDS YOU! As enchanting as the movie billboards were, this one felt like a personal invitation, something he could do and be good at.

———————

Otash brought to Los Angeles a built-in survival instinct
that was embedded in his DNA before he was born. His

parents, Marion and Habib Otash, emigrated to the U.S. in 1895 after fleeing Beirut, Lebanon, to escape tyranny and unrest in the wake of ongoing sectarian conflicts that had ravaged the region for decades. They eventually settled in Methuen, Massachusetts, a picturesque city and textile manufacturing hub that was thriving along the Spicket River in the early twentieth century, where Fred was born the last of six children, four girls and two boys, on January 6, 1922. His father would die young of a heart attack when little Freddie was only five years old. When the Great Depression hit two years later and continued to devastate the U.S. economy throughout the 1930s, Methuen would become so riddled with crime and poverty that it was commonly referred to as "the most godforsaken place in Massachusetts."

It was during this period of personal and economic adversity that Freddie's only brother ran away. Having lost his peer support system, he began to subconsciously act out in ways that masked his underlying fears and anxieties. Freddie was expelled from every public school in the city, and when he made a habit of sneaking out his second-story bedroom window to swipe the family car and go joyriding with his pals in the middle of the night, his mother had no alternative but to send him to Mount Saint Charles Academy in Woonsocket, Rhode Island, a private Catholic school where the Brothers of the Sacred Heart eventually managed to turn the troubled teen around for the better.

In 1938, as the American economy took a steep downturn for the worse and his family struggled to make ends meet, Fred left school in the middle of his tenth-grade year to help financially support his mother and four sisters. He joined the Civilian Conservation Corps, one of the earliest New Deal programs established by President Franklin D. Roosevelt to relieve unemployment by providing national conservation work, primarily for unmarried young men. They transferred him to Estes Park, Colorado, the base of Rocky Mountain National Park along the Big Thompson River, an incredible land of breathtaking wooded and mountainous vistas where he worked as a forest ranger at the age of sixteen. Two years later, he returned to his home state to work as a lifeguard in Salisbury Beach, a longtime summer playground for Massachusetts beachgoers, until the United States entered World War II in December 1941.

Despite the fervid objections of his mother and sisters since, in effect, he was the only man left in the family, Otash volunteered to join the U.S. Marine Corps. A natural athlete with a penchant for wrestling, boxing, and swimming, he excelled at the Marine Boot Camp in Parris Island, South Carolina, where he was eventually assigned as a physical education instructor to teach Marine recruits the art of self-defense, combat swimming, and jungle warfare. He was then transferred to the Marine Corps base in Quantico, Virginia, assigned as an instructor in the FBI Academy to train candidates in the art of self-defense before being deployed overseas as a staff sergeant in the Solomon Islands campaign until his discharge in 1945.

And so, the day after seeing the billboard, Otash visited LAPD headquarters at Los Angeles City Hall, approached the front desk inside the drab, windowless main office, and greeted the inexpressive civil service Bureaucrat sitting behind it.

The Bureaucrat's insipid disposition flickered to life as he eyed Otash in his Marine uniform with four stripes on the upper shirt sleeve indicating his rank as staff sergeant. His strapping six-foot-two frame, sturdy jawline, and upright posture projected the confidence and physicality of a man you didn't want to mess with, while his ruggedly handsome looks, with dark wavy hair and charcoal eyes framed by thick brows against his olive complexion, projected the self-assurance of a man who could do the job.

Men like Otash were exactly the prototype the department desired to fill their depleted ranks following a mass exodus of cops who had left to fight overseas before choosing different lines of work when and if they returned. Others were over-the-hill officers who needed to be pushed into retirement and replaced as soon as possible to handle a surge in population.

"Tell me, Sergeant Otash, where did you serve?" the Bureaucrat asked.

"I fought in the South Pacific," Otash answered with pride.

"Well then, I salute you," the Bureaucrat said, gesturing in kind. "Where exactly?"

"Treasure Island, Bismarck, the Northern Solomon Islands . . . I was part of a physical training unit, keeping soldiers fit and helping them in hand-to-hand combat," Otash explained. "I studied judo and close-combat techniques."

"Well, you sure look like someone who can hold his own in combat," the Bureaucrat observed with a smile.

Otash figured his hiring was in the bag, especially when the Bureaucrat began touting LA's moderate climate and the LAPD's career advancement opportunities as a final selling point. What he failed to disclose was the fact that postwar

Los Angeles was a crime-infested bubbling cauldron ready to explode, its police force steeped in corruption.

Just as he was about to hand Otash a pen to fill out his application, he touched upon one last formality. "Do you have a high school diploma?"

"No, sir, I don't," replied Otash, thinking nothing of it.

The Bureaucrat slightly withdrew his pen before probing further. "How far did you go in high school?"

"I left in the tenth grade . . . joined the Civilian Conservation Corps to help support my family. Is that a problem?"

The light left the Bureaucrat's face. Although he admired the young Marine's devotion to family, the regulations were clear. "A high school diploma is required before you can even apply to be an LAPD officer, much less be accepted," he said.

Otash countered that he got his education working as a forest ranger in the Civilian Conservation Corps, not to mention everything he learned serving his country during the war. "That should count for something," he argued.

"I didn't write the rules, Sergeant," the Bureaucrat stiffly replied. "I'm just following them."

This was going nowhere . . . a dead end, Otash thought. He was about to turn and leave when a middle-aged man who had been observing the entire exchange from his back-office desk intervened.

"Hey, Sergeant, come on back here. Let me talk to you," he said, motioning him over.

The man introduced himself as Mr. Hawthorne, head of the Civil Service Commission.

"When are you getting discharged?" he asked.

"Next thirty days," answered Otash.

"Why did you decide to apply, Sergeant?"

Trying to sound like he would be devoted to the cause, Otash explained. "It feels like the right thing to do," he said. "To serve my new city."

Hawthorne sized him up like a proud general about to send a fine soldier to the front lines. The staff sergeant stripes and campaign bars on Otash's uniform indicated leadership ability and performance under pressure in combat—an ideal police recruit if there ever was one. In showbiz terms, he was right out of Central Casting.

"How long were you in the service?"

"Almost four years."

Hawthorne lowered his voice and his eyes quickly scanned the room to ensure their discretion. "All right then, Sergeant, here's the deal," he began. "I'm going to make an exception in your case because I think you'd make one hell of a police officer. I'm going to let every year of service count as a year of high school. Now you have a high school diploma."

"You can do that?"

"I just did," he assured him. "But you must promise me that, under the GI Bill of Rights, you'll go to Judge Frickey's Police Course."

Otash hadn't a clue about Judge Frickey or his namesake police course but nodded without missing a beat.

"Welcome to the LAPD," Hawthorne said, offering his hand.

Otash's large, thick, combat-seasoned hand wrapped around Hawthorne's and shook it with a grip so firm that the supervisor could barely keep from wincing, a final affirmation he had made the right decision. A new police rookie was born. His pay: a very decent $67 a week (about $1,130 in today's dollars).

The next day, Otash began Judge Frickey's six-week training program. He was also obligated to attend a seven-month
night school course in police science before he'd officially be
certified as a cop, giving him a chance to bone up on his reading and writing skills. But his real education into the city he'd
be serving and the ways of Hollywood came just three weeks
into his LAPD training in October 1945 when a strike by two
major Hollywood labor unions escalated into all-out war.

––––––––––––––

The strike had started seven months earlier on March 12,
1945, after Columbia Pictures, RKO, Universal, 20th Century Fox, Warner Bros., MGM, and Paramount Pictures
refused to negotiate with the two mob-controlled unions, the
International Alliance of Theatrical Stage Employees
(IATSE) and the Conference of Studio Unions (CSU), over
wages, prompting set decorators, designers, and illustrators
to walk off the job and picket the studios. Members from a
dozen different industry guilds soon joined the crusade, and
suddenly the jobs of twelve thousand film workers ground to
a screeching halt.

On October 5, the frayed nerves of picketers across the
city came unraveled. At sunup IATSE and CSU members
turned out in huge numbers in front of Warner Bros. Studios.
Nonstriking IATSE members were hell-bent to go to work
and the CSU strikers were equally determined to stop them.
Something had to give. When IATSE members tried to break
through the picket line, the CSU mob charged them from
behind the barricades. Yelling and screaming swiftly escalated to pushing and shoving and a wild, out-of-control street

fight broke out with a flurry of swinging knives, chains, battery cables, baseball bats, flying beer bottles, smashed windshields, and overturned cars.

Three hundred cops stormed in wearing full riot gear, smacking people around with billy clubs. They ultimately turned two high-powered fire hoses on the strikers while Warner Bros. studio police tossed canisters of tear gas from the roofs of buildings near the Gate 3 entrance. Two hours later, it was all over. Everyone, banged up and bloodied, had either dispersed, were sent to the hospital, or been carted off to jail. Miraculously, no one was killed, and the day was burnished in Hollywood history as "Black Friday."

Five days later, on October 10, CSU and IATSE took their act on the road with brutal clashes in front of all the major studios. There weren't enough cops on the force to handle the massive uprising at so many different locations. They needed backup and reinforcements—and fast. Otash and his rookie class were yanked out of the training program, issued khaki fatigues, pistols, batons, and badges, and ordered to enter the fray across the city. After all, they *were* war combat veterans, supposedly able to handle out-of-control situations.

Otash found himself wading into a bloody melee at Columbia Pictures, where each side used an assortment of brass knuckles, swinging chains, hammers, battery cables, and assorted pipes to beat the shit out of the other side. His Marine instincts triggered, Otash and his fellow rookies finally beat back the mob and put an end to the violence. For his first day on duty as an LAPD cop, the event had proved to be a harsh initiation for Otash, who showed that he was up to the task.

That night, in his one-room apartment in the Selma Hotel, Otash unwound with a bottle of cheap scotch. He opened a fresh pack of smokes and turned on the radio. The hit song "I'm Beginning to See the Light" by Ella Fitzgerald and the Ink Spots was playing as images of post-traumatic stress danced in his head. What the hell had he gotten himself into? Nothing he couldn't handle, he reasoned, and it was easier than war.

As he pulled on the fifth of scotch, Otash couldn't help but wonder what was going on behind the scenes. He had stopped the workers from killing each other while the real forces behind the entire dispute—the mob bosses who ran the unions and the studio bosses who locked them out—watched from the sidelines as the workers were pitted against one another and left the police officers to stop the violence.

From this experience, Otash became fascinated with the Hollywood power structure and would soon learn that while movie stars were considered America's royalty, the place was run by the studio bosses who moved the stars around like pieces on a chessboard and the mob who controlled the labor that the studio chiefs relied on to make their movies.

The mob, he learned, had come to Hollywood for the same reasons that businessmen relocated there from the East Coast—the weather was good and there was a boatload of money to be made if you were smart, savvy, driven, and ruthless. Many of the movie moguls, like most gangsters, were European immigrants who had arrived penniless in the U.S. at the dawn of the twentieth century. As kids, they clawed and scraped inside their respective Irish-only, Italian-only, and Jewish-only neighborhoods to make a buck, determined to escape their respective ghettos and broaden their horizons. They figured out early on that to get ahead in America it was a good idea to change their ethnic names to ones sounding more American. Hence, Szmuel Gelbfisz and Lazar Meir, both Jews from Poland, became Samuel Goldwyn and Louis B. Mayer. In 1924, the two merged their respective production banners with Metro Productions to rebrand themselves as the iconic Metro-Goldwyn-Mayer Studios, known to the cinema-loving world as MGM with its roaring lion logo encircled by the Latin idiom *Ars Gratia Artis*, or "Art for Art's Sake."

Otash concluded that what he didn't know about the relationship between the Hollywood moguls, organized crime, and his brothers in blue might hurt him. For the sake of both self-preservation and career advancement, he knew that he would have to figure out how this town *really* worked.

TWO

THE OTASH TOUCH

Main Street, the once bustling and beautiful heart of downtown Los Angeles, had been in decline for quite some time. The twenty-one-mile main artery stretching north to Lincoln Heights had seen better days since its heyday in the early 1900s, when luxe hotels, grand banks, the finest department stores, and over twenty-five theaters and cinemas like the Bijou, Hippodrome, and the Grand Opera House graced its hallowed ground. By the time rookie Otash completed his training and was assigned the beat in March 1947, his first after graduating from the police academy, it was a virtually unrecognizable, odorous cesspool reeking with vice. His job was to clean up Main Street, and damned if he wasn't going to deliver.

Otash quickly learned that the city had a dark underbelly that didn't square with the golden, sunshiny façade most Americans bought into. Behind the storefronts and in the alleyways there were petty thieves, bookies, pimps, con men, and other lowlife hustlers. Otash saw it as his duty to help clean the place up, to give the city its money's worth. He didn't care if a whorehouse was paying one of his superiors for protection, he'd bust it all the same, because that was his job. Bookies who were doling out bags of cash to corrupt officers to stay in business were a favorite target, and he went out of his way to target businesses that were making payoffs to police and politicians.

Otash liked patrolling, walking the beat, talking to merchants and shoppers to ascertain a general sense of the problems they were facing. Justice was simple. Catch someone breaking the law, arrest them, and book 'em. But if he knew one thing from the bootstrapped years of his youth, the devil was in the details. There would be times when going easy on some two-bit criminal could provide useful information down the line, like that pimp he nailed two times over for hustling a potential john. In the Otash patrol handbook, this strategy was called "trading a hamburger for a steak sandwich."

"I thought I already took out the trash," Otash told the pimp on the second bust as the man begged for leniency.

"Give me something I can use and I'll consider it," Otash bargained.

The pimp eagerly obliged, giving him what sounded like a hot tip on a local drug ring.

"You're not shittin' me, are you?" Otash demanded.

The pimp swore on his mother's grave that it was for real.

"Really? If not, I'm going to bury you alive right next to her. You got me?"

He got it all right, and a satisfied Otash let him go and sprang into action.

The sun was just about to set on that late Tuesday afternoon when Otash rushed through the front door of a liquor store and out the back into the alley where he spotted the go-to dope pusher selling heroin to some schmuck sitting behind the wheel of a ragtag Chevrolet sedan.

"Hey . . . !" Otash called out as he moved in on them, his deep staccato voice cutting the air like a bullet.

The guy saw him coming in his side-view mirror, floored it, and sped away as the pusher dropped his product and bolted. Otash was on his tail now, gaining ground, arms pumping, healthy as a Pamplona bull but breathing hard from all the cigarettes he smoked. The pusher hit a chain-link fence and was hopelessly trying to climb it when Otash grabbed him by the ankles and yanked him to the ground, cuffing him on the spot as he tried to wriggle away.

"He was trying to sell *me* that shit . . . I wasn't gonna buy it . . . I'm just out taking a walk," the pusher said, trying to weasel his way out of being arrested.

"Tell it to the judge, asshole," Otash said. "I'm sure he'll believe you."

Otash picked up the smack for evidence and marched the perp back through the liquor store to make an example of him in front of startled patrons who then gathered at the window to watch the police officer drag his suspect toward his parked squad car. When Otash tried to maneuver him into the back seat, the pusher put up a struggle.

Bad idea. In no mood to dick around, Otash jammed two fingers up the pusher's nostrils and tossed him nose first into the squad car declaring, "You . . . are . . . under . . . arrest."

His buddies from his police academy class laughed their asses off when they heard him recount the story. As time went on, tales of his signature tactics became known throughout the department as "The Otash Touch."

n those days the police system boiled down to graft—good and bad. Bad graft was when a cop was on the take. Good graft was when cops like Otash accepted perks in exchange for better protection, like showing their badges to get free rides on streetcars, free admission to the movies, and comped or half-priced meals in restaurants. For their part, the restaurateurs appreciated having a police officer in their midst; it made them feel protected, a salubrious form of quid pro quo in-house security. The restaurants were also a great place for Otash to meet women who worked or dined there.

He also picked up some extra cash working off duty in uniform at big Hollywood premieres where he got to see all the glamorous leading ladies dressed in their finery, like Joan Crawford in *Possessed*, or Lauren Bacall starring opposite Humphrey Bogart in *The Big Sleep*. They posed for the throng of photographers and newsreel cameras, waving at their legions of fans whom Otash kept at bay. Once the crowd dispersed, Otash would go inside, grab a seat, and watch the picture for free.

But beyond the klieg lights, Otash began to see another side of the rolling hills the stars climbed to get there as he walked his Hollywood beat, a boulevard of broken dreams for most young ingenues who came to town with high hopes of fame and fortune. The most ambitious of these soon discovered that a willingness to have sex with the right person was often more important than any real talent.

After World War II, the studios were desperate to restock their reservoir of young actors following a four-year drought due to an exodus of drafted and enlisted young men. The few who remained behind were disabled, but not necessarily in a way that was obvious, such as Peter Lawford, who had severed nerves in a childhood accident limiting the use of his right arm.

Young women were arriving in droves, fresh, beautiful, and striving as ever. If they had the goods and made the right moves, the studios would sign them to contracts the minute they arrived in Hollywood, thanks to a virtual army of talent scouts they had deployed across the city.

These harsh, boilerplate contracts enabled the studio heads to own and use them in most any manner they pleased, which included pimping them out as evening companions for visiting dignitaries, or to movie star leading men they were trying to keep happy. It was all illegal, of course, but was seen as no harm, no foul if the studios encouraged it and the actresses bought in. However, if the girls stepped out of line in any way, or if the studio simply wanted to get rid of them for any reason, their respective legal departments were just a phone call away to invoke the ubiquitous morals clause in their contracts and have them kindly escorted off the lot.

Vice laws were very strict in postwar America. Being a consenting adult meant nothing and it was against the law to trade sex for money. Regardless, while lending out girls was equal to extortion and sexual blackmail, it was standard practice for many studios at the time. If their spirits were broken, the actresses never uttered a complaint, at least not publicly, because there was too much at stake.

Mobster Mickey Cohen, the patriarch of his LA crime family, also got in on the act. He arranged for handsome young gangsters to seduce movie stars on the rise and recorded their most intimate moments of ecstasy. Then Cohen blackmailed them into forking over a percentage of their earnings as their careers advanced. If they didn't agree, recordings would be released, sinking promising careers. And so, they did. The studios had no choice but to stay out of it, as Cohen controlled much of their labor through his mob-run unions.

Because information was power, when Cohen was building his house on Moreno Drive in Brentwood, the LAPD sent Otash and a couple of officers to the property at night dressed as contractors. They brought along a soundman who would run extra lines under the floorboards and through the skeletal frame. The end result was that every room in Cohen's house was bugged, even the bathroom.

Otash also became a master of disguise to suit the assignment, posing as a pimp, a hood, or just another face in the crowd. He once even prowled the city streets in drag, trying to catch the elusive "Red Light Bandit," Caryl Chessman, a robber, kidnapper, and rapist who accosted his victims in the dark. While he didn't nab Chessman, Otash got points for his effort.

Otash often worked cases where actors and actresses got caught up in minor compromising positions, but he sometimes looked the other way because he didn't want to go too far in risking the Hollywood relationships he was forging, nor the extra dough he earned working off duty at premieres and on location shoots. But thanks to what he learned observing the inner workings of the LAPD, he began keeping "shit" files on these incidents in case he might need them for future counterintelligence. He did, however, maintain an inherent compassion for those who couldn't protect themselves.

One day, a distraught mother walked into the LAPD with her daughter, who couldn't have been more than twenty, her eyes red and swollen with tears. Otash gave the girl a soda and sat them down to find out what happened.

The mother explained that her daughter was in acting school and had answered a casting call in the *Hollywood Reporter*. When she arrived, the movie producer told her all the roles had been cast but that he might be able to find her some extra work, provided they get more acquainted on his couch. This was the type of scumbag Otash couldn't stand. He felt compelled to try to straighten things out, or at least let these bastard producers know such bullshit was unacceptable, so he decided to set up his own sting operation.

He partnered with a policewoman and waited outside the studio gates while she posed as an actress showing up to audition. She too had come to LA with dreams of stardom, but her high moral values wouldn't tolerate success at any price. Instead, she joined the force and put her skills to use for the greater good. The policewoman answered a casting call like the girl, and when the slimeball producer offered her the same deal, she promptly pulled out her badge and busted him for extortion.

Otash then joined her in the office of the now-irate producer. He was a first offender, so they decided to let him off so as not to embarrass the studio. They came to an understanding wherein the producer could still have sex with whichever cast members he pleased, or take them on his yacht to "rehearse," but he could no longer *advertise* auditions as a shill to seek sex. He would have to legitimately cast one of the starlets before ever trying to seduce her.

Otash then left him with the sort of ominous warning only he could deliver: "Listen, you little prick," he began. "Next time you pull any out-of-bounds shit, I'm going to book your ass." Ironically, in the stifling moral climate of 1940s Hollywood, this was sadly considered progress.

Otash next moved in on a group of actresses working in a clandestine prostitution ring out of Paramount Pictures. He now lived across the street from the studio in an apartment on Marathon Avenue, which gave him easy entrée to the studio. Many of the women were part of Mickey Cohen's stable, while others were actually under contract at Paramount—like Betty Sullivan, whose day job was teaching school in Pasadena.

Otash later recalled in recordings made before his death: *"Anytime Paramount had some hotshot people out here from any part of the world, and they wanted a date, the studio would arrange for her to be available. The guys wouldn't pay her, the studio would."*

Posing as an out-of-town film buyer, Otash arranged for Betty to meet him at a suite he booked at the upscale Plaza Hotel on Vine Street. She arrived in a chauffeured car, looking all high-class wearing a full-length mink coat.

"A mutual acquaintance told me we were going to get together and have some dinner," Betty said as she closed the door behind her and removed her rhinestone encrusted clip-on earrings. "So . . . your wish is my command."

She began to undress with the seductive ease of a seasoned professional, and Otash followed suit, unable to ignore her beautiful body as he took off his trousers. He was down to his boxer shorts when the closet door burst open and out sprang a man flashing his police badge.

"Police!" Pinky Meade, Otash's partner, announced with great enthusiasm.

Betty's face dropped quicker than her teddy as she reached for her mink coat to cover up her naked body.

"I'm awfully sorry to do this, Betty, but uh . . ." Otash said, glancing down at his obvious excitement. "I mean . . . I really would have enjoyed spending the evening under different circumstances, but uh . . . you're under arrest."

Betty started crying hysterically. "I'm a schoolteacher," she wailed. "I'm going to lose my job in Pasadena. I have a husband . . . two kids . . . we're just trying to buy a house . . . I'll be ruined."

Otash later recalled: *"Shit. She almost died. She wasn't a world-famous prostitute. She was just a special girl who worked for Paramount Pictures as an 'entertainment director.'"*

Otash told her that he would let her loose if she would become an informant. Betty agreed without hesitation, and Otash wrapped up another "steak sandwich."

Betty turned out to be a reliable informant. If she got a call to meet some guy or heard of another girl getting a gig, she'd tell Otash. With her help, he wound up quietly busting the prostitution ring at Paramount Pictures.

Otash's undercover work busting prostitutes who operated through popular hotels, like the famed Hollywood Roosevelt and the Biltmore, was executed with an alternate strategy. For those, he wore his Marine uniform with his discharge button on the lapel and checked in as Marine Sergeant Otash. He'd get a room, go upstairs, and call the bell captain.

"Hey, Cap, this is Sergeant Fred Otash in room 711," he would begin. "I just came back from the Solomon Islands. Is there some place I can buy a bottle of booze and get some company?"

"Yes, sir, Sarge," the bell captain would answer with alacrity. "We'll work it out for you right away."

Within minutes, the bell captain would appear with a cheap bottle of booze. Minutes later, a hooker would show up and ask for another hundred. This was Pinky Meade's cue to pop out of the closet or from under the bed, and they'd make the arrest. They'd then nail the bell cap and the hotel manager for procuring prostitutes and selling liquor without a license.

Otash also focused on the rash of hustles and scams pulled on GIs by older crooked patrolmen. They would troll the bars looking for soldiers too soused to know which end was up and arrest them. On the way to transporting them to the drunk tank, they would steal all their cash. Once dried out, the GIs would realize they'd been ripped off but nothing could be done about it. They had no proof of when or where the money was stolen, or any way to pin it on the arresting officers.

Whenever Otash got wind of these shakedowns, he'd recruit some buddies from his rookie class to put on their old uniforms and soak themselves with booze to look and smell like stinking drunks. Then they'd go to a nightspot, pretended to be passed out, and let themselves get rolled by the uniformed cops. Once inside the station, Otash and his gang dropped the drunk act and thoroughly enjoyed exposing the scumbag officers, who were shocked to find that the stolen money was all in carefully marked bills.

O tash liked the fact that the LAPD could use its power to do good in the community. He became involved in the LAPD's annual fundraising police show designed to help families of officers injured or killed on the job, as well as raise money for developing recreational programs for kids on the street. Sold-out audiences were treated to a variety stage show extravaganza with singers, dancers, and comedians, headlined by stars like Frank Sinatra and Bob Hope, who entertained for free. Many performers volunteered their talents because they appreciated the LAPD's work, while some just did it to bolster their public personas. Others had reasons to fear law enforcement, so compliance was sort of mandatory, but it was all for a worthy cause.

It was also where the cozy kinship between the LAPD and Tinseltown paid dividends all around. The studio moguls purchased buckets of tickets and provided performers, who in turn got good ink in the gossip columns for their philanthropy.

Columbia's Harry Cohn took it one step further. He tipped the police officers selling tickets on the lot a hundred dollars each (nearly $1,300 today), which was damn good money for anyone, let alone a cop in those days.

"What do I need with all these tickets?" Cohn would tell them. "I see these jackass performers all the time. Take the hundred bucks, keep the tickets, and give them to some poor kids who'd love to see the show."

Some honest officers donated them to an orphanage or church group, while others pocketed the dough and resold the tickets. Cohn knew he was beholden to them, so he bought a little extra protection in case he got caught in illegal gambling, or if the name of one of his people appeared in some busted hooker's trick book.

During off hours, Otash showed his softer side by volunteering to be the scoutmaster of the LAPD-sponsored Boy Scout Troop 174, even going camping with the diverse group of adolescents. They were mostly wards of the court, rebels and misfits like he had been at that age, which made him feel compelled to help them.

One day, he heard that the MGM production of *The Bride Goes Wild*, a comedy starring June Allyson and Van Johnson, was looking for a hundred kids as extras. Otash knew his boys would be perfect and wanted to parlay the police/studio connection to make it happen by finagling a meeting with Louis B. Mayer, who loved to show his sympathy for the less fortunate to help burnish his image.

Mayer was a mercurial man at best—either a mean bastard or a nice guy, depending on what day it was. Otash arrived at Mayer's office and announced to his secretary that he was a member of the LAPD. Mayer, unsure of what this officer might want, told his secretary to show Otash in.

Mayer was seated behind a large desk the size of a dining room table that was elevated on a platform so that when his visitors sat in front of it, they'd always be looking up at him.

"What can I do for you, Officer?" Mayer said pleasantly.

"I hear you're doing the Johnson and Allyson film . . ."

Mayer nodded. "But I may change the title. *The Bride Goes Wild* seems to lack a sense of family, don't you think? What did you say your name was, Officer?"

"Otash . . . Fred Otash. I'm a policeman but I'm here as the scoutmaster of a Boy Scout troop in Central Division."

One of the most powerful men in Hollywood raised his eyebrows wondering what the angle was. "Yes?"

"Well, you see, these kids are all disadvantaged, mostly wards of the court, and I'm trying to help them out, sir," Otash said.

"A noble venture, son," Mayer said, adding as he no doubt often did, "that might make a good movie script."

"Yes, sir," Otash continued. "We need money to buy the boys uniforms and equipment, and I'd like them to work for it, to give them a pride of ownership they don't get when they swipe things."

Mayer nodded pensively, contemplating what good press this would be.

Otash then drove the pitch home. "I heard you need about a hundred extras, and I'd really appreciate it if you'd give these boys a chance and hire them."

Mayer jumped to his feet and pounded his fist on his desk. "You've got it, Officer," he said.

It was smiles all around as Fred stood up and shook Mayer's outstretched hand.

"I like you, Otash," he said intently, looking him straight in the eye as they sealed the deal. "We are like-minded."

Yeah, right . . . but Otash didn't argue the point as he scored a real victory. The boys were each going to receive sixteen dollars a day (about $200 in today's dollars), plus a box lunch.

When the movie premiered at Grauman's Chinese Theatre, the troop entered on the red carpet along with all the movie stars and their guests to a barrage of popping camera bulbs. But there was a slight problem when the picture played. Every time the boys spotted themselves on the screen, they shouted, hollered, and stomped their feet, drowning out the dialogue in those scenes. But everyone felt so good about giving the boys such an experience that no one seemed to care. Otash himself left feeling proud he had pulled it off for his kids without having to trade any favors with Mayer.

———————————

I n such a complex environment, the art of cultivating informants now played a key role in Otash's success. Not only did they help him nab suspected criminals, but any intel garnered could prove beneficial down the line.

Atop this growing list were the city's mobsters. Mickey Cohen, whose prostitution and extortion rackets fell just outside Los Angeles where Otash had no jurisdiction, became one of his most valued sources. It was a symbiotic relationship, with Cohen naming names of competing gangsters and madams vying for his clientele. In turn, they too made deals and became informants.

Even bartenders were cultivated. One night in a dive lounge frequented by alleged homosexuals at a time when such behavior was a crime, an undercover Otash sat alone at the bar nursing a scotch rocks like any other lonely out-on-the-town bachelor might as Nat King Cole's hit song "Nature Boy" played on the jukebox. It wasn't long before a guy in his early twenties with perfectly coiffed hair sidled up next to him and started making small talk. When Otash pulled out a cigarette and rummaged for a match, the guy eagerly obliged with a gold-plated lighter that he lowered several inches below the cigarette, sending a six-inch flame into the air that provided a better view of Fred's chiseled good looks in the dimly lit bar.

A few minutes in, Otash felt an open hand with what seemed unusually long fingers move up his thigh and toward his crotch. Reacting quickly and discreetly as to avoid resistance and attract any attention from the other patrons, Otash calmly pulled out his handcuffs and gently manacled one of the guy's wrists to the barstool's metal frame. He signaled over the bartender.

THE OTASH TOUCH 45

"Another round, boys?" the bartender asked, noticing the flop sweat on the patron's forehead.

Otash politely leaned in. "Not for me, thanks. I need you to call the police station for a squad car to take this guy in."

A knowing look of resignation crossed the bartender's face. He knew Otash, and he also knew that one guy making a pass at another was a crime.

"Can you not book him here, Fred? It's bad for business."

Otash figured he owed him a solid since the bartender had been a reliable tipster in the past, so he freed up the guy and took him outside, where he cuffed him again.

"If it's any consolation, I sincerely apologize for offending you," the guy began, his anxiety mounting as he continued to explain. "I'm new in town and just starting my career and, I, uh . . . well, there's no excuse."

Otash could tell he was genuinely remorseful for his actions, but he seemed oddly out of place and too refined and sophisticated for a dump like this.

"What do you do for a living?"

"I'm a pianist."

"A pianist? Yeah, well . . . next time, don't pee where you drink."

Otash was surprised when he laughed out loud despite his predicament. Something told him he should give this one a warning.

"Fuck it. I've got bigger fish to fry tonight," Otash said, uncuffing the guy once again, who thanked him profusely for letting him loose. "I expect good things from you and I'm gonna keep tabs. What's your name?"

"Valentino," he began, smiling. "Valentino *Liberace*."

Liberace was just one of many young entertainers that Otash would meet unexpectedly in those early days working vice. One afternoon in 1948, he was filling in for a hungover buddy, directing traffic downtown in front of the Million Dollar Theater, when he noticed the headliners on the marquee—the Will Mastin Trio featuring Sammy Davis Jr.—whose amazing talents had dazzled Hollywood audiences and critics alike. Later, when Otash went into the drugstore across the street to grab a bite, none other than Sammy himself approached.

"Hey, Officer," he said, flashing his megawatt smile. "Come sit at my table."

"Yeah, I saw your picture in the paper," Otash said, accepting the invite.

After making easy conversation between bites of their burgers, Davis asked, "You know, Fred, I'd sure like to learn how to shoot. Is there any chance you could teach me?"

"Of course, Sammy. Sure, why not?"

"Do I have to shoot in the colored section of the rifle range?" Davis asked.

"Nah, not with me you don't," Otash said. "But when you leave make sure you keep your gun drawn." He winked and Davis's raucous laugh filled the drugstore diner.

The two arranged to meet at the Police Academy in Elysian Park, where Otash gave shooting lessons to the future global sensation. Davis returned the favor by giving Otash house seats for his show. Neither of them knew at the time, but it was the beginning of a friendship that would last the rest of their lives.

Otash later recalled in a taped interview: *"I had bodyguards on Sammy for years. When he married the white Swedish-born actress May Britt, both the blacks and whites hated him, and the marriage hurt their careers. Someone pistol-whipped his mother, and he was very concerned about her well-being so I had men up at his house around the clock."*

On and off duty, Otash's life began to intersect with Hollywood's rising and established stars. He'd eat late dinners in the same Vine Street restaurants as the local entertainers, using these places as stakeouts in a neighborhood rife with illegal activity of all shapes and sizes, where he gleaned a more acute pulse of the city. On any given night, he'd hear a buzz on myriad subjects—which stars were sleeping with whom, Joe Kennedy selling RKO Pictures to Howard Hughes, chatter about the congressional witch hunt for suspected communists in the movie industry during the House Un-American Activities Committee hearings, or Robert Mitchum getting busted for smoking marijuana, a dramatic arrest in which Otash played a part.

It happened when the rookie police officer heard that illicit shit might be going down at a house on Vine. After a stakeout that lasted about an hour or so, he saw Lana Turner exit the house with some guy in tow. A few minutes later, Ava Gardner did the same. When they all got into the same car and drove off, Otash tailed their vehicle to the El Bonita Apartment House a few blocks away. Lana didn't go in, but Ava did. Otash then got out of his car, squeezed his burly frame between the hedges lining the stucco building, and peered inside the first-floor window where he witnessed a few people rolling joints at the kitchen table before watching Ava leave as hastily as she'd arrived.

Otash quickly moved back around the building and jotted down the license plates of all the cars parked in front before calling Narco Squad to take over. From his lead, they busted four people for smoking marijuana, including matinee idol Robert Mitchum. No one learned of Otash's role in the bust, an anonymity he preferred as not to jeopardize his burgeoning celebrity relationships. In cases such as these, he was more than happy to do his job without notoriety.

Another night, Otash and his vice squad partner were staking out the Hollywood Studio Club, a chaperoned dormitory run by the YWCA to provide safe and available housing for aspiring young women seeking a career in motion pictures. Located at the corner of Lodi Place and Lexington Avenue, the three-story Mediterranean-style sorority compound designed by renowned Hearst Castle architect Julia Morgan was opened to much fanfare in 1926, subsidized in large part by a well-publicized *UNESCO* of movie studios and luminaries eager to mitigate a growing public sentiment that the film industry was rife with moral turpitude and systematically exploited young and virtuous women after a series of public scandals severely tarnished Hollywood's otherwise glamorous façade. Ironically, twenty years on, Otash and his partner were acting on a tip that a number of Studio Club actresses were working as "escorts" to pay bills or advance their careers when they saw a shiny new Chrysler pull up in front of the building. Moments later, a young lady hurried out and jumped into the car.

Their interest piqued, Otash and his partner followed the Chrysler to Ciro's, where the man and the young lady dined. Both looked familiar to him, but he was parked too far away to make a positive ID. After dinner, they tailed them to another apartment building in Hollywood where the couple then entered. When the lights went on in one of the apartments, Otash got out of the car, peered at the window through binoculars, and saw the young lady, now naked, get into bed as the man pulled down the window shade, making it impossible to spy on them further.

When Otash ran the Chrysler's license plate, it confirmed his hunch that the man looked familiar—the car belonged to Milton Berle Enterprises. He also knew that Berle was too prominent a figure in the entertainment industry—and therefore important to police brass—to bust, so he left it alone.

Years later at a dinner party, he told Berle, whom he now knew socially, about the night he tailed him during his Studio Club rendezvous. He also revealed how he had eventually learned the identity of his escort that evening, none other than Marilyn Monroe herself. Berle, a serial womanizer, said laughingly, "You . . . son of a bitch!" before thanking Otash for his discretion.

Otash was learning that virtually everyone was, or could be, compromised in some way, shape, or form. He concluded that he needed to work both sides against the middle just in case one or the other became disenchanted with him. What happened next would integrate a cop on the fringes of Hollywood fame even further into this elusive world. He fell in love and married a gorgeous studio actress.

THREE

THE STARLET

O tash walked past the crowd filing into the Broadway department store at Hollywood and Vine for his Tuesday night ritual. With its neoclassical architecture of ground-floor colonnades, pilasters, and Corinthian capitals all crowned with a larger-than-life art deco neon metal sign that graced the skyline, the Broadway was the epicenter of postwar retail consumerism, and on Tuesday nights the first floor turned into a public theater courtesy of a massive display of TV sets, each one tuned to the *Texaco Star Theater*, starring Milton Berle.

With the advent of television, Berle had become a national treasure, as viewers from coast to coast dropped whatever they were doing to watch the one-hour live vaudeville and variety show extravaganza hosted by the former radio super-star that showcased his signature slapstick comedy, jokes, gags, and costumes. While the medium was still in its infancy, Berle was now its hottest ticket, known throughout the land as "Mr. Television."

When the show was over, Otash would watch with envy as many in the crowd lined up to buy TV sets so they could watch Berle in their living rooms. Unfortunately, Fred was not one of those customers. He couldn't afford it on his rookie salary.

It was tough to make a good living as a cop unless you were on the take, which for Otash was not an option. He was fine with coloring just outside the ethical lines, but he stopped short of taking any payoffs. For him, it wasn't about living like a movie star. All Fred wanted was the ability to enjoy some of life's simple pleasures . . . *like a TV set, for chrissakes.* But that wasn't going to happen without a little extra cash on a regular basis. Working the odd Hollywood premiere was nice and flashy enough, but the jobs were sporadic and an RCA Victor television set that cost $450 (nearly $5,800 today) was going to require something a bit more substantial.

The answer to his dilemma came in the spring of 1948 in the form of an off duty job working security detail for Eddie Nealis, a fifty-year-old San Antonio, Texas, oilman turned "businessman" who owned the Clover Club casino on the Sunset Strip, the Agua Caliente racetrack in Tijuana, and—if that wasn't enough—the Mexican Lottery. Needless to say, Nealis had his fingers in a lot of dubious pies, with a love for gambling so notorious that it had inspired the 1943 film *Mr. Lucky*, starring Cary Grant.

Nealis also tried his luck in the movie business, producing the 1947 film noir crime drama *Johnny O'Clock*. A lifetime member of Mickey Cohen's ultimate crime family, Nealis got a little juice in Hollywood from the picture, as did palling around with heavy hitters like Columbia Pictures' Harry Cohn and his Clover Club business partner Johnny Roselli.

All things considered, for Otash there was nothing exactly illegal about working security for a businessman-cum-mobster, even if he did have to conjure a modicum of ethical flexibility to justify his means, which he did. Nor was there anything illegal about having an affair with Nealis's twenty-six-year-old starlet wife, Doris Houck, though it would require major discretion as their romance ensued.

Doris was a heart-stopping beauty with an hourglass figure and eyes so seductive they could slay you at a glance—and she was smart as a whip. A high school valedictorian with a Mensa IQ, she was also well educated in the transactional ways of Hollywood. Nealis, who had married her a year earlier, draped her in diamonds and furs, ensconced her in a gated mansion on Bentley Avenue in Bel Air with a chauffeur-driven limousine, and protected his investment with a full-time bodyguard.

In Otash's eyes, Doris was an American version of Vivien Leigh, the British actress who took the world by storm in 1939 with her Oscar-winning portrayal of Scarlett O'Hara in *Gone with the Wind*. A former dancer and showgirl born seven months apart from Lana Turner in the same small town of Wallace, Idaho, Doris started her career as one of the scantily clad performers at Hollywood's popular Florentine Gardens, the same nightclub where a sixteen-year-old Norma Jean Baker met her first husband, defense plant worker Jim Dougherty. Time and tenacity had been good to Doris. In just a handful of years she was married to a millionaire and under contract to Harry Cohn at Columbia Pictures, where she ultimately appeared in thirty-eight films. The marriage was a bit of a salvation for her, as her filmography up to that point consisted mostly of B-movies and Three Stooges comedies like *G.I. Wanna Home* and *Brideless Groom,* where she was known as the femme fatale who threw Shemp Howard's head into a vise until he decided to marry her.

Nealis was understandably irate after his bodyguard came to him and told him that Doris was having an affair with Otash. When he confronted her, Doris chose and delivered her words carefully with the same natural believability she had honed in countless acting classes. She admitted it was true, explaining how her feelings for him had already diminished before she met Otash, that it was nothing that he said or did . . . it just happened. She still cared for Nealis dearly, she just didn't love him anymore. Unfortunately, the sincerity of her impromptu monologue failed to soothe the mobster's ego, let alone assuage his seething anger. When Doris pleaded with him not to take it out on Fred, Nealis simply flashed her a stone-cold smile and nodded insincerely.

A pragmatic tough guy, Otash took it like a man when Nealis accosted him in the grand foyer of his Bel Air mansion. After all, he *did* steal his wife. Taking your lumps is one thing but taking them from a gangster who didn't like to be crossed was a whole other ball game. Otash was cocky enough to believe he could handle any crisis, so he had no fear when Nealis got in his face. While Eddie never uttered the words *I'm going to kill you,* the implication was crystal clear when he exclaimed, "I hope you have eyes in the back of your head *and* your asshole, you piece of shit!"

Otash acted as if he didn't get the drift. "Why would you hope that?"

"It's a dangerous world out there, Otash, even for a cop!" Nealis raged.

Unruffled and unflinching, Otash took a beat to examine Eddie's drool now sliding down the front of his coat before wiping it away with a hanky from his back pocket.

"Thanks for the warning," Otash replied before explaining how many of his close buddies at the LAPD knew about the romance, and if something . . . anything . . . unexpected were to happen to him, they'd pin it on Nealis.

"And then you wouldn't be 'Mr. Lucky' anymore," he quipped with a sanguine smile.

"Get the fuck out of here you son of a bitch before I get someone to throw you out!"

Otash obliged without further discussion.

Nealis eventually came to accept that it was all over with Doris and moved on to other women. They made it official by going to Mexico, where they had been married a year earlier on May 21, 1947. As part of the divorce settlement, Doris got to move back into his palatial Bel Air estate with all the trimmings, including a new car and full-time chauffeur.

———————————

When Fred wasn't working, he was with Doris. Wildly in love, they wanted to live together, but Otash couldn't hack the idea of shacking up with his girlfriend in a house still owned by her ex—who wanted him dead—so he persuaded her to move into his one-bedroom apartment.

Doris had given up acting and her contract with Columbia Pictures not long after marrying Nealis, and while she didn't miss it much, she still felt most at home in the Hollywood community. One Sunday morning after church, while having brunch at Coffee Dan's, a popular twenty-four-hour

diner on Vine Street known as *the* place for actors and industry players to network due to its close proximity to the studios, Fred and Doris couldn't help but notice a tall, handsome,
powerfully built man with a pencil-thin mustache staring at
them from a nearby table. It looked like it might be actor John
Carroll, but they weren't sure until the man in question walked
over and slapped his business card on their table.

"My name is John Carroll," he said, introducing himself
with authority.

Otash and Doris followed suit, with Doris adding that she
recognized him as the guy who played Zorro in *Zorro Rides
Again*.

Carroll, now in his early forties, nodded in satisfaction.
He then delighted in noting his other career highlights that
included costarring with John Wayne in *Flying Tigers* and
appearing in *Go West* with the Marx Brothers.

Otash bragged that Doris was also an actress, but she
shrugged it off, saying her credits were less impressive than
Mr. Carroll's.

"Doris was under contract at Columbia," Otash said
proudly.

"Ah, the inimitable Harry Cohn," Carroll said. "A real
sweetheart."

Doris laughed.

In truth, Carroll was more of a working actor than he was
a movie star, one who knew the studio system like the back of
his hand and parlayed his leading man looks into a successful
acting career. Like most Hollywood folks who encountered
Fred in those days, Carroll made the blanket assumption he
was also in the business, until Otash flashed him his police

badge. Carroll raised his eyebrows. Now he was even more intrigued.

"My wife is Lucille Ryman, head of talent at MGM," Carroll said, his eyes shifting back and forth between Fred and Doris. "You two make a very attractive couple and I want her to meet you."

Fred and Doris were all smiles, flattered by the compliment. As they started to thank him, Carroll stood up from the booth and outstretched his arms, his palms open as if trying to stop traffic.

"Stay right there and don't move," he instructed. "I'm calling my wife from the house phone to tell her to get in the car and drive over here right now. I mean it, don't go anywhere." Then he pointed his finger at Fred's face. "We've been looking for a guy like you for a movie."

"We'll eat slowly," Otash promised.

The charm offensive continued when Lucille arrived a half-hour later and saw Otash face-to-face as she sidled up next to her husband. "Oh, John, you're right," she gushed. "He's about the most handsome thing I've ever seen . . . exactly what we're looking for."

"Toldja!" Carroll replied, slapping the table again.

A former actress whose career was as short-lived as her "Jane Starr" stage name, Lucille didn't have the glamorous looks the studio chiefs wanted so she had pivoted her profession into becoming one of the first women to attain a position of executive power in Hollywood, first as head of talent at Universal Pictures and now at Metro. Stylishly dressed, she was energetic, elegant, and had all the right Hollywood mannerisms and affectations, but Otash couldn't help but feel she was sizing him up like a slice of prime rib. On the other hand, her reputation for discovering stars like Lana Turner and June Allyson, and advising the likes of Katharine Hepburn, Spencer Tracy, Judy Garland, and Mickey Rooney, was legend.

Lucille asked if Otash would come over to the studio to meet the head of casting soon.

"Sure, I can swing it," Otash replied, thoroughly interested in where this might lead.

"Wonderful," Lucille said, fishing through her purse.

"Maybe I'll say hi to LB while I'm there . . . haven't seen him in a while," Otash quipped as Lucille retrieved a smoke from an expensive gold case engraved with her initials.

"You know Mr. Mayer?" she asked matter-of-factly, looking into his eyes as she gently tapped the case with her cigarette.

Fred promptly offered a flame from his lighter, as if christening their newfound alliance. "Yep, we're like this," he indicated with crossed fingers.

Lucille's eyes smiled with mischief as she neatly let the smoke drift out her mouth and into her nose.

"Well," she exhaled, "you will be if I have anything to do with it."

To alleviate any possible concern that the cop and the studio head might be into something untoward, Otash explained how he had convinced Mayer to hire his Boy Scout troop as extras.

"How wonderful . . . what a small world," she mused.

Back at their apartment, Otash sought Doris's opinion about changing professions. She schooled him on the pros and cons of life as a contract player. On the surface, signing the standard seven-year studio contract seemed to provide stability, but the fine print told a much different story. Seven years of employment didn't mean guaranteed paychecks, thanks to boilerplate renewal options every six months, with small bumps in salary if the option were picked up. But, Doris explained, the reality was, unless you were a star, an in-demand character actor, or somebody's "favorite," chances were you'd eventually get kicked to the curb.

Nevertheless, Otash kept his word with Lucille and met with her head of casting. While the dapper gentleman was enthusiastic and encouraging enough, Fred resented his sexual overtures and let the man know. They not only conflicted with his macho sensibility, but also served as a stark reminder of the same pervasive casting couch abuse of power in Hollywood that had previously brought a distraught mother and weeping daughter to the police station, the result of a dubious movie producer pimping roles for sexual favors. In the end, the uncomfortable encounter proved anything but fruitful, and Otash decided this acting thing wasn't for him. He thanked John and Lucille for the opportunity, but respectfully passed.

Regardless, by now they were quite taken with Otash. They invited him to their ranch in the San Fernando Valley for one of their regular weekend gatherings, which he gladly accepted, and he and Doris became frequent guests at John and Lucille's sprawling spread, which included a five-mile-long horse-racing track. The kid from Methuen, Massachusetts, was now hobnobbing with their rich and famous friends and cohorts like Gary Cooper, James Cagney, Mario Lanza, and fellow Camel cigarettes chain smoker John Wayne.

One afternoon, the conversation turned to the Red Scare enveloping Hollywood, who had been targeted, and who might be next. The Hollywood blacklist had been instituted in 1947 after ten filmmakers had refused to testify before the House Un-American Activities Committee (HUAC), leading to criminal charges and convictions for the group dubbed "The Hollywood Ten." Branded as communist sympathizers, they were formally condemned by a group of compromised studio executives, which ended their ability to work, at least under their own names.

The Hollywood Ten also railed against the tactics of Richard Nixon in his U.S. Senate campaign victory over Helen Gahagan Douglas, one of their own. Gahagan Douglas, the wife of the popular actor Melvyn Douglas, had herself been an actress and opera singer. In 1945, she became just the third woman from California elected to the U.S. House of Representatives, a point of pride for Hollywood. But in her run for the Senate, she had been smeared as a communist sympathizer and given the nickname "The Pink Lady" by the editor of the *Los Angeles Times*. Nixon upped the character assassination ante in a vicious general election campaign, calling her a "communist traveler" and rallied the antisemitic voters to oppose her because her husband was Jewish. The smear tactics worked as Nixon, who probably could have won without them, ran away with the election.

Otash, a staunch anticommunist, opposed the HUAC hearings because he felt the government was persecuting those in Hollywood just because they were well-known. He did listen closely to these political debates, absorbed which side each person took, and filed away the information in case he needed it someday, but he didn't engage in political banter. He had a knack for reading people and knowing what and what not to say about all topics. That's why at Carroll's ranch he never asked Clark Gable if Doris resembled his *Gone with the Wind* costar Vivien Leigh. Who knows? Maybe he'd agree. But more likely, Gable would either shine him on with a "yes" to be polite, think he's a knucklehead, or blow him off with a "Frankly, my dear, I don't give a shit."

During one Saturday barbecue at the ranch, Otash met an attractive brunette John had recently discovered. Her name was Norma Jean Baker, previously known by her married name, Norma Jean Dougherty, and now known as Marilyn Monroe.

Two years earlier, Norma Jean was living in a small house in Burbank, trying to make it as an actress, but having difficulty cutting it in large part because she had little to no formal training. Things hit rock bottom one night when a man broke into her house and tried to rape her after she got home late from a party. Thankfully, she managed to escape by running out of her house screaming for help in her torn nightgown.

Frightened, she moved out the next day without any real place to go. Fatefully, her and John Carroll's paths would cross that very afternoon at a nearby drive-in diner, where Carroll approached the distraught young beauty holding on for dear life to a canvas bag filled with all her worldly possessions. Of course, she immediately recognized him and, sensing his empathy, proceeded to pour her heart out. She told him that Columbia and 20th Century Fox had both dropped her after six months, and she was now planning to move to San Francisco. Even in a town drunk with aspiring beauty and potential, it was obvious to Carroll that there was something extraordinary about Norma Jean that went beyond the physical. He handed her his card, gave her a hug, told her to hang in there, and said he'd try to help her.

Norma Jean did hang in there, but the best she could do in the short term was a part-time modeling gig as the "Starlet Caddy" for a celebrity golf tournament at the Hillcrest Country Club just east of 20th Century Fox on Pico Boulevard. The first of its kind serving the city's rich and famous Jewish community, the Hillcrest attracted many of Hollywood's stars, such as Milton Berle, Jack Benny, Danny Kaye, George Burns, and the Marx Brothers, to name a few. Providentially, John and Lucille were also at the tournament, which led to them giving Norma Jean rent money plus some extra cash to supplement her modeling earnings so she'd be free to go on casting calls.

Not long after moving into a new apartment, she caught a boy on a ladder peeping into her window, an event that prompted the Carrolls to invite her to move into their home.

John enjoyed living the good life, which was subsidized with Lucille's generous steady income while he did whatever he could to help her spot potential talent. Together they signed Norma Jean to a contract and bankrolled her acting, singing, and dancing lessons. Taking her into their home was not out of character for the couple, who had an "open" marriage. Still, John did it without any thoughts or expectations of having sex with her—at least not initially.

Hollywood lore posits that she and John were a serious item, rendezvousing in an apartment he kept in Hollywood that served as their love nest, with John plotting ways in which to leave his wife. However, those in the know like Otash say the sex ended after a few trysts, mainly because John knew which side his bread was buttered on, and how far he could stray while still keeping his marriage afloat.

Whether she knew about their brief fling or not, Lucille was all business. Thinking Norma Jean, who by now had adopted her new stage name of Marilyn Monroe, might be right for a small but flashy role of a dizzy blonde, she persuaded writer-director John Huston to give her an audition for his upcoming 1950 MGM picture, *The Asphalt Jungle*. Marilyn, who was now also being represented by powerhouse William Morris agent Johnny Hyde, had left the Carrolls' home to live with him in his sprawling Beverly Hills mansion, and he too pressed the famous filmmaker to take her seriously. Huston would see something in Marilyn that others hadn't—he liked her moxie and cast her in the first important role of her career.

———————————

D oris grew less and less enamored living with Otash and his steadfast, of-the-time belief that it didn't matter how much money a woman had, as long as she lived within the means of her man's income. Doris did her best to pretend that living in his small apartment was romantic, but try as she might, his cop lifestyle was getting to her. So were his unpredictable work hours, all of which added up to him working for peanuts. Hell, her dinnerware service was worth more than what Fred earned in a year, plus overtime.

Their still-potent love and sex life aside, Doris needed other comforts to keep it going, and clearly, none were forthcoming. In January 1949, seven months after moving in with Otash, she called it quits and returned to the Bel Air mansion and to Nealis. But that was short-circuited when she discovered that she was pregnant with Otash's child.

Otash was over the moon—*he was going to be a father*! But he wanted his baby to be legitimate, so he made the case to

Doris, who was equally thrilled for her impending mother-hood, that it would be best to have their child raised under the same roof by both parents. Doris agreed, and on July 12, 1949, Colleen Gabrielle Otash was born. Fred then asked Doris to marry him so they could establish themselves as a legitimate family. She accepted, vowing to make things work this time. They were pronounced man and wife by Ruth Rice, minister of unity at the Beverly Hills Courthouse on January 6, 1950, one day before Fred's twenty-seventh birthday.

Otash was as proud and as doting as a father could be. Doris was surprised when he brought home a guard dog, a Border collie mix named "Ruffy," to protect his wife and child when he was on duty. But not half as surprised as Fred when he found the dog sleeping in his newborn's crib early the next morning before he left for work. He was baffled even fur-ther when it happened again the following day even after Fred had moved the crib to the center of the room. Surveillance that evening revealed Ruffy stealthily crawling into the bed-room, where he bounced himself off the wall to land in the crib and snuggle with Colleen.

Being a mother suited Doris well, but regrettably, other than their red-hot physical attraction for each other, the same problems that existed before failed to evaporate with their wedding vows. This soon led to Doris and Colleen moving in with her mother in Mar Vista. While Otash was hurting, he accepted it was for the best. He wouldn't be with Colleen as much as he would like, but he saw her as often as possible.

Then something shocking happened to Otash that felt like a dagger stabbed into his heart. Through a source in the clerk's office, he discovered that Doris had placed Nealis's name on the birth certificate as Colleen's father. While he knew that Colleen was Doris's middle name, he soon learned why Colleen's middle name was Gabrielle—Gabriel was Nealis's middle name. Coincidence or conspiracy?

Otash was furious. "There's no fucking way she's going to get away with this!" he growled to anyone who would listen. Many other guys would've been relieved to be off the hook, but Otash wasn't like other guys. He took Doris to court to publicly acknowledge his paternity of his thirteen-month-old daughter.

Nealis, who still hated Otash for stealing Doris away in the first place, now reveled in sticking it to him good. He hired Jerry Giesler, one of the most powerful heavyweight star attorneys in Beverly Hills, with a client list that included Errol Flynn, Robert Mitchum, Charlie Chaplin, and Bugsy Siegel, to represent Doris and his interests in court.

Otash couldn't afford such an expensive, high-profile lawyer, but he did find a newcomer pit bull of an attorney and fellow World War II veteran named Arthur Crowley, who saw this as an historic case. Back in the day before DNA tests, it was unheard-of for a man to sue for his right to be declared the father of a child, and Crowley couldn't wait to sink his teeth into this David-versus-Goliath battle between an LAPD cop and a millionaire mobster.

Crowley knew it would be catnip for the newspapers and capitalized on the opportunity. "Husband Sues to Establish Claim to Paternity of His Wife's Child," read the *Los Angeles Times* headline on August 21, 1950.

The *Los Angeles Mirror* assigned several reporters to cover the story. They ran a photo of Otash in his policeman's uniform next to the classic cheesecake starlet photo of Doris swinging in the breeze on a ladder overlooking the ocean.

In court, Giesler claimed that Doris's Mexican divorce wasn't legal. Therefore, her marriage to Otash wasn't legitimate, and Nealis should be considered Colleen's father. Crowley called witnesses on Otash's behalf, many of whom were Doris's close friends, to set the record straight. Before the baby was born, Doris had told them all that Otash was the father of her child. When Doris took the witness stand, she admitted under oath that she had lied and that Otash was indeed Colleen's father. She avoided adding that Nealis couldn't be the father because, euphemistically, he shot blanks. But she did confess that she put Nealis's name on the birth certificate because he could financially support Colleen better than Otash could.

The judge reached a quick verdict. He ruled that Doris's Mexican divorce was legitimate and declared Otash the father of the child, granting him custody of Colleen. Further, he said that there was no evidence that Nealis and Doris were intimate after their divorce. His final zinger: "Unless Mr. Nealis has some psychic means unknown to this court, it is difficult to see how he could be the child's father."

Doris felt that it was best for Colleen that the three of them be a family under the same roof, even if it meant a compromise in her living standards. Otash bought a modest tract house on Lake Street in Venice Beach on January 1, 1951. The price tag was $9,950 (nearly $117,000 today)—far more than he could afford with his LAPD salary and moonlighting jobs. As Otash often did, he worked the angles and obtained a VA loan through the GI program. He even bought a new TV set for the family.

Otash adored Colleen, but unfortunately his union with Doris just couldn't transcend their differences and they would eventually divorce in 1953. They loved each other dearly beneath all the drama, but the same issues came up again and again. Furthermore, and perhaps more importantly, they were unable to establish the type of stability, trust, communication, and selflessness a committed marriage needed in order to survive the long term—especially as Otash continued to pursue the hard and fast life of a Hollywood player that beckoned at every turn.

FOUR

RENEGADE COP

When William Henry Parker III was named chief of police in 1950, three years into Otash's LAPD tenure, Otash reacted to the news with a loud "Oh, fuck!" The two men had a history of butting heads as Parker rose up the ranks, and while Otash knew he was in for a tough time, he had no idea of the extent to which Parker was about to make his life a living hell.

A bespectacled, humorless man with a square head and a receding hairline, Parker was a fifteen-year veteran of the force. He had left during World War II to join the Army, where he served in Europe and earned a Purple Heart before resuming his duties at the LAPD, where his ambition continued its upward trajectory. Otash thought Parker carried himself like a Prussian army general, all spit-and-polish brass, while concluding that Parker regarded him as a brash kid who snubbed his nose at proper police procedure.

One major difference was that Parker was far less tolerant and accepting of racial minorities. The year after Parker took the reins as chief of police, seven men (five of whom were Hispanic) were badly beaten by LAPD officers while in custody in what became known as "Bloody Christmas." Parker attempted to sweep the atrocious human rights violation under the rug, until he was pressured to act against the officers.

The dichotomy of their opposing sensibilities served as the construct for the personal animus each man held for the other. Parker had a one-size-must-fit-all mentality for his officers while Otash was bespoke, custom-made, and unlike anything you could grab off a rack. In fairness to Parker, the new chief was dealing with a city exploding in every area: population, diversity, infrastructure, and crime. His anticorruption stance put him in direct conflict with the city's controlling mob operations, as well as the movie moguls, whereas Otash felt there needed to be more give-and-take with the commanding forces outside the police department to keep the peace. He was all about getting the job done, even if it meant cutting a few corners.

Otash's animosity toward Parker had begun two years prior when Parker, then a deputy chief, had brought charges against Otash for shooting craps in uniform. In actuality, Otash had been rolling dice with penny-ante lowlifes in the hopes they'd divulge the names of bigger fish he could bust for gambling. But Parker didn't approve of such unconventional tactics, and based on his recommendation, the Police Board suspended Otash for sixty days without pay.

Luckily, in the interim, Otash found a moonlighting job working security for the Hollywood Ranch Market, something that would ultimately draw Parker's ire.

ocated at the corner of Fountain and Vine with a giant neon clock sign atop its sprawling ramshackle complex that declared WE NEVER CLOSE, the Hollywood Ranch Market was indeed open twenty-four hours a day, seven days a week. Patronized by local residents, the market was particularly popular with members of the film community who had to be on set before dawn and often worked until midnight. It sold just about everything you could imagine, from a five-cent cup of coffee to expensive caviar. The place was always hopping, and business was good, except for the shoplifters who couldn't resist stealing anything that wasn't nailed down. That's where Otash came in, ensconced as their head of security in an office at the back of the store.

Otash had the store owners utilize a then-novel approach to surveillance that he devised on his own: five two-way mirrors strategically installed across one wall, so he could look out onto the floor and watch a customer's every move. Legendary crooner, radio star, and actor Rudy Vallée was one such customer. Otash often witnessed him using clipped coupons to pay for his goods, even though he was loaded. No crime there, but a comical piece of gossip that Otash could share with his drinking buddies.

Another was an unknown nineteen-year-old regular, a struggling hopeful named James Dean who always paid for his food until the day he decided to stash three cans of expensive caviar in his tattered bomber jacket. Not wanting to create a scene, Otash waited until Dean was outside the store. He walked over to him, put his arm around his shoulders like they were pals, and escorted him back to his office. Dean's hands were shaking when Fred offered him a smoke before leaning back in his chair to give him the standard stare-down. As he let him sweat it a beat for good measure, Otash was impressed how Dean's piercing blue eyes stared back at him unwavering.

"Look," Fred began, "I know life as a struggling actor isn't easy so I'm going to cut you a break. But try pulling this shit again and I'm calling you in."

Relieved, the sultry, mischievous grin that would soon help propel Dean to stardom slowly emerged.

Otash saw something unique in the young man, a one-of-a-kind charm and swagger that he didn't want to compromise with a petty theft charge. He took a liking to him, and whenever Dean came into the store, Otash invited him back behind the two-way mirrors where they'd watch for thieves together. Turned out the kid had a talent for reading human behavior and a sharp eye for thieves. With eyes glued on the action while Otash did his paperwork, Dean would grow animated when spotting a shoplifter. "Aisle three!" he'd exclaim. "Guy just stashed a package of lunch meat in his pocket."

A few years later, Dean reached cultural icon status for his star turns in *East of Eden* and *Rebel Without a Cause.* Otash was proud of his young friend and planned to congratulate him in person with a ceremonious tin of Russian caviar, but never got the chance. He was heartsick when he heard the news that Dean, on a day off from shooting *Giant* with Elizabeth Taylor and Rock Hudson, was killed in a car accident on September 30, 1955. He was only twenty-four.

Many young actresses shopped at the Hollywood Ranch Market, including Marilyn Monroe, whom Otash knew from his weekends at John Carroll's ranch. One day when he saw her in the store, he went over to say hello. After some friendly small talk, he invited her into his office, figuring she'd get a kick out of looking through the two-way mirrors, but he was wrong.

Marilyn got mad when Otash spotted a shoplifter and then excused himself to apprehend the man. When he returned, Marilyn was crying, saying that she felt sorry for the poor soul who probably didn't have enough money to pay for groceries.

Otash surmised that the guy stole things for kicks, citing his well-heeled appearance. He tried to enlighten her about profit margins and bottom lines, but Marilyn had no interest in his balance sheet rationale and abruptly left the store upset with Otash. He wouldn't learn how much until a few weeks later.

Late one night, Deputy Chief of Police Roger Murdoch, a close ally of Parker's who commanded the Hollywood Vice Squad, put the word out at the station that he wanted to see Otash as soon as he finished his graveyard shift. Otash knew something was up, as he would normally be allowed to go home and get some sleep after checking in at headquarters.

Murdoch cut to the chase when Otash showed up at his office door. "You're in some deep shit this time, Otash," he said. "Some actress named Marilyn Monroe filed a complaint against you for extortion."

"What the fuck?!?" Otash exclaimed.

"We showed her a dozen mug shots of the men on the force, and she picked you out of the photo lineup," he said, already presuming Otash's guilt.

"I've never extorted anyone in my goddamn life!" Otash railed. "I don't know what the hell she's talking about."

"C'mon. Cut the shit, Otash. You're always stepping up to the line. Looks like you crossed it this time," Murdoch said before ending the meeting abruptly.

Otash couldn't make sense of Marilyn's bogus charge. Was it out of spite for arresting that shoplifter? That would be insane. Whatever the reason, it could cost him his job.

He toyed with the idea of confronting her for an explanation, but Murdoch would probably nail him for interfering with the investigation, which would only make matters worse. Plus, it turned out that Marilyn was in nearby Cedars of Lebanon hospital having her appendix removed, so the timing was bad. Still, the clock was ticking if he was going to quash this charge.

After catching a few hours' sleep, Otash was driving down Sunset Boulevard back to the station to get his next assignment when a Philip Morris billboard caught his eye. The male model in the ad reminded him of a detective who also worked out of the Hollywood station, someone who looked a lot like Otash himself. He recalled their having a recent conversation where he asked Otash if he knew Marilyn. Otash explained their brief history and never thought about it again . . . until now.

Otash speedily weaved in and out of traffic all the way to the station and marched straight into Murdoch's office without knocking. Murdoch was miffed by the intrusion, but Otash pleaded his superior to hear him out, insisting he could prove his innocence in the Marilyn Monroe matter. Murdoch was skeptical, but he cared about his men so he acceded to Otash's strange request to pull both his and the detective's personnel files. Otash then pulled out both their photos and placed them side by side, revealing the rather uncanny resemblance.

Murdoch agreed to show Marilyn the photos, and that afternoon from her hospital bed she confirmed her mistake and identified the detective as the true culprit.

Otash was greatly relieved the charges against him were dropped. Days later, Marilyn sought him out at the Hollywood Ranch Market to apologize, blaming it on the anesthesia. Fred accepted her apology, knowing that their paths would likely cross again, and chalked it up to her neurotic personality. A rather ruffled start to their nascent friendship had been remedied. As Marilyn was leaving his office, she turned around and blew Fred a kiss.

As far as Parker was concerned, Otash's off duty gig was yet another example of his pushing the outside edge of the rulebook. He knew he couldn't change him, so he set about breaking him. To drive home his alpha-dog status, Parker began transferring Otash each month from one trying beat to the next. He assigned him to the prison farm to work as a guard, gave him traffic duty, sent him undercover on the docks of San Pedro, and then, worst of all, put him on patrol alone on the night beat in Watts.

Back then, a lone white police officer patrolling Black neighborhoods was unheard-of, and very dangerous. That was precisely what Parker had in mind, delighted at the prospect of Otash getting his ass kicked by some Black dude. But Fred wasn't worried. He was keenly aware of the community's deep-rooted and accurate belief that the LAPD was racist, so he took the opposite tact.

Otash despised Parker for putting him on this patrol merry-go-round, but he didn't let it get to him, if for no other reason than to deny the bastard any satisfaction. He certainly didn't let it put a crimp in his social life as he continued dating many young starlets.

"I understand you're living it up with a lot of the Hollywood prostitutes," Parker railed at him one day.

"Starlets, Chief," Otash corrected. "They're starlets, not harlots."

Parker disagreed on the semantics and accused Fred of developing a playboy reputation, a bad image for a policeman.

Otash responded that there was nothing wrong with getting laid. In fact, it was rather fun and he encouraged Parker to try it some time.

Parker took offense, calling him an impudent asshole. He suggested that in the best interests of the department, Otash should consider moving out of the Hollywood area to be less conspicuous. Otash would have none of it. He had resided in Hollywood since the day he hit town after the war, and he wasn't about to give up his apartment, located within a mile of Schwab's drugstore, in the thick of all the action he so craved.

Then he turned the screw on Parker to rub it in. "Besides, all the lovely ladies like spending the night there with me," he said.

Parker was determined to have the last laugh when it came to Otash's womanizing, which he considered his true weakness.

Not long after the exchange, Otash found himself getting acquainted with a raven-haired looker sitting next to him at the bar in the Frolic Room, which in cases like this meant asking questions for answers he already knew. This style of examination that he honed to perfection while interrogating suspects as a police investigator proved equally effective when pursuing young ladies in his personal life. Years later, he would liken the scenario to the chorus line from his good friend Sammy Davis Jr.'s recording of the Cheshire Cat in the animated version of *Alice in Wonderland*: "What's a Nice Kid Like You Doing in a Place Like This?"

The Frolic Room was a cavernous former speakeasy on Hollywood Boulevard known as "Freddy's" during the days of Prohibition before being rechristened and reopened to the public in 1934. The historic dive bar next door to the Pantages Theater, now owned by Howard Hughes as part of his purchase of the entire complex in 1949, was a fan favorite to locals and celebrities alike and a popular watering hole for everyone from Frank Sinatra and Judy Garland, to Elizabeth Short— aka the Black Dahlia, a now-infamous twenty-two-year-old waitress-cum-aspiring actress last seen there alive before her gruesome murder in 1947. The storied haunt held a certain dark mystery that appealed to Otash, a place pregnant with possibilities, for he never knew what or who he'd encounter when dropping by for a stiff drink after a long day at work.

"I'm an actress, or at least trying to be," she answered, taking a generous sip of her waning Gibson.

Otash responded with the same enthusiasm he had mustered dozens of times before. "Really? That's great!" he said.

"Thanks." She smiled coyly. "I know it takes time, but I'll do my best."

Not wanting to appear discouraging, he gently cautioned her to be wary of the predatory producers lurking in the cracks and corners of Hollywood, a line of conversation that invariably established his role as protector.

Now it was her turn. "May I ask what it is you do for a living?"

"I'm a policeman," he said.

Her eyebrows arched slightly, as Otash expected they would. She threw back the remnants of her Gibson and placed the empty glass on the bar. Otash signaled the bartender for a refill, and over the next couple of rounds filled with flirtatious small talk and suggestive body language, she agreed to give him her phone number.

A few nights later, she came on strong but backed off when Otash tried to get more affectionate. She liked him, but she indicated she was an old-fashioned girl who wanted to take it slow. Fred was frustrated by all the mixed signals, but this one seemed different: more grounded, natural, less self-obsessed than all the other ingenues he dated, and genuinely interested in him and his stories of working undercover as a cabdriver, or at Douglas Aircraft, or dressing as a pimp. So as much as he wanted to drive this girl home, he gently tapped on the brakes.

On their third date at the Shangri-La nightclub, Otash was surprised to hear his name being paged and excused himself to take the call. It was one of his buddies on the force, a fellow officer who spotted Fred with his beauty as he walked into the club. But rather than say hello, he made a beeline to the telephone booth to give Otash some all-important intel: the girl was actually a policewoman working as an undercover informer for LAPD chief Parker.

Son of a bitch! Now it all made sense. She was having him regale her with stories in the hopes he'd divulge some stinking incrimination that Parker could use as ammunition. Well, two can play at that game. Returning to their cozy corner table facing the room (the seasoned cop always kept his back to the wall), he readied himself for a performance that would make Lucille Ryman and that "charming" head of MGM casting proud.

"That was my babysitter," Otash lied. "I always leave her the phone numbers of my whereabouts in case of an emergency. Nothing's wrong, but my little girl—her name is Colleen, well . . . she wouldn't go to sleep until she heard her daddy say 'good night.'"

"Aww, that's so sweet, Fred," she said sincerely.

Fred immediately suggested they go somewhere nice for dinner. As she slid her arm through his as they left, Otash played along all lovey-dovey. What followed was an intoxicating night at the Mocambo on Sunset Boulevard, replete with dining, dancing, and copious drink, each hoping the other would inevitably come clean. The gal had a high tolerance for alcohol, but it paled by comparison to Otash's. In the end, her only confession was a desire to sleep with him, and while he knew she was trying to screw him over, it was a screw he couldn't resist.

That morning, Otash made sure to wake up first. He quietly slipped out of bed and into her living room, where he searched her purse and found her contact card with the internal affairs phone number on the back. He then grabbed a pen and paper from her desk, wrote out a note, and taped it along with her card to the mirror above her dresser that read: "*You're one of the best police informer lays I've ever had. Please thank Parker for me. Love, Fred.*"

Otash's policing merry-go-round continued when Parker put him back on the vice squad. Otash didn't mind, as this time he was teamed up with one of his favorite old partners, Pinky Meade. The two had similar sensibilities about when to obey Parker's rulebook, and when to throw it out the squad car window.

Shortly thereafter, Fred and Pinky were staking out a ground-floor apartment one night that served as a known makeshift brothel when they spotted a husky man in his early fifties step out of an expensive Chrysler Town & Country two-door Woodie convertible and head inside. They quietly exited the squad car and moved in toward the bedroom suite housing the two prostitutes. Through the slightly ajar window, they could overhear the john requesting services of both girls. Sliding a piano wire through the Venetian blinds gave them just enough gap to briefly glimpse the threesome in progress.

Their rudimentary methods worked and they had seen enough to make a bust. When the man emerged an hour later, Otash arrested him while Pinky went inside to apprehend the two women. The well-heeled john produced a driver's license identifying him as S. P. Eagle. He also produced a business card signed by Chief Parker himself that read: "This man is a friend of mine. Please grant him all courtesies." Fred was well aware that such courtesy cards were commonly used by cops to trade favors they could call in down the road, as he himself had handed out similar versions to John Carroll and Lucille Ryman's friends during his weekends at their ranch.

Normally, Otash would honor the courtesy card and move on. But he was sick of Parker's crap, so as payback, he politely denied Eagle his *Get Out of Jail Free* card. Then Eagle fessed up. He explained that "S. P. Eagle" was a pseudonym he had used earlier in his career to combat antisemitism in the industry. The producer was now using his real name, Sam Spiegel, after the success of *The African Queen*, the critically acclaimed box-office hit starring Humphrey Bogart and Katharine Hepburn that had just earned Bogart the Best Actor Academy Award.

Otash was certainly impressed, but unfortunately, this was about getting back at Parker. He offered to book Spiegel under another assumed name and have him pay a fifty-dollar fine in exchange for cooperation to expose the prostitution business in the apartment building. If not, he'd book him under his real name, at which point word would eventually leak out, causing him the inevitable embarrassment. Spiegel took the deal and Otash booked him under the name Sam Schwartz, then waited for the situation to play out, which it did.

The following day, the police chief called Otash into his office and reamed him—Do you know who this man is . . . blah-blah-blah?!? For Otash, the dressing-down was worth it knowing that Spiegel had ripped Parker a new one over his courtesy card not working as promised.

In early 1954, Otash received an out-of-the-blue telephone call from Paul Coates, the former actor turned crusading columnist for the *Los Angeles Mirror* who became the widest read man in the city before parlaying his popular personality into hosting the syndicated tabloid-style television series *Confidential File*. Coates wanted to do a piece on Otash at the Hollywood Ranch Market, and Fred was happy to oblige.

Coates and his camera crew spent five days at the Market following Otash around. He and Coates talked about how market owners were losing money due to shoplifting. The camera crew even captured Otash nabbing suspected shoplifters who, ironically, were then happy to be interviewed on camera.

Of course, Parker was incensed when he got word of the piece. He summoned both Otash and Coates to his office. While he was deferential to the TV personality with no knowledge of proper police procedure, Parker lectured that Otash should have known better than to collude with Coates in exploiting suspects to appear on television, conceding their guilt without any due process.

"Colluded?" Otash mocked. "Oh, for chrissakes, Chief, they practically fell over themselves to get on camera."

Parker said nothing. He just stared down Otash with a palpable contempt that wasn't lost on the *Confidential File* host.

Coates explained that from his professional experience, most people, including shoplifters, can't resist being on camera regardless of their circumstance. "After all," he affirmed, smiling, "everyone wants to be on TV."

This cavalier defense was all too annoying for the stoic Parker, but he remained diplomatic for Coates's sake, "Well . . . that may be true, Mr. Coates, but it's not the way we do things around here. Could you please refrain from these sorts of stunts in the future?"

Stunts? Now Coates was annoyed. Bristled by Parker's reference to his reporting style, he couldn't wait to get away from this killjoy, so he simply stood up, vowed to be more mindful next time, shook Parker's hand, and left the room.

Otash followed him out. When he reached the door, Fred looked back and told Parker he couldn't offer any such promise. Then he walked away without waiting for a response.

Parker wasn't about to let it go. The next day, he called Fred in to tell him that his subpar record of booking shoplifters at the Hollywood Ranch Market was a dereliction of his sworn duty as an officer of the law. Otash refuted Parker's pretext, claiming that he caught hundreds of criminals, booking one out of every ten and always the most hardened. Even traffic cops didn't book every driver they pulled over, he rationalized. They scared most of them with a warning; otherwise the jails would be full of red-light runners and petty thieves.

In addition to busting his butt at every turn, Otash was certain that Parker was jealous, if not altogether envious of the young and handsome police officer whose lifestyle, social life, Hollywood connections, even his ability to get a better table at the Mocambo, Ciro's, or any other hotspot nightclub in town eclipsed his own. Hell, Fred owned twenty-five tailor-made suits and drove a brand-new Cadillac convertible gifted to him by the owners of the Hollywood Ranch Market as a Christmas bonus. And if that wasn't enough, Fred's annual LAPD salary, coupled with the extra seven hundred bucks a month he was making from the Market, meant he was pulling in more than the chief of police himself. All this roiled Parker incessantly, and when he found out how many hours a week Otash was working off duty, he called Fred on the carpet.

"You're working far more than the sixteen off duty hours authorized by your permit for a second job," Parker accused.

"Okay . . . well, you let me know when all the deputy chiefs, inspectors, and captains can prove they're working within the guidelines," Otash pushed back. "Until then, this is all a bunch of horseshit, and you know it."

Parker got in his face. "Let me remind you, I'm still your superior officer. I set the rules and regulations around here."

Otash stood his ground. "I'm not gonna obey that one," he said. "Hell, it probably isn't even legal."

"If you don't like it, you can leave the force anytime you want," Parker advised. "Nobody's going to stop you."

"Not a chance, Chief," he said. "You want me off the force? Take me up before the board and try proving I'm not a good cop. I'll make you push it all the way."

Parker's problem was that he couldn't fire Otash because he reported to Thaddeus Franklin Brown, Otash's friend and confidant who respected his unique style of policing. Brown served as the deputy chief of detectives at the LAPD until July 18, 1966, when he was appointed chief of police two days after Parker's death. A celebrity in his own right, his real-life persona had been frequently name-checked on the hit series *Dragnet* by creator Jack Webb's "Detective Joe Friday," who tagged him as the boss during his self-introduction on both the TV and radio programs, and actor Raymond Burr would portray him on the 1951 premiere episode.

So Parker called Otash's bluff and took him up before the board, hoping they would do his dirty work for him. The following day, Otash received a last-minute notice that an emergency hearing of the LAPD Investigative Board had been called for 8 p.m. that evening to address his off duty work permit.

Otash was now in a tough spot. The renegade cop was beginning to feel like he was running out of room. An emergency meeting like this had never been done before, and if he didn't appear to defend himself in person, Parker could can his ass for cause. He had to hit this head-on.

The LAPD Investigative Board, composed of three deputy chiefs and two police inspectors—all of whom were in Parker's pocket—was caught off guard when Otash showed up with his lawyer, Arthur Crowley. Now, *that* had also never been done before, but there was no rule against it, so they had to allow it.

A young upstart attorney who had made a name for himself working divorce cases, including Otash's well-publicized paternity suit, Crowley saw this as another juicy case he could sink his teeth into and once again exploit in the press. With a flair for the theatrical, he opened by demanding to know why the hearing had been called at night, and why his client was given such short notice.

One by one the board members explained that it was the only time they could all meet.

Using information that Otash and other department insiders had given him, Crowley exposed the real reason why the hearing hadn't been scheduled during the day: because everyone on the board had off duty night jobs just like Otash! Then, he lowered the boom.

"Chief Parker's vindictive personal animus toward Officer Otash is common knowledge within the police department," Crowley intoned with a trace of pleasure. "As a result, my client intends to file a lawsuit against the chief for harassment, for attempting to revoke his work permit, and for putting him on the so-called merry-go-round."

Unsure how they should respond, the board sat tongue-tied. No cop in LAPD history had ever sued the chief of police. Crowley went on to advise them that unless Parker stopped the merry-go-round, Otash would go to court and obtain a restraining order against him for harassment. Furthermore, he said that if Otash's work permit was revoked, his client would ignore the revocation and continue working at the Hollywood Ranch Market. And should they suspend him for that, Crowley promised to see them all in court to address the legality of their regulations—if necessary, all the way up to the Supreme Court.

"These regulations should clearly be tested before a jury in the court of law," Crowley said.

Not wanting a fight that could bring them all down and subject them to public criticism, the board ended the hearing without any action against Otash. But Parker refused to back down and revoked Otash's work permit anyway. So, on October 6, 1954, Crowley announced to the press that he was filing a test case to challenge Parker's authority to control off duty employment.

Otash kept working, and Parker didn't try to stop him, most likely due to all the bad press in every local paper, from the *Mirror* to the *Times*, blasting him for his vendetta against Otash. Still, Parker was able to get a stay against the restraining order, and once again assigned Otash to patrol Watts. Fred complied, and as he walked the streets of the working-class Black community, he spent a lot of time thinking about his future, and picturing Parker checking the daily death and injury reports, disappointed not to see his name on it.

Eventually, the war with Parker took its toll on Otash. Even if he could withstand it for the long haul, to what end? The very basic satisfaction he once had from a hard day of policing was over now, and the reality that his entire career could be sabotaged by an egomaniac superior lay heavy on his mind. He sure as hell wasn't going to be promoted anytime soon.

Just when he needed a Plan B, one dropped into his lap.

By now, Fred had garnered a reputation as someone who was both tough and discreet when it came to movie stars. And so it wasn't surprising that high-power attorneys Melvin Belli and Jerry Giesler, his adversary from his paternity case, both separately offered to hire him nonexclusively as their private investigators. This was exactly the type of opportunity and career move the thirty-three-year-old Otash was looking for, a place where he could ply his trade, his way.

He accepted each of their offers and, after ten years on the force, decided to turn in his badge.

Parker tried to hide his glee at the news when he caught up with Otash at the personnel office signing his resignation papers.

"What's this I hear about you quitting?" Parker asked, smugly.

"Yes, Chief. It's true," Otash confirmed. "I'm through, finished. I figured it would make you happy. But believe it or not, even after all the shit I got from you, I still respect you because you're an honest cop. I never doubted that."

Parker was momentarily disarmed, until Fred hit him with a final parting blow. "But I'll tell you one thing . . . you are the worst man for managing officers this city has ever seen."

Parker seethed, "Well, that's your opinion, Otash."

"It's also the truth," Otash said. "Now if you'll excuse me, I've got a meeting in San Francisco with Melvin Belli, one of the greatest attorneys alive, about a lucrative new job."

FIVE

IT'S CONFIDENTIAL

n January 1955, Otash launched his eponymous Fred Otash Detective Bureau in an office building on Fairfax Avenue in Hollywood. He assembled a staff of nine, mostly ex-cops and ex-FBI agents who, under his tutelage, became masters of what Otash coined "creative surveillance." At considerable expense, he retrofitted a 1950 Ford F1 panel delivery truck with a state-of-the-art electronic surveillance package and had 24 HOUR TV REPAIR SERVICE, INC. painted on its side, a move that immediately set him apart from other detectives who relied on more old-fashioned techniques to ply their trade.

His team's MO was to park near a target's home within reach of their long-range cameras and parabolic microphones. If that wasn't an option, they'd climb up the nearest telephone pole, carefully tap into the telephone wires, and run them back into the truck. If a target suspected something fishy about the TV repair truck, Otash had it repainted ROOFING

COMPANY or FURNITURE MOVERS or his favorite, OTASH PLUMB-
ING: WE CLEAN CESSPOOLS.

Otash's go-to gadget was the Stephens Tru-Sonic Transmitter. Created by Robert Lee Stephens, a former draftsman
at MGM Studios whose namesake Stephens Manufacturing
Company became a pioneer in theatrical sound systems, it
could be hidden along with a tiny microphone in an actor's
clothing so that no matter where or how they moved, the sound
quality remained consistent. The transmitter, which was actually a miniature FM radio, could broadcast three to four
blocks before it was picked up by a receiver and wire recorder.
Adapted versions could be placed inside an office or residence,
plugged into an existing wiring system, or hidden inside the
base of a table lamp, a phone, or any other electronic appli-
ance to be had. A voice activator triggered the recording whenever anyone spoke near the microphone, and the system could
broadcast for months if need be with the recorder concealed
inside the trunk of a car, in an adjoining room, apartment, or
anywhere else where it could be kept indefinitely.

Otash used the Stephens whenever a movie star, power
broker, or wealthy businessman sought his services to determine whether or not their spouse was cheating. Sometimes he
got the goods on their not-so-better half; other times the concerns were groundless. But despite its sophistication at the
time, the Stephens did not have a brain. It could not be selec-
tive or programmed to distinguish between one sound or
another. Once the mics were activated, *everything* was
recorded. In more comical scenarios in which the clients
themselves were having an affair, those infidelities (much to
their chagrin) would be documented in kind. Otash referred
to such incidental data collections as a *by-product*.

These surveillance techniques were highly illegal. If convicted, each incident carried a five-year prison sentence. But Otash rationalized the risk, calling it "equal justice," the only way investigators could compete with tools already at the disposal of law enforcement. As it turned out, they also paved a profitable avenue for him when the groundbreaking, no-holds-barred *Confidential* magazine hired him as its "fact checker" shortly after he opened his business.

Otash and *Confidential* magazine were made for each other. Each was astutely attuned to the times and unafraid to confront or disrupt the business-as-usual Hollywood establishment. In movie parlance, they were perfect casting. *Confidential* disregarded the unwritten rules that had governed Hollywood since the dawn of the movie business and, in the process, gave studio bosses and big-name stars the middle finger, metaphorically. Its norms-busting founder and publisher, Robert Harrison, had heard that Otash was not dogmatic about protocols or proprieties and willing to operate in the gray areas of the law, all of which appealed to Harrison.

A native New Yorker, Harrison always had a cigarette strategically dangling from his mouth. He was a dandy in his matching white suit and fedora that contrasted his deep tan, a fashion style known as "please notice me." He felt invisible after a series of failed attempts publishing tame girlie magazines. But at age forty-eight, he was certain the world would take notice of him with his new concept. Through a confluence of watershed cultural events, including the maiden issue of *Playboy* magazine hitting the market, plus the riveting televised U.S. Senate Kefauver Committee hearings putting the mafia on display, he had his aha moment—sex, sin, and violence sells.

In his mission statement, he asserted: "The lid is off! The bunk is going to be debunked! In its first issue, *Confidential* will open your eyes and make them pop! It pulls the curtain aside and takes you behind the scenes, giving facts, naming names and revealing what the front pages often try to conceal! Here, you will read about the famous and the infamous; about the glamorous who are deglamorized; about the mugs and the mobs. . . . Yes, you will be shocked, but at least you'll get the truth without any trimmings. . . . You'll get the real stories behind the headlines—uncensored and off the record."

Confidential had hit the newsstands in December 1952 as a quarterly publication, with red and yellow covers and a vow that it "Tells the Facts and Names the Names." Inside the magazine were embarrassing stories and scandalous exposés, written in cliché-ridden and campy prose, about the private lives of movie and television stars, famous figures outside of show business, and even gangsters.

With an initial run of 150,000 copies, the racy stories in its first two issues barely caused a stir in Hollywood. But the August 1953 issue was a game changer with an explosive story about the ballyhooed romance between Marilyn Monroe and baseball legend Joe DiMaggio. That was also the year Marilyn became a bona fide movie star, graduating from flashy supporting roles to receiving star billing in three box-office hits in a row—*Niagara*, a noir thriller, and the splashy musical comedies *Gentlemen Prefer Blondes* and *How to Marry a Millionaire*. Her screen presence was magical, electric, and the camera loved her. So did audiences, who flocked to movie houses to see the newly christened blonde bombshell radiate sex appeal and charm them with deft comedic talent. Otash had followed this closely and was genuinely happy that Marilyn's dream of movie stardom had finally come true.

DiMaggio, the recently retired New York Yankees superstar, had become a household name in 1941, the summer before the nation went to war, when he captured the public's imagination with an incredible fifty-six consecutive games hitting streak, a record that still stands today. He was the highest-paid professional American athlete in a team sport, earning $100,000 a year (more than $2 million today), unheard-of at the time, but worth every penny because he filled stadiums and led the Yankees to nine World Series championships.

They were American royalty: DiMaggio the tall, handsome hero of the country's national pastime, and Monroe the beautiful, glamorous movie star lighting up the silver screen. Readers took every word blurbed about their romance in gossip columns or trumpeted in fan magazines as gospel, breathlessly wondering when they would be tying the knot. Otash was also curious about it himself.

Robert Harrison had the answer to the question, puncturing a hole in this fairytale courtship with *Confidential*'s blockbuster third-issue story headlined: "Why Joe DiMaggio Is Striking Out with Marilyn Monroe!"

Written under the not-so-pseudonym Harrison Roberts, his opening paragraph read: "He put the wood to the best fastballs ever served up in the American League, but 'Joltin' Joe' DiMaggio kept swinging and missing these lovely curves in his world series of his heart—that gallant attempt to make Marilyn Monroe his wife."

He then blamed 20th Century Fox cofounder Joseph Schenck for opposing the marriage. Thick with innuendo, the story reported that Schenck had a Svengali-like influence over Marilyn because he was her "daddy" and whatever he says goes. Now the studio's hottest "single" commodity, Marilyn had added millions of dollars to its coffers and become a household name in the process—and he wanted to keep her that way.

Harrison struck gold with the Marilyn-DiMaggio issue. Virtually overnight, *Confidential* jumped from a circulation of 150,000 issues to 800,000 and went from a quarterly publication to bimonthly. When *Time* magazine called it "success in the sewer," Harrison knew he had tapped into a scandal-hungry tabloid mentality readership that had barely existed. Unlike editors at fan magazines like *Photoplay* and *Modern Screen* who depended on studios to give them access to their stars for puff pieces, Harrison didn't need access. Nor did he want it.

From that issue on, Harrison was called a smut-peddling menace or worse a thousand times over by Hollywood, while the community laughably pretended the magazine didn't exist. As Humphrey Bogart put it: "Everyone reads *Confidential*, but they deny it. They say 'the cook' brought it in the house."

———————

Technically, Otash didn't work for *Confidential*. He was on the payroll of Hollywood Research Inc., the intelligence-gathering front for the magazine run by Harrison's niece Marjorie Meade and her husband, Frederic. Otash often worked out of their offices located on the ground floor of a luxury Beverly Hills apartment building, where tough-looking surveillance agents and goons manned the fact-checking command center, some of whom were ex-cops that had traversed into the gray areas. Phone recording and listening devices were often used, and files and photographs were scoured over to prove or disprove the accuracy of every story.

In his and Harrison's view, if public figures didn't want their dirty laundry aired, they should live a clean lifestyle so magazines like *Confidential* would have no reason to exist. But since that would never happen, *Confidential* wasn't going anywhere. It was causing a collective headache for Hollywood, but there were bigger problems afoot. The movie business was losing ground to television. The number of feature films released by the eight major studios went from 263 in 1950 to 215 in 1955. Americans only spent 9.4 percent of their recreation dollars in 1955, compared to 12.3 percent in 1950.

Paranoia also still lingered and nerves were still raw within the Hollywood community from the Red Scare, even after it finally faded away. Friendships were fractured and careers were in tatters after friends and colleagues testified in front of the House Un-American Activities Committee (HUAC) and publicly named names of people they knew or thought were communists in order to take the focus off of themselves. Many of them were not immune to *Confidential* publicizing their political affiliations, even if the evidence was unproven or merely guilt by association.

———————

Otash was able to compartmentalize his personal and professional lives, never allowing one to interfere with the other. He also never talked about his work for *Confidential* because he enjoyed hanging out with Clark Gable and other stars at John Carroll and Lucille Ryman's ranch. But that didn't stop him from fact-checking a July 1955 *Confidential* plum story headlined "The Wife That Clark Gable Forgot."

Gable's first wife, Josephine, a former Broadway actress, discovered him in 1923 while she was running a theater group in Portland, Oregon. He was working as a telephone repairman but interested in acting. Dazzled by his handsome looks and the twinkle in his eyes, she taught him to act, talk properly, and carry himself with a newfound confidence, as well as cooking for him when he was broke. Despite being ten years his senior, Josephine Dillon became Mrs. Josephine Gable. She eventually took him to Hollywood, where he was cast in a series of small roles until he made noise in 1931 as the villain in *The Painted Desert*, after which he dumped her to marry another woman, Maria Langham.

Confidential got a tip from one of Gable's recent jilted lovers about Josephine now living in a run-down North Hollywood barn, with Gable ignoring her after their divorce and telling her to stop using his last name. She complied. But when she became ill, she reached out to him to help pay her hospital bill. He refused.

Once Otash confirmed the facts with Josephine, the story opened like this: "Is it wrong to ignore the woman who launched you on your way to the top, while showering gems, furs, gowns and money on a little French model? Is it wrong to hand one wife a million-dollar settlement [meaning Maria Langham, whom he had since divorced]—and let another grub to pay the grocer?"

The story's impact was seismic. Newsstands could barely keep enough issues in stock, and it sold 3.7 million copies, the biggest newsstand sale of *any* single magazine issue in history.

MGM's publicity department went into damage control. Though this was nearly twenty years after *Gone with the Wind*, Gable remained a big earner for the studio, having recently starred in director John Ford's 1953 Technicolor romantic adventure drama, *Mogambo*, opposite Ava Gardner and Grace Kelly. The flacks arm-twisted newspaper columnists to call the allegations a pack of lies and allowed respectable magazines like *Look* direct access to Gable to induce them to publish glowing pieces about him.

Confidential editor Marjorie Meade fought back, persuading Josephine to write a first-person follow-up to the original story. Josephine pointed out the factual holes in Gable's spin, like their actual age difference, which Otash considered to be basic fact-checking.

Gable needed to make a countermove fast, so he agreed to buy Josephine's dilapidated house from her at a discount price, fix it up, and let her continue living there. MGM publicity convinced reporters to gush about Gable's magnanimous gesture, which was nothing more than a good real estate deal and a way to put the story behind him.

Seven years after Robert Mitchum's drug bust, his and Otash's lives would intersect again when *Confidential* dug up a doozy. Wasted after guzzling down a quart of gin at a wrap party celebrating the completion of principal photography on *The Night of the Hunter*, Mitchum stripped naked in front of everyone and slathered ketchup all over his body.

"I'm a hamburger," Mitchum joked, thinking he was being hilarious. While his crude attempt at humor horrified and offended all in attendance, the occurrence made for great raunchy reading in *Confidential*. A public relations nightmare ensued, prompting Mitchum to file a lawsuit seeking $1 million in damages.

Under a plan hatched by his lawyer, Mitchum sent his younger brother John on a mission to infiltrate Hollywood Research. The plan was for John to tell Otash that he had some real dirt on his brother, but he first wanted to find out what they had on him so he could confirm the sordid stories. Otash smelled a rat and sent John Mitchum on his way.

In fact, Mitchum's lawyer was Jerry Giesler, who was working *with* Otash on divorce cases at the same time he filed Mitchum's lawsuit. But Giesler and Otash shrugged off any conflict of interest as nothing to see here, just business as usual in Hollywood, where you sometimes ended up on the same side as your adversary.

Giesler had grown disgusted by the passivity and ineffectiveness the movie studios had against *Confidential* dragging their stars through the mud. The problem would only get worse unless someone took them on.

In 1955, after filing suit for Mitchum, Giesler convinced smoky-voiced fashion model turned actress Lizabeth Scott to sue the magazine for $2.5 million after it reported that she was a lesbian. The outcome was never made public, but it was believed the case was settled out of court for an undisclosed sum.

―――――――――――

Confidential developed a rhythm for producing stories. Once a report of some chicanery came in, Otash would investigate. If he could confirm the dirt that was being shoveled, Harrison would then send his niece Marjorie Meade to visit the subject of the hit-job article. She'd present a copy of the article with an offer to deep-six it for better dirt on another celebrity. Everyone was fair game and everyone gave tips to Hollywood Research—maids, bellmen, waiters, caterers, janitors, journalists, and cops. Some did it for money, others for revenge. And there was always room for a trade.

Cohn's mobster pal Johnny Roselli wanted to make an upcoming story in *Confidential* about comedy giant Jerry Lewis disappear. He had a soft spot for the biggest comedy box-office draw at Paramount Pictures because Lewis always treated Roselli and his cohorts with respect and gave them free tickets to his shows. But the problem was, the mercurial comedian-actor-director had just fired his errand boy for no apparent reason. Feeling wronged, the gofer tattled about the abortions Lewis had been responsible for, and how he sexually forced himself on a female costar. Lewis appealed to Roselli, who then sat down with Otash and asked him to mediate.

"That guy he fired is full of shit, Fred," Roselli declared.

"He's convincing, John," Otash replied. "I recorded him for three hours and I have a pretty good bullshit meter."

"Look, Jerry's married . . . he's got a family . . . he makes people laugh," Roselli explained. "So he fucks around a little, so what?"

"A little?" Otash quipped. "He's lucky I haven't reported him to the cops or slapped him around myself."

"Okay, okay, I'll get him to calm down, tell him to use a fucking rubber," Roselli promised. "How do we make this go away?"

"It's not up to me. It's up to Bob Harrison," Otash answered. Then he started thinking out loud because his job required it.

"Maybe if the gofer retracts everything and uh, I don't know, somehow gets his job back, and Jerry stops treating girls like shit, Harrison will reconsider."

After the magazine was reimbursed for investigating the story and Roselli, through intermediaries, sent a tip Harrison's way, the story was killed. The errand boy got his job back and Lewis escaped marriage and career-ending exposure. Sixty-five years would pass before the ugly truth about Lewis's sexual assaults of multiple female costars was made public.

Marilyn and DiMaggio were the gift that kept on giving for *Confidential,* which would also turn out well for Otash. After two years of dating, and with Joe Schenck's tight grip loosened, Marilyn married DiMaggio on January 14, 1954, at San Francisco City Hall. They were mobbed by reporters and fans after Marilyn accidentally revealed her wedding plans to someone at 20th Century Fox who leaked it to the press.

Their honeymoon in Japan was interrupted when she was asked to perform for American soldiers stationed in Korea. She couldn't say no to our boys in uniform and left her angry new husband alone in the hotel suite to stew while she wowed the soldiers with her warmth and outsize sex appeal.

After the newlyweds returned to the States, Joltin' Joe decided that he didn't like his wife's sexpot image. One night in September, Marilyn was in New York shooting the iconic scene in *The Seven Year Itch* of her standing over a subway grate with the air blowing up her skirt. Press photographers snapped pictures and onlookers cheered take after take after take, unlike DiMaggio, who was on set watching. And fuming. He became so irate that he stormed off without telling Marilyn, then emotionally abused her when she came home.

The two separated in late September and Marilyn filed for divorce. On October 28, 1954, she stood in a Santa Monica courtroom and testified that DiMaggio had treated her with "coldness and indifference" when she had expected "love, warmth, and affection." The presiding judge granted her petition on the grounds of mental cruelty, and she walked out of the courthouse with an uncontested divorce. Her lawyer was, of course, Jerry Giesler.

Otash's good friend and Marilyn's close confidant, gossip columnist Sidney Skolsky, gave him the skinny one day over lunch at Schwab's—the romance was more myth than reality, as Otash had suspected. DiMaggio was in love with Marilyn, but her feelings weren't reciprocal. She never intended to make DiMaggio more than a brief relationship. He also bored her to tears with his desire for her to be a housewife by day and watch TV at home with him at night.

But DiMaggio couldn't get over her. His obsession was revealed in the powerhouse September 1955 issue of *Confidential* headlined "From a Detective's Report: The Real Reason for Marilyn Monroe's Divorce."

During their marriage, DiMaggio was certain that Marilyn was having a love affair with her friend, actress Sheila Stewart. He believed that if he caught Marilyn and Sheila in bed together, she'd come back to him rather than risk him publicly exposing her sexual proclivities. And so in November 1954, he hired Barney Ruditsky, a top-notch, fifty-year-old gumshoe, to bug Marilyn's home, and tail her and call him immediately whenever she and Sheila were together.

Ruditsky, along with his young associate Phil Irwin, kept close tabs on Marilyn. One night, Irwin determined that Marilyn was heading to Sheila Stewart's apartment on Kilkea Drive, a quiet street in West Hollywood, where he spotted Marilyn's black Cadillac convertible in front of the two-story building. He then drove to a phone booth and alerted Ruditsky, who in turn raced over to join him.

When it was determined they couldn't see into Sheila's apartment, Ruditsky told Irwin to stay put while he went to a phone booth to alert DiMaggio, who it turned out was having dinner with Frank Sinatra at the nearby Villa Capri restaurant in Hollywood.

Ten minutes later, DiMaggio arrived with Sinatra, along with Villa Capri owner Patsy D'Amore, the restaurant's maître d', and Sinatra's manager/bodyguard as reinforcements. With booze clouding DiMaggio's judgment, he began threatening to go inside and kill Marilyn.

Sinatra grabbed him by his shoulders. "Are you out of your mind?!" he implored. "She's not worth going to the electric chair over. No broad is."

But DiMaggio was hell-bent. Ruditsky feared the worst, especially since Sinatra's bodyguard was packing heat. Desperate to defuse the situation, he came up with a sordid plan—they'd storm the apartment together and catch the two women in the act. Everyone bought into it.

The seven men snuck upstairs to the apartment Ruditsky identified as Sheila's. Then he kicked the door in. They went inside the dark apartment and into the bedroom. Irwin took flash pictures with his camera. A woman screamed. Sinatra turned on a table lamp, revealing a woman named Florence

Kotz. She was on her bed, wearing a nightie and scared out of her mind. They had broken into the wrong apartment!

Panicked, the men got the hell out of there, ran down the stairs to their cars, and drove away before the police arrived.

The police did an investigation, but Florence Kotz was too frazzled to know who had broken in. The landlady claimed she saw a man who looked like Sinatra leaving the scene of the crime. The cops wrote it off as an attempted robbery and left it as an open case.

But there was another corroborating witness—Marilyn. As soon as she heard the scream, she went onto Sheila's balcony to see what was going on. Once she spotted the cars and watched them flee in terror, she knew who was there and why. But she stayed mum, not wanting to call any attention to the situation.

Everyone went on with their lives, except for Irwin whose life was unraveling. His excessive drinking and womanizing had ended his marriage, plus he was in a financial rut and needed a way to climb out. So, he stole the case folder that Ruditsky created to document the raid, showed it to the Meades at *Confidential*, and told all.

Ten months after the break-in debacle occurred, *Confidential* broke the story and printed over four million copies of what was infamously called the "Wrong Door Raid," the most explosive story in that publication's history. Otash had to go out of town on business for Giesler, so the Meades turned to Polly Gould, a PI they had used in the past to vet the story, which checked out.

DiMaggio was embarrassed, but his reputation was only temporarily sullied. His loyal baseball fans forgave and forgot. Sinatra hated being ridiculed for his bumbling actions, but his standing quickly recovered when his new recording rose to the top of the charts.

Ruditsky wasn't as fortunate. He lost his private investigator's license. Irwin's penalty was getting beaten up and then deposited in a phone booth by Sinatra's friends—at least he assumed it was Sinatra's guys.

Sinatra didn't know it then, but the story would set off a chain of events that would have far-reaching consequences for him and for *Confidential*. It would also thrust Fred Otash into the national spotlight.

SIX

THE WEE SMALL HOURS

B y the 1950s, Wheaties had gained massive popularity as the "Breakfast of Champions." Packaged in a bright orange box with famous sports figures on the cover, the iconic breakfast cereal was marketed to consumers as a healthy way to nourish a fit and active lifestyle. According to a tip to *Confidential* from one of Frank Sinatra's lovers, the megastar always ate a bowl of Wheaties before sex, then consumed three more between encore performances. That tidbit inspired the magazine's May 1956 story headlined "Here's Why Frank Sinatra Is the Tarzan of the Boudoir." Otash joked that Sinatra's face should grace every box. Still pissed-off at *Confidential* for the 1955 "Wrong Door Raid" story, and no doubt annoyed that his latest album, *In the Wee Small Hours*, failed to hit No. 1 on the *Billboard* album chart, the thin-skinned Sinatra threatened to sue.

S inatra wasn't the only celebrity getting fed up with *Confi-dential* for tarnishing their polished personas. Stars were growing litigious and the lawsuits were piling up. Tobacco heiress and socialite Doris Duke sued for $3 million after a story reported she had an affair with a former Black handyman and chauffeur. In the lawsuit filed by Jerry Giesler, she claimed that *Confidential*'s implication of "indecent acts" was "completely and entirely false and untrue," exposed her to "disgrace, contempt and ridicule," and that the sole purpose for her suit was "to defend her good name against the ugly, unfounded and scurrilous attack" and "to discourage this magazine and others of its ilk from making similar unfounded attacks on innocent people." In 1957, the case was settled for a substantial sum.

In the wake of these and other lawsuits, Harrison began giving way to his original policy of never settling a claim. Otash, who was receiving ample praise from clients for his meticulous investigations, reassured Harrison that the stories he investigated had enough backup to withstand legal challenges. But nobody bats a thousand, not Babe Ruth, not Joe DiMaggio, and not Fred Otash.

In July 1957, *Confidential* outed Liberace as a homosexual. Ever flamboyant with coiffed hair and custom-made suits, tabloid trouble came after he made unwanted moves on a young and straight male press agent while on tour in Akron, Ohio, and again in Dallas.

Otash must have been overconfident about the story's veracity, given that the self-proclaimed piano virtuoso had hit on him in a Hollywood dive bar while working as an undercover police officer. But Liberace didn't take it lying down and publicly proclaimed he was heterosexual. Otash scoffed at the career-saving move. What he didn't bet on was that Liberace had concrete proof that the dates of the accusations didn't jibe with his touring schedule. He sued the magazine for $20 million. The case was eventually settled for $40,000, which he donated to charity.

Maybe Otash was spread too thin. In addition to *Confidential*, he had taken on a heavy workload to build his business while continuing an active social life. He was also spending as much time as possible with his now six-year-old daughter, Colleen, who looked forward to their weekly outings at Kiddieland. The popular amusement park was frequented by Hollywood elites and Sunday bachelor dads like Fred, who, dressed in tailored suit and tie, somehow managed to squeeze his strapping six-foot-two frame into the small carnival rides with his little girl. What else could explain his sloppy work on the Maureen O'Hara story?

Red-haired and radiant, O'Hara was catapulted to Hollywood stardom in the 1940s after a series of critically acclaimed roles in hit films such as director John Ford's *How Green Was My Valley*, *The Black Swan* starring Tyrone Power, and opposite an eight-year-old Natalie Wood in the Christmas classic *Miracle on 34th Street*. When the magazine uncovered that the Irish-born actress had been more than canoodling with her Mexican lover while seated in the last row of Grauman's Chinese Theatre during a matinee, she filed a $5 million libel suit.

True, she was having a romantic liaison with a Mexico City hotel man who fit the exact description of the man the two Grauman's ushers spotted with O'Hara. But the day they said it happened didn't match the day stamped on her passport, proving that she was in London at the time and not in the famous Hollywood movie theater.

Simply put, Otash had screwed up. He felt terribly that he left Harrison legally vulnerable and wanted to make it up to him. That chance came in 1957 when he got a call from his own attorney, Arthur Crowley, asking him to help Sinatra beat a perjury charge that had resulted from *Confidential's* "Wrong Door Raid" story.

Crowley explained to Otash that a California Senate committee investigating tabloid magazines had dug into the two-year-old story and subpoenaed the records of Hollywood Research Inc., as well as Marjorie Meade, DiMaggio, and Sinatra to testify. DiMaggio was back in New York and out of reach of a subpoena but gave a written deposition stating that the *Confidential* story was sensationalized. Sinatra, however, testified under oath that he stood by the car smoking cigarettes as he waited for DiMaggio and the others to talk with Marilyn inside the apartment, an assertion that both detective Phil Irwin and the landlady contradicted during their sworn testimonies. The committee members seemed to believe Irwin was telling the truth because he had been beaten up for selling the story to *Confidential*. "Right now it is our educated guess that he could be indicted for contempt at least, and for perjury at most . . . he could go to jail," Crowley told Otash.

To make matters worse, the LA district attorney had convened a grand jury to determine if DiMaggio, Sinatra, and the others involved should be indicted for conspiracy to commit criminal mischief.

Crowley needed Otash to corroborate Sinatra's claim that he hadn't been in the apartment. Otash didn't know if Sinatra had committed perjury or not but didn't think he should go to jail over such a trivial matter. If he took the case, Otash would be working for and against *Confidential* and for and against Sinatra—a dicey proposition. When Crowley implied that Sinatra would not sue the magazine over the Wheaties story, Otash saw an opening to use the conflict of interest to his— and the magazine's—advantage. He went to Harrison and explained the symbiotic angle that working for Sinatra would give his boss one less lawsuit to worry about, which was just fine with the besieged publisher.

Otash went to work. He drew up a diagram of the apartment building so he could study its ins and outs. Then, with a court reporter present, he interrogated the landlady. The break-in happened at night, but she claimed she saw Sinatra "plain as day." It was meant as a figure of speech, but Otash felt he could turn it to Sinatra's advantage.

After the interview was over, he did a midafternoon search of the area for any outside lighting. There was none. Nor were there any streetlights near the apartment building. When he returned that night and examined all the doorways, he couldn't see a thing. He still wanted more evidence to bolster his case, so he gathered information from the weather bureau that established there was no moonlight on the night of the raid, making any visual identification impossible. Unless Sinatra was serenading her personally, there was no way the landlady could make a positive ID.

To button things up, he visited his old pal and fellow detective Barney Ruditsky, who, due to poor health, had been excused from testifying. Ruditsky told Otash that Irwin lied to the committee about staking out the apartment all night when, in fact, he was driving around with his wife earlier in the evening, trying to patch up his marriage after she caught him repeatedly lying about his infidelities.

Otash had enough to prove Irwin was a liar. He didn't ask or want to know if Sinatra was in the apartment because he had enough to absolve him. He also knew that Ruditsky would fall on the sword for Sinatra out of loyalty to his well-paying client Joe DiMaggio. But he sensed Ruditsky was holding back information.

"Something doesn't add up, Barney," Otash said. "You had Marilyn under surveillance and knew exactly where Sheila lived."

"So?" Ruditsky replied.

"C'mon, you were too good at your job. How the hell could you not identify Sheila's apartment?"

Ruditsky chuckled. "Of course I knew. I broke into the wrong goddamn apartment to save DiMaggio from doing something crazy."

"You did the right thing, Barney," Otash said.

"A lot of good it did me," Ruditsky said. "I lost my license. Don't be a schmuck like me, Fred. The last thing you need in this job is a conscience."

Otash laughed knowingly.

Although he had privately concluded that Sinatra was indeed in the apartment, Otash cast enough doubt on the landlady's story and Irwin's credibility that the committee exonerated Sinatra, who, thanks to Otash's work, avoided a grand jury indictment. Prior to this, the two men had been friendly acquaintances who always exchanged pleasantries whenever they bumped into each other. Now Sinatra avoided Otash like the plague because he knew he knew the truth. Surprisingly, the committee didn't indict Irwin despite having evidence that he lied. But they did cite Otash with contempt when he wouldn't reveal his sources or turn over his *Confidential* files.

Crowley eagerly sprang into action on Otash's behalf. He accused the committee of violating the state's professional code of conduct, which prohibits a private detective from divulging information except to law enforcement agencies, reminding them that they were not a law enforcement agency nor entitled to the information. He also scorched them for wanting to divulge that information so they could grandstand about it on national television. After a closed-door session, the committee backed down.

The magazine was now clearly in the political and legal crosshairs of state authorities. California attorney general Edmund "Pat" Brown convened a Los Angeles County grand jury and indicted *Confidential* on charges of conspiracy to commit criminal libel, plus conspiracy to publish obscene and indecent material.

Brown believed the magazine was a scourge on society. He was also pressured by studio bosses to do something about it. They made it clear that he'd have their deep-pocketed financial support in his upcoming run for governor if he drove *Confidential* into the ground.

From his own sources, Otash suspected Joe Kennedy as a prime mover on this as well, leaning on and advising fellow Democrat Brown that this was smart politics. It also wouldn't hurt if magazines like *Confidential* were driven out of business to protect his son Jack's philandering from being exposed.

In the September 1957 issue, titled *Hollywood vs. Confidential*, Harrison wrote that the charges were a "determined effort, initiated by a segment of the motion picture industry, to 'get' this magazine." He pointed out the hypocrisy of California accusing his magazine of a crime, the crime of telling the truth, while lying and falsehood was Hollywood's stock in trade.

While his assertion rang true, it didn't lessen the gravity of his situation. He was able to sidestep attempts to extradite him from New York to Los Angeles to stand trial. But Marjorie and Frederic Meade lived in the jurisdiction and faced three years in jail and a $5,000 fine if they were found guilty.

As much as he hated to settle, Harrison began negotiating with the prosecutors Brown assigned to the case to protect the Meades. They were open to it, but Superior Court judge Herbert V. Walker, who once was an extra in a movie called *Bill the Office Boy*, rejected it. He appeared to be angling for the attention this high-profile case could bring him, knowing that newspaper reporters from all over the world would be covering the trial inside his courtroom.

Crowley, the magazine's defense lawyer, announced that he'd be subpoenaing two hundred members of the film industry to force them to testify under oath that what *Confidential* had written about them was true. This, as Crowley explained, "resulted in an exodus from Hollywood that rivaled Moses leaving Egypt," with stars like Sinatra bolting out of town to avoid being served by Otash. Others weren't so lucky and couldn't duck him.

The studio mavens worried that their stars' testimonies would be humiliating. They urged Brown to quash the subpoenas, but he couldn't. The best he could do was pressure California distributors to stop carrying the magazine.

Harrison fretted that *Confidential*'s anonymous tipsters, the lifeblood of his magazine, would be revealed. The tattlers, in turn, were petrified that if their identities were disclosed, their lives would be upended.

Otash felt he was just getting started as a Hollywood PI and was worried that he would be tarred with the same broad brush that was tarring Harrison. The trial was in progress and in the news when he maneuvered his way for an invitation to appear on *The Mike Wallace Interview* show. His logic was twofold: to separate himself from the magazine while promoting his burgeoning detective business.

Before he was a take-no-prisoners award-winning correspondent on *60 Minutes*, Mike Wallace hosted a half-hour nationally televised one-on-one interview program on ABC aptly called *The Mike Wallace Interview*. On it, he grilled controversial guests with gotcha questions, but Otash was confident he could handle himself on the hot seat and not undermine the magazine's trial defense—especially since Wallace's secretary, who knew Otash and had brought him to the attention of Wallace, gave him the questions in advance. All in all, he felt the appearance could boost his profile and result in more business.

Wallace opened the episode by plugging his sponsor, Philip Morris, and then, with the two men seated across from each other smoking cigarettes, grilled Otash about what he did for a living.

Wallace first questioned Otash about money, with Fred revealing that he earned about $25,000 a year from *Confidential* and about $100,000 a year overall from his PI business (more than $1 million in today's dollars).

"Aside from the money, Fred, what other reason do you have for working for *Confidential*? What satisfaction, if any, do you get out of working for them?" Wallace asked acidly.

"I get no personal satisfaction. I've no axe to grind with anyone that's exposed in an exposé magazine. I get an assignment to do a certain job, and I do a certain job," he answered calmly.

"Pure and simple, a job. No personal satisfaction whatsoever?" a skeptical Wallace asked again.

"To me, it's a job," Otash answered. "I look at it very objectively and try to determine if the facts and the items are true."

Wallace drilled down. "You don't feel it's an invasion of privacy? Let's not talk about legality here, Fred, but about morality. How do you square that with yourself with just plain human decency?"

Otash cleared his throat, then measured his words. "I look at it through a different set of eyes probably, Mike, like you would or maybe a reader would. Being a private investigator is a dirty job. There's no two ways about it because you're always dabbling into the life of an individual. But I just take it in stride."

"But you take any case that pays you money, is that not so?" Wallace asked pointedly.

"Well, no, not any case. Now, I won't take a case for a member of the Communist Party or a communist. I sort of draw the line there," Otash replied, still unruffled.

Wallace tried to trip him up by asking loaded questions such as what Otash thought about *Confidential's* tipsters, about the junk stories in the magazine and about the people who read them. Otash said he didn't respect kiss-and-tellers, that he preferred *Reader's Digest* over exposé magazines, and had no opinion of people who read *Confidential*, but noted that there was clearly a market for them.

Otash held his own as he parried with Wallace, even when Wallace brought up his bogus suspension while on the LAPD, which Otash blamed on his spat with the straightlaced Parker in a world where straightlaced didn't get it done. His appearance garnered one of the highest ratings in the show's history, a 22.2 percent share of the audience that eclipsed Wallace's interview with mobster Mickey Cohen, whose appearance generated a paltry 17.1 percent share by comparison. "We don't think to go after ratings," Wallace told *Newsweek* on September 16, 1957. "Not a thing. There is nothing in the world you can do, except to try to get people about who the country is curious. That is the big factor." Undoubtedly, the appearance was a big factor in cementing Otash's status as the go-to PI in Hollywood.

––––––––––––

The trial turned out to be the kind of spectacle that, if *Confidential* weren't the defendant, Harrison would have loved to cover. It had everything—a showboating judge, witnesses who were red-faced with embarrassment, and strange trial-related coincidences occurring outside the courtroom.

Clark Gable's former jilted lover, who gave the tip that led to "The Wife That Clark Gable Forgot" story, tried to kill herself before testifying. It wasn't clear if it was the pressure of the trial or other issues, but when it was all over she fled the country to parts unknown.

Retired boxer Chalky Wright, Mae West's purported Black lover, died mysteriously in his bathtub on the eve of his testimony.

Prosecution witness Polly Gould, who fact-checked the "Wrong Door Raid" story, died from an apparent overdose of sleeping pills before she could testify.

Otash also made headlines when a prosecution witness, actress Corinne Calvet, accused him of threatening her outside the courtroom, an accusation he vehemently denied.

The bottom line, however, was that things weren't looking good for Harrison. *Confidential*'s distribution system was in shambles and news dealers feared prosecution for selling obscene material. Though he was still in New York, the daily reports from LA weren't encouraging. Crowley was putting up a fierce defense, but the prosecution was able to expose the names of tipsters. Even Frederic Meade was forced to confirm the accuracy of the tipster list.

Paul Gregory, who produced *The Night of the Hunter*, testified that Marjorie approached him sub rosa at a Hollywood restaurant and offered to kill a seedy story about him for a thousand dollars.

"It's not true! He's lying!" Marjorie cried out from the defense table, then collapsed dramatically and fainted.

After a doctor attended to her, the judge granted Crowley's motion to recess for the day. Otash used the time to find a witness Crowley could put on the stand to refute the bribery claim—the press agent for the Beverly Hills Hotel. The press agent testified that Marjorie had been in the hotel's Polo Lounge having a drink precisely when Paul Gregory alleged that she was bribing him in at a restaurant miles away.

Marjorie's friend Jackie O'Hara corroborated under oath that she was having a drink with Marjorie at the time of the bribery claim. Perhaps it was mere coincidence, but Miss O'Hara was also Otash's former girlfriend.

During Crowley's summation to the jury, he argued free speech First Amendment rights, citing great works of American literature that included passages, which in the eyes of the beholder, could be deemed as obscene. But mainly he tried to plant a seed of reasonable doubt in the jurors' minds and muddy the waters. Otash felt that the muddier the waters, the better for all the accused. It worked. On October 1, 1957, after a record two-week deliberation, a hung jury emerged unable to reach a verdict, with seven voting to convict the Meades and five to acquit. A mistrial was declared, but prosecutors vowed to retry the case.

Faced with a costly retrial, Harrison entered into an agreement that *Confidential* would no longer publish stories about the private lives of celebrities. Because he relented, all charges were dropped except for one count of conspiring to publish obscene materials, which carried a fine of $5,000 (nearly $55,000 today). Hollywood Research closed its doors forever and the Meades went into the real estate business.

In April 1958, Harrison announced that *Confidential* was "quitting the area of private affairs for the arena of public affairs." But without the magic ingredient of scandal, readership plunged to 200,000—a far cry from its heyday just three years earlier when the magazine broke all newsstand records with sales of 5 million copies, making it one of the best-selling publications in the nation and netting Harrison Publishing $1.2 million to $1.4 million a year (about $8.5

million to $10 million today). A month later, Harrison sold *Confidential.*

Undoubtedly, Harrison had ushered in an entire genera-tion of seamier tabloid publications like the *National Enquirer,* whose stories could be vicious and reckless—and oftentimes simply made up with no basis in fact. They would become even more crafty in couching their stories to prevent lawsuits. *Confidential* seemed quaint by comparison.

Though Harrison faded into obscurity, Otash's career continued on the upswing. In just two years after setting up shop, the publicity garnered from the *Confidential* case and Mike Wallace interview had capitulated Otash to becoming one of the nation's top private detectives, working for approx-imately one hundred law firms all over the country. Within the Hollywood community, who had seen him walk through the raindrops and come out clean during the biggest tabloid scandal in U.S. history, Otash was now *the* PI to call whenever you got into a jam, because chances were he'd get you out— that is, if you needed something done surreptitiously.

Above: The warranty for an Oriental rug dated February 17, 1919, handwritten on the original, official stationery for Habib F. Otash & Son, the Otash family's Oriental rug and carpet business at Marston's Corner in Methuen, Massachusetts, established in 1895.

Right: Marion Otash with her six-year-old son Freddie outside their home in Methuen, Massachusetts (circa 1928).

Above: Twenty-two-year-old Marine Corps Staff Sergeant Fred Otash at 53rd NCB Camp, Bougainville, British Solomon Islands (circa 1944).

Left: Twenty-year-old Private Fred Otash in his Marine Service Uniform (1941).

Below: Twenty-year-old Marine Corps Private Fred Otash at the Fraternity House in New York City (1942).

Above: Twenty-one-year-old Marine Corps Private Fred Otash in Honolulu before deployment to the Solomon Islands during World War II (circa 1943).

Above: Marine Sergeants Fred Otash (*left*) and Doyle Nigh at El Toro Marine Base, California (1945).

Below: CSU strikers and nonstrikers clash outside the employee entrance at Warner Bros. Studios in Burbank, California, on October 5, 1945. (Credit: *Los Angeles Times* Photographic Archive, UCLA Library Special Collections)

Above: Fred Otash's LAPD head shot (circa 1947).

Above: Fred Otash LAPD Assistance Card (*front and back*).

Below: Rookie police officer Fred Otash at Los Angeles
Police Department headquarters (circa 1946).

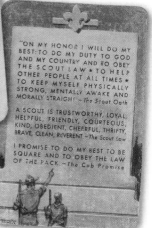

Above: Assistant Scout Master Fred Otash (*far right*) with his LAPD Boy Scout Troop 174 (circa 1947).

Left: Fred Otash Boy Scoutmaster Card (1947) (*front and back*).

Opposite: Doris Houck photographed at the Savoy-Plaza Hotel in New York (circa 1946).

Above: Doris Houck acting head shot (circa 1945).

Below: Fred and Doris at Tom Breneman's famous Hollywood Restaurant, inscribed "To My Darling Little Baby Doll, Love Fred" (circa 1948).

Above: Doris (on "Freckles") and Fred (on "Topper") while vacationing at the Pan Hot Springs Hotel in Big Bear, California (August 1948).

Below: Doris and Fred on the deck of the Houck family's cabin in Big Bear, California (August 1948).

Above: Doris and Fred sit on the wall by the outdoor pool at the Pan Hot Springs Hotel while vacationing with Doris's parents in Big Bear, California (August 1948).

Below: Doris and Fred sitting with their dogs on Ocean Park Beach in Santa Monica, California (July 7, 1948).

Above: Doris and Fred sit underneath the tree at her home on North Bentley Avenue in Bel Air, California (Christmas Eve, 1948).

Left: Doris and Fred embrace on New Year's Eve at her home on North Bentley Avenue in Bel Air, California (1948).

Above: A photo taken by Doris Houck of Fred riding atop "Red Boy" at Du Brock's Riding Academy near Griffith Park (circa 1948).

Right: Fred poses in front of Doris's car with their dog (circa 1948).

Above: Fred (*right*) and best friend Frank Mancini hold five-month-old Colleen on Christmas Eve 1949.

Below: Fred poses with six-month-old daughter Colleen (December 1949).

Above: Fred, Doris, and Colleen in the backyard of Doris's
parents' home in Mar Vista, California (June 1951).

Below: Fred Otash's license to carry a pistol (1951).

Above: Two-year-old Colleen holds hands with her parents outside their VA home on Lake Street in Venice, California, on Mother's Day 1951.

Below: Fred with Colleen by the pool at his apartment on Kings Road in West Hollywood (April 1953).

SEVEN

A MARILYN MONROE PRODUCTION

t was a Saturday morning in early 1956 when Otash arrived promptly at 9 a.m. for a hastily arranged breakfast at Nate 'n' Al's in Beverly Hills. The small, unpretentious, namesake Jewish deli on North Beverly Drive, renowned for its authentic kosher fare and too-big-to-bite corned beef and pastrami sandwiches, had long been a popular local haunt with a litany of loyal showbiz patrons since Nate Rimer and Al Mendelson first opened its doors in 1945. Rita Hayworth, Ava Gardner, and James Garner were among its myriad movie star regulars, as was Doris Day, who, as legend has it, stopped by early every morning in her bathrobe to grab breakfast.

A favored regular since his early days as a police officer, Otash was known simply as "Freddie" to the troop of long-standing waitresses, one of whom instinctively led him to his unofficial booth where he always sat with his back to the wall to catch all the action. His old buddy Sidney Skolsky, the famous gossip columnist and radio personality who helped champion his close friend and confidante Marilyn Monroe to stardom, joined Fred moments later. But what really turned heads was the arrival of E. Maurice Adler— "Buddy" to his friends, the famous silver-haired forty-nine-year-old producer of the seminal World War II romantic drama *From Here to Eternity*, which nearly swept the Academy Awards and was one of the highest-grossing films of 1953. As he anxiously made a beeline for Fred's table, all eyes were on Adler, who should have been in a better mood, considering he had recently replaced Darryl F. Zanuck as head of production at 20th Century Fox.

Adler was knee-deep in principal photography on *Bus Stop*, the romantic dramatic comedy headlined by Marilyn Monroe and directed by revered Broadway and motion picture writer-director Joshua Logan, whose many accolades included a Pulitzer Prize and Tony Award for cowriting and directing *South Pacific*. *Bus Stop* would mark a pivotal point in both their careers. For Marilyn, it was the first film produced under her new Marilyn Monroe Productions banner, which she established shortly after her divorce from Joe DiMaggio in 1954 before announcing it to the world via a statement she read to eighty journalists and friends from her lawyer's home on East Sixty-Fourth Street in New York City on January 7, 1955.

Monroe had grown tired of being systematically typecast in the blonde-bombshell roles that had made her famous in previous films and the $1,500 (about $17,000 in today's dollars) a week salary she was still earning under her current contract, a paltry sum compared to fellow stars of her caliber. She wanted more dramatic roles, more freedom to control her own destiny, and to be paid her worth. After a year of negotiations and legal maneuvering, she ultimately prevailed by leveraging her huge success the previous summer in the monster box-office hit *The Seven Year Itch*. Marilyn secured a new contract with 20th Century Fox, who, in addition to forking over a substantial check for past earnings, would pay her $100,000 per film (about $1.1 million today) over a seven-year period, with the studio granting her story, director, and cinematographer approval, revolutionary for an actor of that era.

Monroe would comment on the impetus behind her maverick move during an interview on Edward R. Murrow's popular *Person to Person* television show on April 8, 1955, broadcast live from the kitchen of famed celebrity photographer Milton Greene's home, a 150-year-old converted barn in Weston, Connecticut, where Marilyn had been staying with Greene, his wife, Amy, and one-year-old son Joshua. It was also the same location where she and Greene, the newly named vice president of Marilyn Monroe Productions, had first hatched their plan to form her own production company a few months earlier after Marilyn had fled Hollywood for New York in the middle of the night to forge a new life and career far and away from the tight grasp of the long-established studio system. When Murrow asked her if it was fair to say that she got rather tired of playing the same kind of roles all the time and wanted to try something different, Marilyn gently replied, "Well, I . . . it's . . . it's not that I object to doing musicals or comedies—in fact, I rather enjoy it—but I would like to do also dramatic parts, too."

Otash studied Adler's demeanor as he approached the table. He could tell he was nervous. After a swift introduction by Skolsky and a brief exchange of pleasantries, Adler got straight to the point.

"Marilyn has disappeared," he said quietly, almost under his breath.

"What do you mean she disappeared?" Otash asked.

Adler explained they were now filming interiors at the studio and Marilyn hadn't shown up for work the day before, nor called in to explain her absence. Nobody had seen or heard from her in the last twenty-four hours, not even her newlywed husband Arthur Miller, the famous Pulitzer Prize–winning playwright and supposed love of her life who was in New York and worried sick. When she was on set, Marilyn's erratic behavior had already cost Adler too much time and money, and a recent hospitalization while on location in Idaho for nervous tension had pushed the film way over budget.

Adler said he would have fired her and recast the role if he could, but they were now halfway through the shooting schedule and there was no turning back. The production had crossed the Rubicon, and the studio was losing about forty grand every day she was MIA. Adler needed Otash to find Monroe as soon as possible and get her back on set. If not, they would have no choice but to shut down the film, which would cost the studio an unprecedented amount of money. Otash asked why they thought Marilyn would suddenly disappear like this. Skolsky hypothesized that perhaps the pressures and challenges of her first major dramatic role had taken its toll. Adler said that it didn't really matter, but if she didn't return to work soon, he would have to scrap the film—which Otash knew could result in Adler losing his job.

Still, Otash could sense that Adler was different from most studio honchos. Despite the corporate grandstanding, his tone indicated he genuinely cared about Marilyn's well-being, not just the bottom line.

Otash promised he would make this his priority—a priority that would soon establish him in his new Hollywood role as "the fixer."

When he got to his office, Otash began rifling through his many files and multiple Rolodexes, searching for clients and people he'd investigated to see if there was a connection to Marilyn. Through an attorney client, he got a tip on a witness who had been close to Monroe, but he didn't seem like someone she would be sexually attracted to, which would imply there might be something else going on. Otash had a job to do but he was also concerned that, given her current state of mind, Marilyn might be vulnerable enough to do something stupid, and he didn't want that to happen on his watch.

He called an LAPD detective friend who he knew had access to Chief William Parker's files on known associates of celebrities. The detective was able to find the name Otash had given him. It was not good news—the guy was a junkie who was heavily into heroin. Even though Marilyn, despite all her booze and pills, had never been into hard drugs, this guy could spell trouble for her.

Otash then hired Barney Ruditsky, DiMaggio's private investigator, partnered him with one of his own nine investigators, Norman Placey, and had them set out to find this lowlife—and hopefully Marilyn. They started by checking railroad, bus, and airline records, but came up empty. Otash knew from the gossip columnists that when movie stars wanted to travel under the radar, they would often use a travel agency that booked the trip under an alias and kept the itinerary in a confidential file, as the columnists would often pay off the low-level agency clerks for the information. He then called his travel agency mole with whom he had a trusted relationship, but rather than reveal the name he was looking for, Otash paid for two weeks of bookings up front, so the guy would have no idea whom he was trying to tail. He then combed over the agency lists again and again, looking for "Marilyn Monroe" or some similar name, an alias, or a maiden name she might have used, but nothing stood out. However, every time he looked over the list the name "Pearl Baker" caught his eye, though he didn't quite know why, so Otash called Skolsky to see if that name rang a bell . . . and it did. "Gladys" Pearl Baker was Marilyn Monroe's mother.

Otash ran point from his office as he sent Ruditsky and Placey to the Santa Barbara address he had found in the travel agency's booking list, a cheap, run-down, off-the-beaten-path motel. Before Barney acted, he called Fred from a nearby phone booth to ask if he should bust into the room.

Otash was faced with a dilemma. Marilyn was a grown woman, responsible for her own actions. If she wanted to shack up in a fleabag hotel room with some deadbeat, that was her right. The PIs had no legal right to enter her room and, essentially, take Marilyn against her will and return her to the studio to complete a film. He decided it was a small risk. Since the studios had so much power over their actresses—Marilyn included—he was certain she wouldn't go to the police, so he told Barney to go ahead.

When Ruditsky knocked on the door saying that he had a delivery, a man's voice said he'd be right there. A moment later, he heard the interior door latch unhook and the drug addict in question opened the door wearing nothing but a pair of boxers.

Ruditsky announced that he was looking for Marilyn Monroe, shoved the man aside, and barged into the room with Placey right behind him. As the man fell to the floor, Ruditsky almost couldn't believe what he saw. Marilyn was lying naked on the bed frozen in a fetal position, and there were needles, syringes, and other drug paraphernalia strewn about the room. After quickly checking for a pulse and determining she was unconscious, he covered her body with a sheet. He then picked up the phone and apprised Otash of the situation, as Placey ordered the bewildered druggie to get dressed.

Otash told them to make sure Marilyn didn't need immediate medical attention and directed them to stand by while he phoned Adler and explained what they had found. Adler wanted her taken away from the motel safely and indiscriminately with all traces of her presence there erased. He told Fred that he would dispatch an ambulance to the scene to take her to a safe hospital for detoxing.

Back on the line with Ruditsky, Otash ordered him to clean up the place and take the lowlife to the nearest bus stop, where he was to buy him a one-way ticket to San Francisco and impress upon him that none of this ever happened—or it would be the last thing that ever happened to him.

The situation fixed, Marilyn would return to the set a few days later. When the press asked about her absence, a studio publicist explained that she had relapsed from her earlier hospitalization and merely needed a few more days' rest.

———————

When *Bus Stop* was released on August 31, 1956, Marilyn received some of the best critical raves of her career.

Bosley Crowther, the veteran film critic for the *New York Times* whose discerning reviews played a critical role in helping shape the careers of many actors, directors, and writers, praised that her new acting skills had transcended her previous bombshell roles, and that "Marilyn Monroe has finally proved herself an actress in *Bus Stop.*"

It was her breakthrough movie. Marilyn had given a performance that delivered on her latent talent, had gotten her wish, and her star would shine more brightly than ever. For Otash, the end result more than justified the means of helping get it there.

EIGHT

FOR THE LOVE OF LANA

O tash could tell it was personal from the tone of his voice. It was late 1957 when Steve Crane, the second of Lana Turner's seven ex-husbands and father to her only child, called Otash to meet him for lunch at the Tail o' the Cock. He said he wanted to talk business, but Fred figured that was bullshit given the not-so-secret, much-gossiped-about goings-on in Lana's personal life. And while he knew Crane didn't much give a damn anymore who his movie star ex-wife spent her leisure time with, how those affairs affected daddy's little girl was another story.

Had business been on the menu, Crane would've met Fred at the Luau, the popular Polynesian restaurant Crane owned on Rodeo Drive where A-list patrons dined on the "Feasts of the Seven Seas," served up with Crane's inimitable personality and signature style. There could be only one reason, Otash surmised, why Crane chose the Tail o' the Cock: discretion. For compared to his nearby Kon Tiki hotspot in Beverly

Hills, asking Fred to schlep an hour over Coldwater Canyon to an old-school steak house in the San Fernando Valley was equivalent to crossing state lines.

Freddie O, as he was now coined by clients and confidants, enjoyed hanging out with the beautiful people at the Luau where he forged a simpatico relationship with its hands-on proprietor. Handsome and charismatic, Crane's youthful attempts to forge an acting career at Columbia Pictures yielded little more than mediocre roles in B-movies due to his self-admitted lack of talent. Dreams of stardom notwithstanding, the now-successful forty-two-year-old Crane still received ample notoriety for his off-screen romances with Ava Gardner, Rita Hayworth, and Lana Turner.

An all-American beauty of the blonde-bombshell variety whose shapely five-foot-three figure personified larger-than-life sex appeal when projected on the big screen, the twenty-one-year-old Lana Turner was well on her way to becoming MGM's highest-paid leading lady when she met Joseph Stephenson "Steve" Crane at the Mocambo nightclub three weeks before their impromptu marriage on July 17, 1942. Four months later, when the tabloids trumpeted the shocking revelation that Crane was still officially wed to his first wife, a furious and humiliated Lana would seek an annulment to minimize the scandal. But when she later learned she was pregnant a month before his divorce was finalized, the ill-fated lovers remarried in Tijuana in March 1943.

MGM was not amused. But as long as Lana's legions of fans kept bringing in the box office, the general consensus among studio brass was to look the other way and hope for the best. Meanwhile, the publicity department went into overdrive to hastily announce the joyous news that their beloved screen goddess was expecting, and on July 25, 1943, daughter Cheryl Crane was born. A year later, however, citing Crane's incessant gambling and unemployment, Lana would end their marriage twice and for all.

In 1948, Crane would again become engaged to another MGM starlet, Lila Leeds, until the Lana Turner look-alike got busted along with rascal movie star Robert Mitchum for the then-serious criminal offense of smoking marijuana during a well-publicized narcotics raid on her Hollywood Hills home. Unbeknownst to the newly minted beat cop on the scene that night, Otash saved Crane the pain of what would have likely been his third divorce.

Indeed, that honor went to twenty-eight-year-old actress Martine Carol, yet another flaxen-haired femme fatale whom Crane wed while rebounding in Monaco later that year. Martine would become one of French cinema's top box-office draws during their marriage, but by 1953, the newly anointed Gallic version of Marilyn Monroe, as renowned for her beauty as she was for her tumultuous lifestyle, would be Crane's third divorce. Fourteen turbulent years of fame, fortune, three more husbands, drug abuse, and a suicide attempt later, she would die unexpectedly of a heart attack in a Monte Carlo hotel room at age forty-six while shooting her final film, *Hell Is Empty.*

Crane looked like ten miles of bad road when Otash found him tucked away in a secluded corner booth at Tail o' the Cock.

"Jesus Christ, Steve, you look like shit," he bluntly remarked as he slid inside the red tufted-leather booth. The generous pour of scotch whiskey he ordered en route to the table now arrived.

"You're right, Freddie," he admitted. "I look like shit, and I feel even worse, which is why I needed to see you."

An empathetic Otash pondered what had or was about to happen. "Well . . . I'm here now, my friend. How can I help you? I hate seeing you like this."

"Freddie . . . Lana's having a fling," Crane disclosed. "Christ, I hope it's only a fling. He's one of Mickey's boys. You know who I'm talking about?"

Otash lit up a Camel and took a long pull on his whiskey, waiting to hear what was needed of him.

"Johnny Stompanato," he confirmed. "Yeah, I heard."

"How bad is he?" Crane dared to ask.

"He's a complete piece of shit," Otash summated. In light of Crane's lugubrious state, there was no point adding salt to the wound by revealing Stompanato's record for physically abusing his women.

"What the hell is she doing with him?" he asked rhetorically.

"Beats the hell outta me," Crane bemoaned from the end of his tether. "I stopped trying to figure her out years ago. Honestly, Freddie, I don't care. She's a big girl . . . headstrong, she can take care of herself. It's Cheryl I'm worried about."

Crane still kept in touch with Lana out of his love and devotion for their daughter and was unabashedly candid how she was the best thing to come from their two blink-of-an-eye marriages. Now nearing her fifteenth birthday, she was young, beautiful, and impressionable, an easy target for a scumbag like Stompanato. When he learned she was enjoying many weekends with her mother and her new lover, Crane became deeply troubled that his little girl was spending quality time with a dangerous and unscrupulous mobster. But in an era where a mother was routinely awarded custody of a child in any divorce, there was little Crane could do to intervene.

Otash could certainly relate given his own two rapid-fire marriages to Columbia starlet Doris Houck. Protecting his own daughter from the harsh realities of Hollywood life had been a major priority since the day she was born. Fortunately, he and Doris agreed on how best to raise their child, which was certainly more manageable outside the public eye than swimming in a fishbowl of tabloid fodder like Lana.

Being the daughter of a living legend only exacerbated Cheryl's inability to cope with the emotional difficulties of adolescence. When she ran away from the boarding school her parents placed her in to ease the stress, the incident generated heartbreaking headlines when Cheryl was found wandering aimlessly through downtown LA's skid row. It was reported that a man who saw her being followed by three other men promised to find her a hotel room, but instead took her to the police station.

Lana was embarrassed when she picked up her daughter at the station. Her stardom, established in her critically acclaimed performance in *The Postman Always Rings Twice* a decade earlier, was now waning. As a result, she had become hyperaware of her contract's morals clause, and equally wary of any negative publicity that might cost her the next movie role.

Otash was more than happy to take on any case against *that son-of-a-bitch* Johnny Stompanato, with whom he had his own share of altercations as a young beat cop. Had the gangster not been repeatedly arrested by the LAPD, Otash would've also busted him for pimping or embezzling or sadistically bullying numerous victims. Instead, he let Mickey Cohen deal with his problem child in order to keep the whale of a mobster on the hook as a valuable informant. Still, he loathed Stompanato for a litany of reasons, not the least of which was how his fellow ex-Marine and World War II veteran seemed to delight in dishonoring both the military and the uniform at every turn.

––––––––––––––

The son of Italian immigrants, Johnny Stompanato Jr.—he of the many aliases including Jimmy Valentine, John Valentine, J. Hubbard, J. Holiday, or John Steele—began his postmilitary life as an unsuccessful pimp in Chicago. In 1947, after manipulating his way to the wild west of Los Angeles, he set himself up with a nice apartment and a tailored wardrobe to match his good looks and suntanned complexion. The Sunset Strip became his playground, and it wasn't long before he developed a reputation as a cocksman who hustled as a pimp on the side. Two fleeting marriages to marginally successful actresses ended in divorce after they were no longer willing to be grifted into paying his bills or endure his violent temper, which often resulted in bruised flesh, black eyes, busted lips, or all of the above.

But Mickey Cohen, a man who destroyed the lives of countless men and women up and down the Hollywood food chain by mining the depths of sex, power, and blackmail, saw great potential in Stompanato, in whom he found the perfect soldier for his sextortion racket. Cohen made a lot of enemies during his reign as Hollywood's playboy gangster, and after numerous attempts on his life, which included two bombings at his home on Brentwood's monied Moreno Avenue, he fortified the tony residence with multiple alarm systems, floodlights, a well-equipped arsenal, and a small army of bodyguards, led by Stompanato.

At the direction of Cohen, Stompanato, whose official front was selling cheap pieces of ceramic pottery and wood carvings feigning as fine art at his Myrtlewood Gift Shop in Westwood, became a master at the art of seducing an actress into bed, where he would secretly record everything from their pillow talk to their moments of ecstasy. That's where Cohen came in, to hold his victims hostage for substantial cuts of future earnings, dare they risk being ostracized by the Hollywood community and their reputations destroyed in the court of public opinion should the recordings ever see the light of day. Some of his more notable screen star victims would include Kathryn Grayson, Ann Miller, and Marilyn Monroe.

———————

That afternoon, an anxious Crane, desperate to know the truth, gave Freddie O the green light to put Cheryl Crane, Lana Turner, and Johnny Stompanato under surveillance.

Otash could relate. He had a daughter of his own. He also had a horse, a world-class Palomino that he often showcased while riding in the annual Beverly Hills and Palm Springs Easter parades wearing elaborate tack and designer western wear. It was stabled at Dincaro's Stock Farm in the San Fernando Valley, the same place Cheryl kept Rowena, her gift horse from avid rider Stompanato, a coincidence that made his surveillance of the two that much easier.

When he arrived at Dincaro's, Otash positioned himself so that he could watch Cheryl and Stompanato on their horseback ride through high-powered binoculars. They were an impressive yet odd pairing, he thought, the gangster and the movie star's daughter, both donning their matching dressage. But when he observed Stompanato caressing Cheryl at every opportunity, his contempt hit home, to his own daughter, and the visceral disgust of watching a child victimized by an adult male predator.

At his next meeting with Crane, Otash weighed his bias for Stompanato against his objective observations. As much as it pained him as a father to say it, he explained that his intelligence indicated Lana's lover had untoward designs on his fourteen-year-old daughter.

Crane lost it. "That bastard! I'll kill him!"

"Well, you certainly wouldn't be the first one to say that," Otash began before talking him off the ledge and suggesting a more prudent approach that wouldn't land him in jail or find him wearing cement galoshes at the bottom of Lake Hollywood. They concluded the best strategy was to inform Lana of their findings. But Steve knew his wife's famous temper too well and was certain she'd lash out at him for intruding in her love life. So Otash agreed to sit sidecar during the meeting in the hopes she might actually listen to the facts and share his concern.

Whether she was naïve, unaware, or in abject denial of his mob ties and malevolent nature, the reality remained that Lana had fallen hard and fast for the image projected by the entrancing bad boy Stompanato. The fact that he used the alias "John Steele" when first wooing her should have been a huge red flag to the lovesick Lana, but she was too caught up in him to notice.

N ow approaching her thirty-seventh birthday, Lana had four marriages and a laundry list of formidable lovers in the rearview mirror by the time she met Stompanato, which included Frank Sinatra and Tyrone Power, the latter of whom had purportedly left her because she was too temperamental, too high-maintenance, and drank too much. During her torrent affair with the Argentine-born Latin lover Fernando Lamas, her costar in MGM's saucy 1952 musical *The Merry Widow*, Lana was subjected to violent physical abuse. The same was true during her third marriage to businessman Robert Topping. Her four-year marriage to Lex Barker, who starred as Tarzan in five iterations of the eponymous franchise for RKO Pictures, ended abruptly in 1957 with Lana forcing him out of their home at gunpoint after Cheryl accused him of molesting her throughout the course of their marriage, a charge Barker fervently denied.

Through all her romantic vicissitudes, it was Lana's incredible career as a mega movie star that provided the much-needed self-worth that served as a counterbalance to her unfulfilling love life. But when MGM, her studio home of eighteen years, dropped her contract following a string of box-office flops, the separation anxiety left her susceptible to a mercenary and malevolent monster like Stompanato, who liked his women rich, beautiful, and biddable, even if he had to beat them into submission.

Despite a few initial physical dustups, there was no doubt their love affair was passionate above all else. She even looked the other way after learning of his mob connections, opting instead to continue showering him with tender love letters and expensive gifts, like a solid gold bracelet inscribed with his pet name for her, "Lanita." But she was careful to make sure they were rarely seen in public together, insisting she wanted to keep the special nature of their relationship private, despite his objections.

In 1957, a year after being given the heave-ho by MGM, Lana landed an incredible opportunity to salvage her career when 20th Century Fox hired her to star in *Peyton Place*, based on the best-selling book by Grace Metalious. Released that December, its box-office success led to Lana securing a starring role in the British film, *Another Time, Another Place*, opposite Scottish newcomer Sean Connery.

The minute Stompanato heard the rumors reported by the UK tabloids that a romance was brewing on the London set between Connery and his girlfriend, he became so bitter with jealousy that he arrived unannounced and uninvited. Any mixed feelings Lana was harboring were extinguished upon laying eyes on him, and they shared a bed until the day Stompanato stormed on set and waved a gun at Connery. A former body builder and karate black belt, the future James Bond quickly bent Johnny's wrist back until the gangster dropped his gun, then he punched him in the face in front of the entire crew.

Otash took great delight when word of the surreal event filtered its way back to Hollywood. Meanwhile in London, Lana was done with Stompanato and wanted nothing more to do with him. Neither did the film's producers, who swiftly reported the incident to Scotland Yard, who then had him deported. Stompanato would go into hiding until Lana returned stateside, where she took him back after he begged her forgiveness. It was a decision she would live to regret.

———————

When Crane and Otash arrived at Lana's home for their meeting, Crane didn't mince words and confronted her head-on: Stompanato was dangerous, poisoning her life, putting Cheryl in harm's way, and she needed to separate herself from him as soon as possible. Otash then reiterated his investigative findings as Lana stared back at him in cold silence. By the time he finished, she had become so bottled up with rage that it was difficult for her to speak at first, but then she found the words.

"You know something, Otash," she began, unable to contain her anger, "you're an asshole!"

Steve tried to calm her down, but she cut him off.

"You're an asshole too!" she screamed. "The whole thing is stupid. It's not true and it won't work. You two have cooked this up! Whatever you have on your mind, just forget it. I mean, you've done some low things in your life, Steve, but this takes the cake!"

Then she turned to Otash. "And as for you, Mister Private Asshole, why don't you fucking get lost!"

It seemed there was no convincing Lana that Otash was nothing but a paid pawn in her ex-husband's charade. But Fred, who was well versed in the granular details of Stompanato's past, came prepared. He quietly pulled out a folder from his briefcase containing a copy of Johnny's rap sheet, then slid it across the table as Lana continued to exclaim how she knew him in ways they didn't.

"Go ahead, Lana, take a good look," he said calmly. "Find out where he's been and what he's done over the years. See the people he shook down, and all the wealthy women he embezzled."

Embezzled . . . that caught her attention. "What women?"

"You think you're the first?" Otash continued. "Don't kid yourself, sweetheart. You think he wouldn't use your daughter? Think again. This is a man without a conscience. Is that what you want for your life?"

Otash revealed that in addition to his lengthy criminal record, Stompanato had actually been divorced three times, not twice as he told her, and that he had abandoned his first wife and their young son without support years ago in his hometown of Woodstock, Illinois.

After an enervating hour of combing through her lover's past lives, Lana was woefully convinced that her ex-husband and his private detective were right. She needed to get out. But how? Otash cautioned that any rash decision or drastic move could easily backfire, and that the safest route would be to slowly ease him out of her life by spending more time at work and being as unavailable as possible. Hopefully, he'd eventually get the message and move on.

When the two men left, Lana confided in her daughter how Johnny beat her, her plans to get rid of him, and how she needed her help so they could brave this together and make things right again. For her part, Cheryl would stick to the script, pretend everything was fine, and emphasize her mother's busy work schedule whenever Stompanato came around.

In February 1958, when Lana received the Best Actress Academy Award nomination for *Peyton Place*, she decided to attend the ceremony at Hollywood's Pantages Theatre with Cheryl and her mother, Mildred. Though Stompanato was eager to be her escort, to parade down the red carpet before all the cameras, the paparazzi, and the cheering fans on Tinseltown's biggest night with one of the world's greatest movie stars on his arm, Lana gently and carefully made him understand that she was obligated to bring her mother and her daughter out of gratitude for their undying support throughout her career. While he begrudgingly accepted defeat, deep down his reptilian mobster brain felt disrespected, especially after marinating in drink while watching the awards on live television from the massive hotel suite she had booked for the evening.

A twenty-eight-year-old Joanne Woodward brought home the Best Actress Oscar that night for her groundbreaking performance in *The Three Faces of Eve*, but that hardly dampened Lana's delight for her nomination and renewed acclaim. It had been a night like no other at a time in her life when she needed it the most, and she looked every bit the iconic Hollywood movie star as she returned to the hotel dressed in the immaculate formfitting strapless mermaid gown and white mink stole she wore to the ceremony. But all that was about to turn on a dime at the end of the evening when she entered her hotel suite and was greeted by a mean, drunk, and belligerent Stompanato determined to bring her back down to earth despite her restored self-esteem.

Stompanato greeted her by slapping her so hard it caused one of her earrings to scratch her cheek. Terrified her screams might waken Cheryl, who was asleep in the next room, or cause a PR disaster should they be heard by other hotel guests, Lana endured the vicious abuse in silence as Stompanato threw her around the room. He then ended the evening with an ominous threat as he held a razor blade so close to her face that, if she dared to move, it would disfigure her: *if she ever left him or treated him like this again, he'd destroy her beauty forever.*

Over the next eight days, Lana realized there was no turning back. Now well aware of Johnny's close ties to mobster
Mickey Cohen, a man whose powerful and violent reputation
far exceeded that of his loyal apprentice, she had to avoid any
appearance of mistreating him. She managed to keep the
peace as he helped her and Cheryl move into a new home she
leased a week before at 730 North Bedford Drive in Beverly
Hills. But on Good Friday, April 4, 1958, a final heated argument in her bedroom would end as quickly as it had begun—
with the murder of Johnny Stompanato.

No one will ever know exactly what happened that night.
The one man who did ended up dead, so he wasn't talking. By
the time the story went public, Lana and Cheryl were so well
rehearsed that it was almost impossible to believe them. The
fundamental nature of various contradicting accounts by
those on the scene and the individuals who came to their aid
in the immediate aftermath is best described by an unrelated
quote belonging to legendary Hollywood impresario Robert
Evans, who once poignantly addressed the validity of his own
life's recollections by saying: "There are three sides to every
story: your side, my side, and the truth. And no one is lying.
Memories shared serve each differently."

In the official version, Cheryl had retired to her bedroom
that night to watch TV and do her homework. It was only
when she heard the intense shouting that she went to investigate. Standing outside her mother's closed bedroom door she
heard Stompanato, angry with Lana for her attempt to end
their relationship, terrorizing her as he had the night of the
Oscars in a manner that would horrify any woman, let alone
a glamorous movie star: by threatening to carve up her face.
For her part, Lana launched a blistering counterattack that

tallied all the lies he had perpetrated since the day they met, and it escalated from there with Stompanato enumerating all the violent ways in which he planned to destroy her.

Desperate, Cheryl ran downstairs to the telephone to call the police, but she stopped short when she realized that doing so could trigger a scandal, her mother's worst nightmare. Operating on visceral impulse and uncertain what to do or where to turn, she ran to the kitchen, grabbed a large butcher knife, and hurried back upstairs, where she placed it on the floor outside the bedroom. She then knocked on the door, again and again, harder each time, trying to get them to open up and talk to her. But it was no use; they couldn't hear her over their incessant barrage of verbal threats and accusations.

"Cunt, you're dead!" were the last words Cheryl heard Johnny yell out before she knelt down to pick up the butcher knife with her trembling hands. Then her mother screamed, "Get out!"

A split second later, the door flew open with Lana holding it. Cheryl could see Stompanato coming at her mother from behind, arms raised as if to pummel her. She lurched forward over the threshold as Stompanato seemed to rush at her, and the act of their collision plunged the knife into his torso. In the brief moment before he collapsed, Stompanato uttered his final words in the form of a rhetorical question, "My God, Cheryl, what have you done?" Later, the official autopsy would reveal that the single knife wound penetrated his liver, portal vein, and aorta, resulting in massive internal hemorrhaging.

Across town in Hollywood, it had been just another long day at the office for Otash, who had been juggling several high-profile cases involving bold-faced names such as Judy

Garland, Rock Hudson, and mega director-producer Otto Preminger. He was more than eager to step out for dinner with his latest lovely lady, the aspiring actress Susie Woods, when the telephone rang. He picked up on the second ring thinking it was Susie, but instead heard the desperate voice of his frequent client, uber movie star trial attorney Jerry Giesler.

"Freddie, it's Jerry," Giesler said urgently. "I need you right now."

"Now? Jesus Christ, Jerry. It's been a day and I've got dinner plans."

"Cancel! This is an emergency!" Giesler implored. "There's been a death at Lana's house."

Otash feared the worst. "Oh, shit. Who?"

"It's Stompanato."

"What about Lana and Cheryl?"

"They're okay, but I need you here now!"

"Okay . . . I'll be right over."

On the one hand, Otash was relieved that Lana and her daughter were safe. But how in the hell did Stompanato end up dead *in Lana's home*? Was it an accident? An act of self-defense? A crime of passion? Was Steve Crane involved? Did Mickey Cohen know yet? His mind awash in hypotheticals, Otash quickly called Susie for a rain check, slipped his gun into his ankle holster, shrugged on an overcoat, and ran out the door. The April showers were coming down in sheets as he jumped in his car, shifted into damage control, and sped to Beverly Hills.

When Otash arrived, he could see Giesler's limo parked on the street and five other cars parked in the driveway, including Stompanato's white Ford Thunderbird. He bolted upstairs to the master bedroom, where he found the family doctor and her press agent attending to a barefoot Lana dressed in a white blouse and black silk pedal pushers, apparently in shock. A few feet away, a distraught and crying Cheryl was being comforted by her father and grandmother. Just beyond this morbid milieu was Stompanato's dead body lying face up on the floor, with a bloody butcher knife resting on an adjacent marble dressing table.

Otash couldn't help but notice there were only a few drops of blood dotting the plush pink carpet next to him, a clear indication the crime scene had been tampered with.

Giesler, who was now representing Cheryl, pulled Otash aside to fill him in. This was no Technicolor movie set, it was real life, an active murder scene involving one of Hollywood's greatest movie stars, who was now forced to improvise.

According to Giesler, Lana rushed into the bathroom immediately after the stabbing to prepare a cold compress for Stompanato's forehead. She even tried mouth-to-mouth resuscitation, to no avail. She then summoned her inner circle, first by phoning her mother, then her doctor, then Giesler, then her press agent, and then Steve Crane, in that order.

Crane was first to arrive on the scene, followed by her mother. When the doctor got there, he hoped to save Stompanato by quickly administering a shot of adrenaline, but it was no use. He looked up at Lana and her attorney; someone needed to call an ambulance. That's when Giesler called his number one fixer Otash, not only because of his familiarity with the situation, but to help figure out what, if anything, could be done to minimize the impending scandal.

Otash instructed everyone not to touch anything, then he told Lana to call the police. In true Hollywood tradition, the cops were the last to arrive, which did not sit well with Beverly

Hills police chief Clinton Anderson, a man whose reputation for shielding the city's image as a sleepy little town for big screen stars was legend. Anderson was outraged that Otash and Giesler got there before he did, and that Stompanato had been dead a full two hours by the time he pulled up in his squad car. When the ambulance finally arrived, a crowd of neighbors and a handful of press had already gathered outside the mansion.

Anderson, who happened to be a regular at the Luau, where Crane never charged him for a thing, was open-minded and gracious toward the powerful and privileged residents of Beverly Hills whenever they ran afoul of the law. He sat Lana and Cheryl down to hear a full account of what transpired, wherein neither mother nor daughter seemed able to remember the knife entering Stompanato's body. When it was all over, Lana pleaded with him to let her take the blame, but that wasn't an option. Cheryl, who had already confessed to the murder, was then handcuffed and led away to juvenile prison, where she would be held without bond until the coroner's jury inquiry.

A few days later, when Anderson learned that Crane had hired Otash to conduct surveillance on Lana, Cheryl, and Stompanato, he demanded Fred meet him in his office. The two men were hardly friends. Like the rest of greater Los Angeles at that time, Beverly Hills was steeped in mob influence, and while Fred could never quite figure out on what side Anderson's bread was buttered, he knew he couldn't trust him. Once the door was closed, the chief took him to the mat.

"Lookit, Otash," he began. "I don't want a bunch of shit from you, because I could nail your ass to the wall as an accessory after the fact to the murder of Johnny Stompanato."

Otash didn't shock easily but . . . "What the hell, Clint?"

"Don't play coy with me, you son of a bitch!" Anderson continued. "You think you got informants? How the hell do you think I keep the peace in Beverly Hills if I don't have informants? I know *exactly* what went on up in Lana Turner's bedroom that night, and your ass is not clean."

Otash calmly stood his ground. "What the hell are you talking about?"

Anderson thought he had it all figured out.

"I happen to know that you and Giesler were the first two people on the scene," he continued. "That you personally removed the knife from Stompanato's stomach, wiped Lana's prints off the handle, and had Cheryl grip it to make sure it was her prints the police would find there. Then you placed the knife back in Stompanato's dead body. Now that's what I know, you lousy two-bit detective."

Otash knew he was being played so he called his bluff.

"I don't know what kind of information you *think* you have, Chief, and I don't much give a damn, but let me tell you something," Otash said. "If you're trying to connect me to Stompanato's murder, you're nothing but a fucking liar. Personally, I think you're fishing . . . and I'm not biting. So, fuck off!"

Then he walked out the door.

The story garnered major headlines worldwide as the most scandalous murder to hit Hollywood in decades. Mickey Cohen, who usually kept a low profile involving any of his associates, took it so hard that he publicly shared his suspicious grievances with the press. He refused to believe the murder was justified, or that a girl like Cheryl had the strength to kill Stompanato. Without using the exact locution, his implication was clear: the story was a *cover-up* and Lana, who had killed her lover, was being protected.

Cohen made every effort to reshape the narrative so that Stompanato was perceived as a nice young man, a patriotic ex-Marine who was led astray by a movie star and murdered in cold blood. He even had one of his boys burglarize Stompanato's apartment to retrieve Lana's love letters, which he then had published in the *Los Angeles Herald-Express* to show beyond a doubt that far from her being afraid of him, Lana and Johnny were in love. But despite all his efforts, the public embraced Lana as a sympathetic figure, a naïve and hopeless romantic, while Stompanato was correctly deemed a thug.

Otash conducted an additional investigation after the death to show the police and the court the sort of man Stompanato was, and that Cheryl's actions were justified. After twenty-five minutes of deliberation, the jury in the coroner's inquest ruled it to be justifiable homicide. While Cheryl was not prosecuted, she was punished as though she had been, spending months in juvenile jails and reformatories, followed by time in and out of a psychiatric hospital.

On behalf of his family, a fourteen-year-old John Stompanato III, who had been abandoned along with his father's first wife years before, sued Lana and Steve for wrongful death to the tune of $750,000, claiming they were responsible for their daughter's emotional issues by citing the time she was found on skid row. He would ultimately settle for twenty grand. Otash was personally offended that Stompanato was buried with full military honors, which included the customary draping of the American flag over his coffin. He would later muse that his tombstone should have read: Good Riddance to Bad Rubbish.

Years later, Otash would read Turner's 1982 memoir, *Lana: The Lady, the Legend, the Truth*, as well as Cheryl's 1988 memoir, *Detour: A Hollywood Story*. Naturally, Stompanato's death was featured prominently in both their stories, but as far as Otash was concerned both women seemed to go out of their way to ignore the facts. Lana's book didn't even mention her meeting with Otash and Crane, while Cheryl's only noted that "an associate" of her father had intimated something was going on between her and Stompanato.

But there was another, more off-the-record version of what happened that Good Friday night in 1958, one that Otash would only share with a handful of trusted confidants before taking it to his grave in 1992.

After his contentious meeting in Beverly Hills police chief Anderson's office three days after the murder, Otash drove straight to Giesler's law office, where he watched the color drain from the celebrity attorney's face as he gave him the play-by-play of his encounter with Anderson.

"There is no statute of limitations for murder," Giesler solemnly counseled as his skin turned ashen. "Do me a favor, Fred . . . don't ever tell that story to anybody until I'm dead and buried."

With the public on her side, Lana would not only survive the scandal but thrive the following year with her star turn in the 1959 feature film *Imitation of Life*, considered to be one of the great commercial successes of her career. She would also be married four more times. Cheryl would go on to become a successful real estate agent and in 2014 marry her longtime partner, Jocelyn LeRoy, after living together for thirty-four years.

At the time of the murder, word on the street was that Cheryl was framed to save Lana's career, so much so that even

Esther Williams, the former champion swimmer turned MGM movie star, would echo those shared sentiments when the subject was posed during an interview. "Nobody will ever know the entire truth," Williams said. "The bottom line is, there have always been cover-ups here because Hollywood protects its own."

Years later, in a 1999 *Vanity Fair* story, the award-winning biographer of the stars Patricia Bosworth tried to untangle the murky circumstances of Johnny Stompanato's death. She interviewed Turner's longtime hairdresser Eric Root, author of *The Private Diary of My Life with Lana*, who claimed that Turner confided in him that she—not Cheryl—had stabbed her lover. "I killed the son of a bitch and I'd do it again," Root says Lana told him. She made him promise, he adds, to "tell the truth so I can rest in peace. Don't let my baby take the rap all her life for my mistake." Root said he never pressed for more details, but when he published *The Private Diary* after she died, he maintained that he had been able to piece the story together with the help of Otash's old friend Raymond Strait.

According to Otash's recollections to Strait reported in the story, Jerry Giesler took Otash to the mansion before the police arrived and together they persuaded Turner to let her daughter take the blame for the stabbing. Root quotes Otash as saying he "wiped the prints off the knife and replaced Lana's prints with Cheryl's. (The police reported only smudged prints on the knife.) The bed looked as if a hog had been slaughtered in it."

Cheryl Crane, in the story, called Root's account "far-fetched."

NINE

BETWEEN A ROCK AND A HARD PLACE

On September 5, 1969, the Golden State emerged from the dark ages of legal separation after Governor Ronald Reagan signed his autograph to the revolutionary no-fault Family Law Act, which recognized irreconcilable differences as sufficient grounds to terminate a marriage for the first time in U.S. history. No stranger to divorce, the former Hollywood actor and two-time president of the Screen Actors Guild could have used such groundbreaking legislation twenty years earlier when his marriage to movie star Jane Wyman went bust over his nascent political ambitions. Fortunately, love would prove more encouraging the second time around.

A year after starring in Universal's 1951 romantic comedy *Bedtime for Bonzo*, a box-office success in which he was often upstaged by his chimpanzee costar, Reagan hitched his wagon to Nancy Davis, a young actress under contract at MGM, where she was routinely typecast as the loyal housewife. True to form, the future first lady was very supportive of her Ron-nie's aspirations for public office, and when he was elected the fortieth president of the United States in 1980, the Gipper (as he was affectionately known for his first big role as football legend George Gipp in the Warner Bros. classic *Knute Rockne: All American*) became the first divorced leader of the free world.

Married couples seeking a divorce before 1970 were bur-dened with oppressive old-world legalities rooted in colonial law that required witnesses to corroborate a partner's wrong-doing based on adultery, extreme cruelty, willful desertion, neglect, conviction of a felony, or even moral turpitude. Nowhere were the stakes higher than in enclaves of conspicu-ous consumption like Hollywood and Beverly Hills, where high-profile divorce was as copious as the expatriated palm trees lining the twenty-two-mile stretch of Sunset Boulevard. For those privileged denizens, hiring a private detective to conduct opposition research on an estranged spouse was an all-important strategy if they wanted to get what they believed to be their fair share of joint financial assets.

Into this most propitious milieu stepped Otash, a man so specialized in "Civil, Criminal and Marital Investigations" that he made it the letterhead of his elegantly embossed stationery right under his name. Expensive three-color brochures hyping his proprietary skills for state-of-the-art surveillance, documented reports, and obtaining witnesses, photos, and recordings to secure substantial evidence were dispatched to Jerry Giesler, Melvin Belli, Greg Bautzer, Arthur Crowley, and every other power attorney in town—many of whom kept him gainfully employed with their star-studded clients. Barring the lucrative paydays, Fred derived no pleasure from working these cases. In fact, their very nature often triggered unresolved issues from his own two failed marriages to the love of his life, Doris Houck. But business was booming in Sodom by the Pacific and the art of divorce, in all its repugnant glory, became a major profit center for the Otash Detective Bureau.

Marital and child custody inquiries were conducted on behalf of some of the most celebrated Hollywood wives in town: Bette Davis, Judy Garland, Ann Miller, and Zsa Zsa Gabor, to name a few. But in March 1958, Arthur Crowley handed Otash a doozy of a divorce whose ramifications threatened to decimate the career of one of the most admired and sought-after movie stars of Hollywood's Golden Age: Rock Hudson.

Otash had history with Hudson, vis-à-vis Henry Leroy Willson, the notorious Svengali talent agent who created the matinee idol, literally from scratch. The son of a prominent showbiz family, Willson had earlier stints as a writer for *Photoplay*, the *Hollywood Reporter*, and *Variety*, where he wrote a weekly gossip column and honed his transactional skills for editorial horse trading. As Hudson's star rose, Willson set out to protect Hudson's homosexuality from coming to light, and he invariably sought out Otash's services to neutralize several jilted lovers who would attempt to extort money from his client once their affairs hit the skids.

Years later, Otash clarified what was known at the time in an interview with Janet Zappala, cohost of the Fox syndicated television show *Personalities*: "*Many times, he would be extorted by men he'd gotten involved with sexually. Henry Willson would call me and say, 'Fred, we got another extortion under the mailbox,' and we'd run it down and go to the people on the*

other side, and we'd resolve the conflict they had with Rock,
either by giving the guy some money, or by . . . you know, 'intim-
idation' is a proper word at times when it's an extortion case. We
knew Rock Hudson was homosexual before the world knew it."

Despite an oppressive moral climate in postwar America
dominated by conservative and traditional values, wherein
gay men and women were unduly persecuted as deviant pari-
ahs whose lifestyles threatened to destroy the very fabric of
society, Otash was rather imperturbable when it came to Hudson's orientation. As far as he was concerned, homosexuality
was a cultural reality kept on the down-low behind the powerful and seemingly impervious façades of Hollywood's myth-
making dream factories. But now, in a surreal twist of fate,
Crowley sought out Otash's expertise to secure damning evidence pertaining to Hudson's illicit sexual activities on behalf
of his client, Phyllis Gates—aka *Mrs. Rock Hudson*, who
hoped the dossier could serve as potential kryptonite to pro-
cure a more favorable settlement in their looming divorce.

———————

Hudson and Gates actually met through Willson, who by
then was known in certain circles as the Fairy Godfather
of Hollywood, thanks to his dubious reputation for having
parlayed a penchant for cruising gay bars and nightclubs into
a lucrative career of discovering and grooming mostly handsome young men from the ground up, starting with their
names. In addition to Rock, other noteworthy creations
included Robert Ozell Moseley, aka Guy Madison, a blond
Navy veteran with boyish good looks best known for his titular
role on the long-running syndicated TV series *The Adventures*

of Wild Bill Hickok; brawny Texas footballer Orison Whipple Hungerford Jr., aka Ty Hardin, star of the hit ABC series *Bronco*; and the clean-cut Arthur Andrew Kelm, whom he molded into matinee heartthrob Tab Hunter. While Willson was notorious for taking advantage of his gay, bisexual, or "obliging" male clients, stringing them along with potential acting gigs in exchange for sex, his business model wasn't all beefcake sexploitations.

Willson regularly staked out schools for promising female talent. Five miles east at Hollywood High School, a savvy sixteen-year-old student named Julia Jean "Judy" Turner had tapped Willson to be her first agent in 1937. She had been "discovered" by the *Hollywood Reporter* editor William Wilkerson at the Top Hat Malt Shop, where she was cutting a typing class one afternoon—not at Schwab's Pharmacy by *Wizard of Oz* producer Mervyn LeRoy, as Hollywood mythology long held. It was Wilkerson who introduced Judy to the comedian/talent agent Zeppo Marx, who in turn introduced her to LeRoy. Both Willson and LeRoy would later claim credit for changing her first name to "Lana," and the rest is cinematic history.

In 1944 he found Marilyn Louis, a beautiful and naïve sixteen-year-old Beverly Hills High School student, crossing the street one day after school. After changing her name to Rhonda Fleming, Willson landed her a seven-year contract with David O. Selznick, who gave the hypnotic newcomer with flaming red hair her first substantial role in Alfred Hitchcock's 1945 psychological thriller, *Spellbound*, opposite Ingrid Bergman and Gregory Peck. Her titillating portrayal of a nymphomaniac in a mental institution kicked off an enviable career that included over forty films spanning two decades, where Fleming was considered one of the most glamorous actresses of her time and the "Queen of Technicolor."

In 1947, while working as head of talent for Selznick's Vanguard Pictures, Willson discovered the twenty-two-year-old Roy Harold Scherer Jr., a handsome, strapping, six-foot-five truck driver from Winnetka, Illinois. Inspired by the young man's force-of-nature physique, Willson had his teeth fixed and changed his name to Rock Hudson, supposedly by splicing together *Rock of Gibraltar* with *Hudson River*. Initially, the two men shared an all-inclusive partnership that entailed both personal and professional services, but that changed once Hudson's career took flight and he became Henry's main meal ticket.

After successful leading roles playing the resident hunk in a string of westerns, swashbucklers, romantic comedies, and action-adventure dramas, Hudson's frequent director Douglas Sirk hired him in 1953 to star opposite Ronald Reagan's ex-wife Jane Wyman in the romantic melodrama *Magnificent Obsession*. Like many of Sirk's films, the story explored a then-taboo subtext of a woman's desire for emotional and sexual fulfillment that, unbeknownst to most moviegoers at the time, served as an allegory for what they considered to be the perils of homosexuality. The film was a runaway hit, and when *Modern Screen* named Rock Hudson the "Most Popular Actor of 1954," one of the brightest closeted cinema stars to ever grace Hollywood celluloid was born.

By then, rumors of Hudson's sexual proclivities were commonly known among industry insiders, but now his heightened fame and notoriety was in jeopardy of being seriously compromised by an inconvenient truth that, if made public, could extinguish his on-screen persona and destroy his career.

In what he no doubt believed to be a safe and expedient remedy at the time, Willson, who had already bearded his own homosexuality by becoming engaged to President Harry Truman's songstress daughter Margaret, set Hudson up with his personal secretary Phyllis Gates, a wholesome farm girl and former Sunday school teacher from the tiny town of Dawson, Minnesota. Like most of the adoring fans who shared an almost parasocial relationship with the movie star, Phyllis was enthralled by her employer's red-hot, ten-out-of-ten client. She and Rock would begin dating in haste, with Willson ensuring they were seen and photographed all about town and chronicled in all the right gossip columns.

All seemed to go according to plan until the summer of 1955, when Willson learned that the dreaded *Confidential* magazine was planning to publish an in-depth story about Hudson's homosexuality based on first-person accounts by one or more of his former lovers. It was an impending publicity disaster of biblical proportions, and the clock was ticking. Rock's recent box-office hit with Wyman had all but cemented him as a global movie star, and their second Sirk-directed film together, *All That Heaven Allows*, was set to premiere on Christmas Day. The exposé threatened to be the most earth-shattering in the history of Hollywood's most feared scandal rag and if Willson (who had a shit file on everyone, including his clients) was to make it all go away, he knew it would take more than one virgin sacrifice to appease the gods.

Using Otash as a conduit, Willson cut a deal with *Confidential* whereby two of his less lucrative talents were thrown under the bus to save his megastar from ruin. He provided the dirt on how Rory Calhoun, who had just costarred opposite Marilyn Monroe and Robert Mitchum in director Otto

Preminger's *River of No Return*, was an ex-con who had served
jail time for grand theft auto and robbing a liquor store; and
that Tab Hunter, who recently received critical acclaim for his
breakout role in the epic Warner Bros. World War II drama
Battle Cry, had been arrested five years earlier for attending a
gay "pajama party."

Pursuant to his job description as chief investigator for
Confidential, Otash verified Willson's tips for publisher Robert Harrison and Hollywood Research Inc., the magazine's
newsgathering machine fronted by Harrison's beautiful but
cutthroat niece, Marjorie Meade. While the tabloid printed
both pieces and kept its side of the bargain by deep-sixing
Hudson's exposé, it wasn't long before the more mainstream
Life magazine ran a cover story on October 3, 1955, titled
"Hollywood's Most Handsome Bachelor," which went on to
report, "Fans are urging 29-year-old Hudson to get married—
or explain why not." The hounds were at the gate, Rock's predicament was at an impasse, and Willson gave him two
months to get married.

Phyllis would happily oblige when Rock asked her to
move into his Hollywood Hills home above the Sunset Strip.
When she agreed to marry him two months later, Willson
orchestrated a small PR stunt wedding at Santa Barbara's
Biltmore Hotel on November 9, 1955. Minutes after the ceremony, curated photos of the happy couple perched over their
wedding cake with scripted interviews penned by Hollywood
gossip queens Hedda Hopper and Louella Parsons were
locked and loaded to hit all the morning papers the following
day. The crisis was averted, and Willson was justifiably elated
with his sophisticated skills for using smoke and mirrors to
avoid disaster.

udson's career achieved supernova status the following year with his star turn in *Giant*, the epic western drama directed by George Stevens costarring Elizabeth Taylor and Otash's friend James Dean, who perished in a tragic car accident late in production. The film lived up to its name as an enormous critical and financial success, and Hudson earned an Academy Award nomination for Best Actor with Stevens bringing home Oscar gold for Best Director. Hudson was soon voted the most popular actor in American cinema, but he couldn't say the same for his home life. Not long after they had returned from their honeymoon in Jamaica, Rock began citing protracted film shoots, voice-over sessions, wardrobe fittings, and a litany of other excuses to explain his truancy at home while he spent quality time with a private posse of male friends. As the situation devolved, what little time he did share with his new wife was rife with guilt, stress, and anxiety, with Rock often lashing out at Phyllis and allegedly slapping her on occasion.

After Hudson left for Rome later that year to star in Selznick's film adaptation of Ernest Hemingway's semiautobiographical novel *A Farewell to Arms* opposite Selznick's movie star wife, Jennifer Jones, and the renowned Italian actor-director Vittorio De Sica, Gates became hospitalized with infectious hepatitis. Her doctor sent Hudson an urgent cable informing him of his wife's malaise, but two weeks passed without a reply. When the physician was finally able to reach him by telephone, Rock acknowledged the cable but blamed the film's arduous production schedule for his inability to respond. From her hospital bed, a recovering Phyllis begged him to come home, but Hudson insisted he had to finish the problematic film. Truth be told, *A Farewell to Arms* was indeed plagued with an almost lethal dose of studio setbacks and production delays, but that wasn't the only thing keeping Rock occupied.

Fabrizio Mioni and Franco Rossellini were platonic comrades within the cloistered community of elite gay men in Rome, until jealousy and betrayal over their mutual interest in Rock tore their friendship asunder. Young and handsome, the twenty-six-year-old Fabrizio was a struggling actor with minor, often uncredited roles. Franco, by contrast, was the refined, erudite, and privileged twenty-one-year-old son of successful film composer Renzo Rossellini, and the nephew of world-renowned filmmaker Roberto Rossellini and his Swedish movie star wife, Ingrid Bergman.

Fabrizio had been well acquainted with Rock long before they reunited during the filming of *A Farewell to Arms*. Five years earlier, he had accompanied a lesser-known Hudson to Capri, Naples, and Pompeii, serving as his personal cavalier servente, translator, and tour guide. They spent a time exploring the sun-drenched ancient ruins of southern Italy, where Rock delighted in filming several home movies of their travels that he would later bring back home to Hollywood and the discerning eyes of Henry Willson, who at the time showed little more than a passing interest in his client's fetching Italian conquest.

By the time Rock returned five years later, he had ascended the summit of Hollywood's Mount Olympus, arriving in style and much fanfare to stay at the historic Grand Hotel. A bastion of elegance and luxury in the heart of Rome, the former residence of a prominent Italian family was now a palatial home away from home reserved for an exclusive clientele of visiting aristocrats, nobility, business magnates, powerful politicians, and, of course, the cinema elite. When Fabrizio caught wind that Universal International Pictures was holding a press conference there to welcome Rock to the Eternal City, he wasn't going to miss it for the world.

Inside one of the hotel's ornate public rooms adorned with elegant frescoes, enormous crystal chandeliers, and stained-glass skylights that evoked the resplendent, old-world ambiance of the Belle Époque, Fabrizio stood at a comfortable distance within eyeshot of his former lover, watching patiently for an hour as Hudson was interviewed by journalists and photographed by a clamoring assembly of paparazzi. When it was all over and the press had dispersed, Rock approached Fabrizio, who thought the now big-time movie star would give him the cold shoulder. But he was wrong.

"Fabrizio, I'm so happy to see you," Rock said fondly. "Honestly, as soon as I realized it was you I thought, how wonderful!"

A passionate Italian who proudly wore his heart on his sleeve, Fabrizio almost fainted.

"Oh my God," he replied, "I came here because I wanted to see you!"

"Well, here I am," Rock offered, donning the alluring aw-shucks grin that helped catapult him to stardom. "I'm going to be here for fifteen days. What are you doing? I would like to see you."

"I would like that," Fabrizio eagerly declared. "I'm going to be in a movie in a month or so, but—"

"My room is 221," an impatient Rock interrupted, cutting to the chase. "Call me in thirty minutes."

And just like that, in Room 221 of the Grand Hotel, Hudson and Fabrizio rekindled their special friendship as if no time had passed. Every night after production wrapped around nine o'clock, the two men would rendezvous in his elegantly appointed suite overlooking the Piazza Venezia. Rock soon introduced Fabrizio to a visiting Henry Willson, who befriended him over a patronizing lunch where he indulged the young man's desire to further his acting career.

"Why don't you come to America?" Willson pandered. "Your face and personality, education and attitude . . . I mean, you should be very successful there."

"That's what I want to hear," Fabrizio gladly admitted, "because I really want to go to America, I always wanted to go!"

"If I can help you in any way, I will try," Willson offered.

"That's wonderful, because I heard that you are one of the best agents there, so if you want to help me, I accept!" he ardently replied. "You could be my agent if you like."

"Well, let's see what we can do," Willson tempered, smiling as his small, chubby hand gently caressed Fabrizio's muscular thigh underneath the table.

Two days later, just before Willson returned to Hollywood, he delivered by arranging a meet-and-greet for Fabrizio with executives from Universal International Pictures. When they became transatlantic pen pals after his departure, Willson went even further by booking him a screen test with director Richard Wilson on the last day of filming *Raw Wind in Eden*, starring Esther Williams and Jeff Chandler, on location near the ancient seaside town of Castiglione della Pescaia. Fabrizio made quite an impression on the director and his team, all of whom echoed Willson's sentiment that the young actor should consider going to America.

Fabrizio was on cloud nine as he navigated the three-hour drive back to Rome along the Tuscan coastline in his weathered Fiat 500 Topolino. He was young, handsome, and, most importantly, admired and desired by powerful and influential men who could facilitate his dream of becoming a Hollywood movie star, and he yearned to confide his happiness in Franco Rossellini, a trusted friend and confidant who knew his aspirations and could appreciate the gravity of the moment and the players involved.

Fabrizio considered Franco to be "one of my four or five best friends in the world" who knew everything about him "and when I say everything, I mean the works." As it turned out, Franco was more than enchanted to hear Fabrizio's detailed account of his new prospects and passionate love affair with Rock. What Fabrizio didn't realize was that Franco was willing to patronize, mislead, and malign his good friend with the intent of gaining access to Hudson and seducing him for himself.

"Wow, I would love to know Rock," Fabrizio recalled Franco telling him. "You've said so many beautiful things about him. You are so excited about him, and think he's such a wonderful person, and such a wonderful friend. You've made me so curious to meet him."

In good faith, a naïve Fabrizio arranged for Franco to meet his lover, who then leveraged Rock's admiration for his aunt Ingrid Bergman to lure him into his patrician world.

Soon enough, a solo Rock was enjoying *la dolce vita* in the familial embrace of the Rossellini clan at their nearby villa. Franco wanted Rock for himself. Once a level of trust had been established, Franco launched a methodical smear campaign worthy of Machiavelli. Playing on Hudson's fears of anything that could compromise his stardom, Franco whispered defamatory tales of promiscuity, indiscretion, and deceit so disparaging of Fabrizio that they would ultimately spell his demise—or what the Italians call *la fine del mondo.*

The curtain came down hard on Fabrizio as Rock turned his attentions exclusively to Franco for the remainder of his time in Rome. Meanwhile, gossip of Hudson's affairs with the two men spread like a contagion among the production crew. By the time Rock returned to America on August 15, rumors of his escapades in Italy were the talk of the town within the close-knit gay communities of Hollywood and Palm Springs, which was not wasted on Willson.

With his many letters to Willson now left unreciprocated since Rock's exodus, an impetuous Fabrizio took a giant leap of faith to act on Henry's offer to come to America before it was too late. After booking his own passage to Los Angeles, he sent one last cable alerting him of the date and time of his arrival. For Willson, who was now up to his eyeballs with Hudson's impending divorce, Fabrizio was persona non grata personified, a liability that needed to be contained, lest he bring more harm to an already bad situation. And so, despite having ignored him for weeks, Willson was waiting for Fabrizio when his plane arrived at Los Angeles International Airport, to welcome him with open arms—and keep the starry-eyed Italian away from Rock at all costs. The two men drove north on La Cienega Boulevard in Willson's luxurious

1956 gull-wing Cadillac Coupe de Ville. As they entered the Inglewood Oil Field corridor with its choking sea of sky-high derricks in every direction, Henry lowered the boom.

"You know, Fabrizio, I didn't think you would come because I didn't write back for the last month," he began. "The situation is terrible now and everything is going wrong. You know that I am very much involved in Rock's situation, with the divorce and all these things. He is very mixed up, and I have to look after him all the time. I really can't have some-body else right now. Besides, there's really nothing much to do, and the work is very slow. But I'm here for you and will help you in any way I can."

Even a neophyte Fabrizio knew there was no upside in his cross-examining Willson on the promises he made in Rome. Nor could he afford to alienate one of the most powerful men in Hollywood, one who had already proven his true regard beyond a superficial physical attraction. Willson offered him a room at a hotel, but Fabrizio declined. He would stay with friends in West Hollywood with whom he already made plans. To ensure he stayed away from Rock, Willson continued to nurture their friendship under the guise of a trusted mentor and confidant. He even helped him land an agent at William Morris that would ultimately lead to his landing the pivotal role in *Hercules*.

According to transcripts of a secret, unauthorized record-ing between Fabrizio and Otash operative Jim Terry while trying to get dirt on Rock for his wife's divorce case, a broken Fabrizio exclaimed as he recounted Franco's betrayal: "He's a whore! This boy, who was one of my best friends, went to Rock and told him that *I* was a whore, that *I* was a terrible person, that he should beware of me because *I* did terrible things . . . and Rock was terrified. He had known Franco for fifteen days, and he knew me for five years! This I can't forget! This skunk Rossellini ruined my friendship with Rock—everything—and Rock was disgusted with me and afraid to see me anymore. I couldn't stop it. Oh my God, I missed him all my days and my nights . . . because he was *the* thing."

As for Franco Rossellini, he would write multiple unanswered letters to Rock in care of Henry Willson in the eight months following their last encounter in Rome, each with the same pining refrain: "Dear Rock—Come back to Rome!!" The first letter, however, which Franco had sent directly to Rock's home address, would end up in the hands of Phyllis, who kept it hidden from Hudson until she ultimately passed it on to Otash.

In the first week of January 1958, after her estranged husband's disregard for her physical and emotional needs had taken its toll, Phyllis hired Jerry Giesler to commence divorce proceedings. Arguably the most popular power attorney in town with a list of movie star clients that rivaled most studio call sheets, Giesler's skill for ruthlessly navigating high-profile Hollywood divorce in the court of public opinion was legend. In their first meeting, Hudson came clean about the *Confidential* exposé that would have outed him right before their wedding. While it was no surprise to Giesler, a shaken Phyllis was coming to the realization that their marriage was nothing more than a fanciful farce to cover up his homosexuality.

A few days later, Giesler informed Gates that Hudson's attorney Greg Bautzer had sent over a proposal for the divorce settlement. While Hudson was indeed willing to grant her a divorce, he left little more on the table barring a few measly bucks, her car, and no place to live. That's when Gates fired Giesler and brought on frequent Otash collaborator and personal attorney Arthur Crowley.

For Crowley, the job was rather simple and straightforward: he needed Otash to secure damning and irrefutable evidence that Rock was a homosexual, which he would then threaten to leak to the press if Hudson didn't fork over the goods. Otash felt that Hudson should step up and support his wife rather than kicking her in the teeth with little more consideration than the countless ex-lovers Fred had neutralized in Hudson's past. Willson and Bautzer were already feeding the gossip columnists a steady stream of defamatory items about how Gates was an unfaithful spendthrift who ran up huge bills at major Beverly Hills department stores. As much as he could be a mercenary in his own right, Otash felt this behavior was beyond the pale. As ugly as things might get, he felt the case was a righteous call to action. Fred contacted numerous sources to confirm Hudson's male lovers, and through Jim Terry orchestrated his recorded conversation with Fabrizio Mioni. Along with Rossellini's love letter provided by Phyllis, the evidence was mounting, but what happened next was a game changer.

First, he had Gates debrief him on the nuances of their married life, and what she herself knew about Hudson's affairs. Then Otash set up a sting operation, wherein he wrote Phyllis a script that would include a series of leading questions gently folded into an overall narrative. Phyllis would then personally contact Rock and ask him to their home, which had been wired, for a forthcoming dinner, to see if they could work things out for themselves. If all went to plan, Otash would get Hudson on tape admitting to his homosexuality.

Otash recalled in a personal recording made before his death: *"She didn't want to admit that she knew he was a homosexual before she married him. . . . Paid by the studio? I don't know whom the fuck she was paid by."*

On January 18, 1958, Otash sent his best electronics man, William Lowe, to the Hudsons' house at 9151 Warbler Place in West Hollywood, where Gates now resided alone. With her permission, Lowe installed strategic listening devices to ensure the best pickup and sound quality. Three days later, he hid in a closet just off the living room to operate the receivers as Hudson arrived around 6:30 p.m., with Phyllis waiting for him with dinner set out on the coffee table in front of the living room fireplace, just like old times.

What follows are the extraordinary and insightful, never-before-seen original transcripts of the recording taken that fateful night where Rock Hudson, one of the world's most iconic movie stars of all time, painfully broke down and admitted to his wife that he was gay.

ROCK: I think it would be a good idea if we hired a press agent to stop some of these stories, because it seems you are getting the brunt of it. I know you don't like it, and neither do I. Phyllis, have I ever said one word about money? Have we ever had an argument about money, ever? Have we?

PHYLLIS: No, never.

ROCK: I met a press agent at the studio the other day, a young fellow. I think we should hire him to stop some of this.

PHYLLIS: Maybe, but Rock, in one of the articles printed the formal you bought with me in Amelia Gray, the one for the premiere, was described a black formal with a train, and you are the only person who has seen it. It is still in the store. How do you explain this? Who gave out the description of the dress? Did you describe it to Henry?

ROCK: I don't know, I might have, but I doubt very much if Henry is giving out any of these stories. You haven't talked to anyone have you?

PHYLLIS: No Rock, I haven't.

ROCK: We have never argued about money in any way, and this seems to be the only thing they are saying. With all the things they have already said, God knows what will be printed and said in the next few months.

PHYLLIS: Rock, when you came back from Italy, you told me you were glad I had told Constance so much about you, because it would be difficult for you to tell her, and yet you haven't gone to see Dr. Rankin. What got in the way?

ROCK: It just doesn't seem the time is right. I don't feel I can go as yet. I've been busy. I just feel I would like to go somewhere. Get away.

PHYLLIS: You know Dr. Rankin knows your problems.

ROCK: How?

PHYLLIS: By your inkblots. You told me you saw thousands of butterflies and also snakes. Constance told me in my analysis that butterflies mean femininity, and snakes represent the male penis. Rock, I am not condemning you, but it seems that as long as you recognize your problem, you would want to do something about it. Lots of people go through their entire lives without realizing they have a problem, but you know about yours.

ROCK: I was completely honest in those tests. I didn't try to cover up anything.

PHYLLIS: They wouldn't do any good if you lied. You would only be lying to yourself.

ROCK: I told Dr. Rankin everything. I didn't hedge on anything at all.

PHYLLIS: You mean about homosexuality?

ROCK: Yes, I told him everything, but I told you we were just talking about the movies.

PHYLLIS: Then what kept you from going back to him?

ROCK: Oh, he doesn't say anything. He wants me to do all the talking, and he just sits back and never says a word.

PHYLLIS: Rock, you are supposed to talk, not him. He is there to understand and guide you. There isn't anything glandular about your homosexuality, it is only a freezing at an emotional state, and it's up to the individual to grow out of it. Everyone has to help themselves, Rock. No one can do it for you. Rock, your great speed with me, sexually. Are you that fast with boys?

ROCK: Well, it's a physical conjunction.

PHYLLIS: I don't understand.

ROCK: Well, boys don't fit. So, this is why it lasts longer.

PHYLLIS: You told me once you had an affair with Rick Savage, and after that you went over to his house and had dinner with him and his wife. Did you feel badly? Did you think how awful she would feel if she found out?

ROCK: Yes, I felt badly. I knew if she found out she certainly wouldn't feel good about it.

PHYLLIS: You told me you had an affair with Henry. How long did that last?

ROCK: No time at all. Do you think I would enjoy having an affair with Henry?

PHYLLIS: But you did it. Why?

ROCK: Because of naivety, I guess.

PHYLLIS: That's no excuse. You must have wanted to do it. Did you do it for your career?

ROCK: I don't know. Maybe.

PHYLLIS: You told Constance that you had found great happiness in homosexuality. . . .

ROCK: I don't know why I said that because I haven't. You know there was Jack, that was unhappy.

PHYLLIS: Then there was Bob Preble.

ROCK: Oh, yes.

PHYLLIS: Don't you learn by your mistakes?

ROCK: Yes. Everyone does, for God's sake.

PHYLLIS: Then why do you continue to do it, over and over? Rock, I know everything. I know why I didn't hear from you in Italy, and what you were doing before Italy, and since you got back. This should make you feel better. It should remove some of your guilt.

ROCK: I know where you hear some of those things. I saw Julie at the Racquet Club last weekend, and she told me she had heard about some Italian actor I had an affair with in Italy and then brought him back here. It's the biggest lie, for God's sake.

PHYLLIS: No, I didn't hear that story. I saw Julie for only a minute. Who did you have an affair with in Italy?

ROCK: An Italian member of the crew, a most discreet man, and a girl.

PHYLLIS: He couldn't have been very discreet. All the tales got back. All the people in the "Farewell" company brought back little stories with them.

ROCK: But Phyllis, do you realize how long I was over there?

PHYLLIS: That isn't any reason for having affairs with men.

ROCK: I know where the stories came from. I can tell you. You have some pictures taken at Ingrid Bergman's villa. There was a man there by the name of Franco Rossellini and he went on the make for me. You know those two sport coats I bought before I left, one was black and the other brown. The black one was torn, and he was the same size as me, and unfortunately I gave him the torn coat. He started the rumors.

PHYLLIS: Everyone knows, Rock, that you were picking up boys off the street shortly after we were married, and have continued to do so, thinking that being married would cover up for you.

ROCK: I have never picked up any boys on the street, I have never picked up any boys in a bar, never. I have never picked up any boys, other than to give them a ride. That's their word against mine. For God's sake, there is a story going around that I picked up a boy and raped him on Mulholland Drive.

PHYLLIS: And Everard Baths in New York?

ROCK: Never heard of it. What is that, some fag joint where they all hang out? I have never been in a steam bath in New York other than the Athletic Club.

PHYLLIS: Rock, people don't talk if you aren't doing anything. You never hear these stories about Gary Cooper.

ROCK: Well, I've heard stories about Cooper, too.

PHYLLIS: Rock, the whole town is talking about your activities. I've heard that one of the major studios doesn't consider you a good risk anymore. You have worked eight hard years on your career, and because of your abnormal sex drive, you are destroying yourself. Rock, can you deny that your pattern is that of a homosexual?

Rock: (crying) No, I can't deny it. I guess. But I never felt we were together on anything. I never felt you loved me.

Phyllis: And that is why you never touched me? Rock, when we came back from our honeymoon you never made love to me for one whole month. I was always here, and I always wanted you. At first I would come to bed, and you would have a book in your face. Then you started to cut film until one or two in the morning, hoping I would be asleep. I knew what you were doing, Rock. People sense these things. Did I ever reject you, physically?

Rock: No, you never did.

Phyllis: A man has to have a sexual outlet. You should have picked me up and carried me into bed, but you never touched me. Rock, how long after we were married did you have your first homosexual affair?

Rock: Oh, Phyllis. I don't know. The next day.

Phyllis: You know I wanted babies, and I couldn't get pregnant having an affair once a month. I told you many times how I felt, and that I needed mental and physical love, and you would change the subject. You wouldn't even talk to me unless we had some of your homosexual friends around, like George and Mark.

Rock: Why bring up George and Mark?

Phyllis: Because we spent the first six months of our marriage with them, that's why. People are judged by their associates, and every time you are seen socially with Henry there is another black mark in your book, and more people talk. Do you know how they refer to Henry in Palm Springs? A bitch in heat.

Rock: (laughing) I was only to Palm Springs with Henry one weekend, and he had a date.

PHYLLIS: With a boy?

ROCK: Sure. I feel a sense of loyalty towards Henry, but I don't approve of his activities.

PHYLLIS: Do you think Henry doesn't talk about you? John Smith told me that you had told Henry that you would certainly like to get into that blonde's drawers. I've even heard that Henry has told people that he procures for you.

ROCK: I know he talks about other people, but I never thought he would talk about me that way.

PHYLLIS: What hold does he have on you? Afraid he will talk if you leave him?

ROCK: I don't know. Maybe.

PHYLLIS: Rock, you are guilty without doing a thing. You can't always be seen with homosexuals. You spent most of the time in Italy with Kurt Kasner, then you told me you didn't know he was homosexual. How can you miss that? Then you went to New York to spend New Year's with him. Rock, would you say Henry is a hundred percent homosexual?

ROCK: Yes, I guess so.

PHYLLIS: I was just a doormat to you. Someone to hide behind. Did you ever worry about my physical frustrations?

ROCK: Yes, I worried about them.

PHYLLIS: But not enough to do anything about them. Rock, did the studio tell you you had to get married?

ROCK: Absolutely not.

PHYLLIS: Do you understand how I got sick? A woman needs love and companionship as much as a man. And number one, she needs children. How do you think I feel when people we have known call me on the phone and say, "at least you know." What should I tell them, Rock?

ROCK: The truth, I guess.

PHYLLIS: Have you ever felt that I was disloyal to you?

ROCK: Oh, Phyllis, of course not.

PHYLLIS: I never was.

ROCK: I respect you for that.

PHYLLIS: I couldn't have, even if I'd made the opportunity. It was you I wanted. I tried everything to make you happy. But it wasn't me you wanted, and I don't understand why you married me. I'll bet you right now that if you want to change and will go to Dr. Rankin, that within four months you wouldn't want your homosexual friends. You would see that they are children not past twelve, and that's why they talk. Rock, every time you have an affair with them they will talk. One Sunday afternoon we were at Henry's pool. I had my car and had to leave early. When I left, you were right in the middle of five little boys, and I thought this marriage doesn't stand a chance. When you came home from Italy, I knew about your affairs over there, but I tried to give it a chance. We went to Hawaii and I spent a hundred dollars on a new negligee, and once again you didn't touch me.

ROCK: I know I didn't.

PHYLLIS: It must have been both guilt and lack of desire. Rock, I don't hate you for not loving me, but you can't treat another person like they are void of any feelings, and never want to discuss anything. On top of everything you tried to humiliate me with those fan magazine stories. That was a mistake. People started to help me. They said our marriage was a laugh, and you were making a mockery of it. The phone rang constantly and I got letters.

ROCK: Everyone tells you these stories about me. Why do you always believe these people?

PHYLLIS: I didn't at first. I didn't want to. Until I was sat down
and the facts were printed out to me. I could overlook a
few, but so many people came to me with the same story.
There had to be some truth in it. What about the *Confidential* story? Would they sign affidavits if they weren't true?

ROCK: Yes. They got a good chunk of money for them.

PHYLLIS: Why would so many people say the same thing?

ROCK: You wouldn't believe me, no matter how untrue I would
say they were.

PHYLLIS: No, Rock, I wouldn't. Now now. A month ago,
maybe, but not now. I know much more than you give me
credit for. And your admission. How about that?

ROCK: Then why don't you tell me these things?

PHYLLIS: Oh, Rock, I don't have to. You know. Just for the
record, how long was it really after we were married that
you had your first homosexual affair? Was it a short time
or a long time?

ROCK: It was a long time. How do you resist a temptation
when it occurs?

PHYLLIS: You think about other things. You think about the
person that loves you and turn your back on it. Paint. Read.
Keep busy. In Italy you could have written to your wife.

ROCK: I would like to call you. Would you see me?

PHYLLIS: Yes, if I could help you get started on the right road,
I would only be too happy to help you.

A couple of days later, Otash and Crowley met with Bautzer
to pressure a settlement. Bautzer was no pushover. As the

attorney for Howard Hughes, he was used to getting his way for his clients.

Crowley opened the meeting by saying, "Look here, Greg, I don't think this thing should ever go to trial. If we go up in front of Judge Brand, and we now file affidavits as to his homosexuality, I think it's gonna destroy this man's career. This has to be settled out of court."

Bautzer jumped out of his chair and banged his fist on the desk.

"You two fucking cocksuckers!" he screamed. "You two fucking liars! How dare you call my partner and my client a homosexual! You're going to get your fucking asses sued!"

"Now Greg," Otash began, "before you go crazy, let me play a tape for you."

Fred placed what looked like a small briefcase on Bautzer's desk, opening it to reveal an Ampex 601 reel-to-reel tape recorder, which he then used to play back the conversation between Gates and Hudson. When it was all over, Otash and Crowley watched in amazement as Bautzer calmly stood up, grabbed the tape recorder, and flung it across the room, where it hit the wall and exploded into a million pieces.

"Greg," Otash said, smiling, "that was not my only copy. Do you think I'm stupid enough to bring the original? Now you owe me for a new fucking machine."

Hudson ended up giving Gates the Hollywood Hills house, $250 a week for ten years provided she didn't remarry, which would come to $130,000 (about $1.3 million today) as she did not, as well as stock in his film production company. For his work, Otash was paid $2,500 (about $26,000 today). And, for the moment, Hudson's secret life remained out of the press.

TEN

JUDY IN LOVE

I t was an auspicious Friday the thirteenth in 1935 when Louis B. Mayer first laid eyes on her. Singing "Eili, Eili" during an audition, the veteran stage performer formerly known as Frances Ethel Gumm had just changed her name for the second time. Legend has it the king of Metro-Goldwyn-Mayer was so charmed by her rendition of the popular Yiddish song that he waived the obligatory screen test and fatefully signed the thirteen-year-old phenom to a long-term contract that would change her life, and the history of cinema, forever. Earning a Depression-defying salary of $100 a week (about $2,200 today), the youngest daughter of a vaudevillian family was then thrust into an all-consuming machine that was the largest, most prestigious film studio in Hollywood, refined, and ultimately reinvented into the inimitable Judy Garland. Fifteen years later, however, the woman who had traded in her childhood to become one of the brightest, most revered stars in MGM's celestial firmament would be abandoned by the dream factory that created her when Mayer, a man she considered a father figure, severed ties with his now fragile and problematic protégé as her private life spiraled out of control.

In those latter years leading up to her dismissal, Garland's personal hardships read more like a passage from the Book of Job than the diary of a glamorous movie star: she had suffered a nervous breakdown, been admitted to a private sanatorium, made her first failed suicide attempt, and underwent electroconvulsive therapy to battle depression. In large part, the handcuff contracts that the studios imposed on the stars of the day, and their insistence they be perfect in public lest they diminish their value, took a toll on their mental and physical health. Incapable of fulfilling her professional obligations, MGM fired her off two major musicals costarring Fred Astaire: replaced by Ginger Rogers in *The Barkleys of Broadway*, and by Jane Powell in *Royal Wedding*.

Just a decade earlier, Garland was riding high with a Juvenile Academy Award for her incomparable portrayal of Dorothy Gale, the Kansas farm girl clad in a blue gingham pinny and ruby-red slippers who sang and danced her way along the Yellow Brick Road into the hearts of adoring fans in the iconic musical fantasy *The Wizard of Oz*. One of a handful of films to usher in Hollywood's Golden Age, Garland's trip to the Emerald City crowned her one of Tinseltown's most bankable stars, which led to headlining roles throughout the 1940s in some of the most acclaimed motion pictures in MGM's musical catalogue, most notably *For Me and My Gal*, *Meet Me in St. Louis*, *The Harvey Girls*, *Summer Stock*, and her biggest box-office success, *Easter Parade*. But the seeds of her misfortunes would be sown long before these creative milestones, during Garland's fledgling years in the studio system; cast in a rapid-fire succession of low-budget musicals where excruciatingly long work hours precipitated a lifelong addiction to prescription drugs after MGM kept her on a steady diet of amphetamines and barbiturates to maintain her weight and keep her going as she struggled to meet the frenetic demands of assembly-line filmmaking.

On June 15, 1945, Garland wed second husband Vincente Minnelli, the fledgling filmmaker twenty years her senior who had directed her in *Meet Me in St. Louis* the previous year. Despite being plagued with a plethora of production delays, artistic complications, creative differences, and back-office studio drama, the Christmas musical would emerge triumphant when it premiered the day before Thanksgiving in 1944. Garland, who had grown weary of the teenage sweetheart roles that had brought her signature fame in previous films, would credit Minnelli for helping her transition to a more mature, graceful, and iconic on-screen presence. The following year, the couple welcomed their first and only child together, Liza Minnelli.

Despite her demoralizing exit from MGM, Judy Garland found renewed stardom just a step beyond the rain in 1951 with a string of record-breaking concert tours at the Palace Theatre and London Palladium. One of the greatest personal triumphs of her career, the American Theatre Wing presented her with a Special Tony Award for her contributions to the revival of vaudeville. Then, on June 8, 1952, after the divorce from her six-year marriage to Minnelli was finalized following a protracted separation in 1949, Garland wed tour manager and producer Sid Luft just two days before her thirtieth birthday.

Two years later through their newly formed Transcona Enterprises production banner, the happy couple developed and produced Garland's big Hollywood comeback in the Warner Bros. musical drama *A Star Is Born*. Directed by legendary filmmaker George Cukor and costarring the renowned English actor James Mason, the film would be the first remake of David O. Selznick's original 1937 Technicolor classic, hand-tailored to exploit every ounce of Judy's extraordinary talents. A massive critical success when it premiered on September 29, 1954, she received both Golden Globe and Academy Award Best Actress nominations for her fierce portrayal of an aspiring performer in love with a former matinee idol who fosters her ascent to stardom before he ultimately succumbs to the perils of alcoholism.

For many Hollywood insiders, including Otash, their marriage had appeared on the surface to be a solid one, with Sid serving as Judy's backbone, helping her attain new heights in her career. But less than four years later, on March 4, 1958, Garland filed for divorce once again. She alleged mental cruelty and physical abuse, and that Luft had beaten her up and attempted to strangle her on numerous occasions.

Her attorney, Jerry Giesler, was concerned about Judy and needed a trusted keeper for his troubled client. When Otash got the call, his first thought was that babysitting a movie star wasn't exactly his forte. The job would take Otash out of his PI work and turn him into a bodyguard and, of course, the fixer.

Otash told Giesler that because it was Judy Garland, he would help, and hey, Judy would be paying $500 a day (about $6,300 today), which sure sounded like easy money. Like everyone else in the world at that time, he remembered the legendary Judy Garland for her glory years at MGM. But now the screen siren sitting across from him in her Beverly Hills home was hardly recognizable. Otash was shocked when he met her the first time, no longer the kid who went over the rainbow but a grown, plump, puffy-faced woman dancing on the edge of her emotional spectrum.

"I want you, Mr. Otash, to come here and live at my house," she declared in the same tremulous voice that had given her famous vocal chops their unique, bittersweet quality.

"Do you think that will be necessary, Judy?" Otash asked.

"Yes, I do," she insisted. "You don't know that son of a bitch. He goes into unbelievable rages. I'm afraid to be alone in this house!"

Her defenseless demeanor notwithstanding, Otash soon realized that Judy Garland was a woman who was accustomed to getting what she wanted from those who worked for her. She particularly feared that her husband would kidnap her children, so the first thing he did was serve Luft with divorce papers that ordered him to vacate the family home immediately, along with a restraining order prohibiting him from harassing, molesting, or annoying his wife. From that moment on, he'd need to make an appointment to legally see his children. Fred then moved himself from the relative serenity of his West Hollywood apartment to the bedlam that was Garland's rambling mansion, along with two of his agents, Bob Drummond and Mickey Finn, both former LAPD officers.

A couple of days in, Otash suspected she was heavily dependent on a debilitating combination of alcohol and narcotics, because most of the time she was in her own little world. While her three children—Liza (twelve), Lorna (five), and Joey (three)—were all thankfully well cared for by the nanny, a long conversation with the household staff, all of whom genuinely seemed to care for their employer and wanted to see her get better, confirmed his suspicions.

"I know all about her problems, Fred," an undaunted Giesler declared after hearing his concerns. "You used to be on the Narcotics Squad, right? I'm sure you know how to handle a situation like this. Do whatever you think is necessary."

"I think it's necessary to get her cleaned out of all that crap."

"Great! Then figure it out."

Imposing a moratorium on the booze was easy. Otash simply gathered up all the liquor bottles in plain sight and locked them away in the garage. The drugs, however, were another story. After years of abuse, a very clever Judy had become quite adept at hiding her stash. After an exhaustive search, Fred finally found her surplus of uppers, downers, and some pills he didn't even recognize, either stuffed into a hole she'd cut under the mattress or packed inside rubber glove fingers cut and tied at the top with a thread, which were then anchored around the faucet of the washbasin and dropped into the drain. When she needed a fix, all Judy had to do was pull up a waterproof finger from the crook of the pipe—brilliant by any standard. Even Otash was impressed by her ingenuity before flushing it all down the toilet. As he had expected, it wasn't long before Judy confronted him in a panic.

"What do you mean, Judy?"

"You know goddamn well what I mean, you son of a bitch!" she fumed.

"I got rid of the stuff."

Garland shook her head in dismay. "You . . . you what?"

"I got rid of it. The booze is locked up and the other crap went down the drain."

As he watched her growing indignation, Otash immediately administered his version of a reality check. "Look, Judy, let me tell you like it is," he said. "You've got three beautiful children and you're facing a divorce action that's going to involve a custody battle . . . and Sid won't give up without a fight. He'll use whatever he can to get the kids away from you, and narcotics and alcohol are just about the best evidence he could ever produce in court . . . believe me."

"What the hell do you know about my husband?" she snarled.

"I know Sid Luft from around," he said. "I've even had the opportunity to speak with him, and I know he wants to see you well again, and the two biggest problems in your marriage are your drinking and the pills. It doesn't matter to me whether you love the guy or not, that's your business. And you still have the right to divorce him if you think that will solve everything. But there's something else to think about. You have a big show coming up and your agent wants you to get in shape. And believe it or not, Sid wants you to be a sensation too."

"Bullshit!"

"No bullshit, Judy. But hey, I don't give a damn. Look, I'm here with my men at your behest, and while we're here I'm gonna see that you don't have access to pills unless your doctor prescribes them. And no booze either! That's it, Judy. It's for your own good."

"You . . . you think you can come in here and change my whole way of life just like that?!" she yelled, snapping her fingers in his face for dramatic effect. "Well, you listen to me, mister, I can throw you out anytime I want! You understand?!"

"You want me out, just say so," Otash calmly replied. "I'll pack up my guys and go. But while we're here, we'll do what you're paying us for, to protect you and your children, and ensure nothing goes wrong." Then he gently put his hand over hers in a final effort to appeal to her better angels. "Dammit, Judy, listen to me. You've got problems, kid . . . let's try to straighten them out. I know it's hard, but you can do it."

Otash breathed a sigh of relief when Judy, out of devotion to her children, begrudgingly agreed to his tough-love terms and conditions.

"**G**et up, you son of a bitch!" Judy screamed at the top of her lungs as she pounded on his bedroom door at three in the morning. Scrambling into action from a dead sleep, Otash found her standing in the doorway in her housecoat, sober as a judge.

"What's all the ruckus?"

"The ruckus *is*, you big bastard, that if you won't give me pills to make me sleep and I can't have a drink, I'm going to keep your ass up all night too."

Fred thought she'd flipped out.

"You heard me, Otash. I'm paying you a lot of money, so we're going to sit up and we're going to talk," she ordered, grabbing his arm as if trying to wrestle a gorilla. "Come on . . . let's show some spirit here and see how you like it."

Judy led him to the living room, where they both sat on the couch as Fred rubbed the sleep from his eyes, "So, what'll we talk about?"

"We're going to talk about my life," she said matter-of-factly.

"Okay. I'm all ears, Judy."

And so began their almost nightly rituals, where Otash would listen patiently as a restless Judy Garland waxed poetically of her remarkable life's journey with the wit and timing of a seasoned raconteur: from her childhood years singing and dancing in her father's vaudeville theater to the perilous heights of Hollywood stardom, where MGM made over $50 million on her back while Mayer turned a blind eye to their "slipping me Benzedrine to keep me going on the set when I was so sick and tired I could hardly move." Bit by bit over the course of a month, Otash would bear witness to what he called "a crazy mixed-up kid inside a woman's body, scared to death of living while killing herself with self-doubt, booze, and those shitty little pills." Even if it kept him up all night, he knew it would be good for her.

As the days passed and Fred and his men settled in, they became so fond of Judy's children that they watched over them as if they were their own; even squabbling over whose turn it was to drive them to and from school.

Otash later recalled: *"One day, a terribly shy Liza, caught in that awkward stage between little girl and young lady, came out to the back of the house where I was washing my car, and she thanked me for helping her mother."*

Fred wasn't expecting such wisdom at her age and found himself getting all choked up as he watched her skip back into the house as quickly as she came. On another occasion, little Joey randomly asked, "Why can't I see my daddy?" It was heart-wrenching. Fred didn't know what to say other than to reassure the toddler that he'd see his father very soon. For better or worse, matrimonial cases always disgusted Otash, perhaps because they hit too close to home, especially when innocent children were used as pawns in a chess game between two adults who had forgotten they once loved each other. Most of the time he witnessed it from a distance. But now Fred's intimate daily interactions with Judy's children haunted him as a constant reminder of his own beautiful eight-year-old daughter, Colleen, who was living with her mother in a home he had purchased for them in the San Fernando Valley. While he financially supported their every need, Otash was beginning to realize that a constant, positive presence was the most important thing a parent could provide, and as much time as he did spend with Colleen, he needed to do even better.

––––––––––

All good cops play their hunches and Otash had one about Sid Luft, who seemed to be playing it too cool. He then learned from a trusted source that he had hired Clyde Duber, a fellow PI friend with a good reputation and an office in Beverly Hills, to be his bodyguard. He couldn't figure out why, until one night when the doorbell rang at two in the morning. Smelling trouble, Otash approached the entrance flanked by his two men. Then he swung the door open with a hand on his gun, only to find Clyde and Sid rushing the door.

"Hold it," he warned, forming an impenetrable wall with his men. "You ain't gettin' in here. What the hell are you up to, Duber? You know there's a court order restraining Sid from coming in this house and bothering Judy, and this is going to bother her, believe me. Dammit, Duber, you're an investigator, you might have more sense!"

At that moment, a patrol car pulled up on the street, red lights flashing, its two police officers running up the drive, wanting to know "what the hell!"

Fred took the oldest cop aside. "This is what's going on . . . Miss Garland is seeking a divorce from Mr. Luft and has a restraining order against him, which he's in violation of just by being here."

"All I want to do is see my kids!" Luft screamed.

"Fine, but not at two in the morning, Sid," Otash shot back. "Hell, if you want to see your kids, have your lawyer work it out with Jerry Giesler. You know how it's done. I can't tell you not to visit your kids. You know better than that."

"But that's what you're doing, Otash!"

"Sid, I'm working for Judy, that's all. No hard feelings, but she doesn't want you here and you're not coming in. And dammit, you're gonna get your ass in a sling over that restraining order if you and Duber here don't cut out right now!"

"You're breaking up my marriage! You're depriving me of seeing my children! That's what you're doing!"

"Oh, come on, Sid . . ."

"That's right," Luft continued, "and you're depriving me of seeing my wife. I want to talk to her. Right now! You understand?!"

The situation was about to get out of control when Duber and the police officers convinced Luft to work through his attorney before his "bodyguard" finally led him away. After that, Otash had explicit instructions from Giesler that if Sid called the house, he couldn't speak to Judy, nor was he allowed to talk to the kids. The only calls allowed were from her attorney, her manager, her agent, and her doctor. Fred and his men screened everything as Judy suffered through the worst of her withdrawals . . . and it wasn't pretty. She screamed, yelled, kept him awake most nights, and called Otash things he'd have knocked a man on his ass for. But after thirty long days and nights, Judy Garland was clean.

An exhausted but satisfied Otash then moved out, leaving his two agents behind as twenty-four-hour guards to make sure she didn't relapse. He had other pressing cases to attend to but, more importantly, was looking forward to seeing his daughter Colleen again.

He drove to the San Fernando home and found Doris in the kitchen making lunch.

"Where's Colleen?" he asked.

"As usual, up one of the trees with her kittens, having a tea party," Doris replied.

In the backyard, Otash called out for Colleen as he surveilled their many fruit trees.

"I'm up here, Daddy!" she exclaimed, revealing her location. "Come up and have a tea party with me and the kitties!"

Otash lit up. "Sure, sounds great!" Then he removed his coat and tie, climbed up the huge apple tree, and sat on a limb across from his daughter for one of their make-believe tea parties in the sky with her basket of kittens, as they would do so many times henceforth during those handful of precious, ephemeral years of her childhood.

Back in his West Hollywood apartment that evening, Otash received a call from Luft.

"I'm gonna shoot your ass off," he told him.

"No kidding," Fred chortled. "What the hell did I do now?"

"You broke up my marriage, you son of a bitch . . . and I'm gonna stick your ass in Forest Lawn where you won't do anybody any more harm."

"Hold on," Fred said bluntly. "We've been down this road before, Sid. Even if you do shoot me, it won't get Judy back. That's something you two people need to work out for yourselves. Throwing dirt over me in Forest Lawn isn't going to change anything."

Luft softened. "Well, maybe we better get together and have a little talk," he said.

"Okay. Tell me where and when and I'll be there," Otash agreed. "But you'd better leave the pistol at home."

They met at Dino's, the popular watering hole co-owned by Dean Martin on the Sunset Strip. He knew Sid was not a man to play games with, so he arrived with his trusted .38 Smith & Wesson Centennial revolver strapped to his ankle, just in case. Luft looked uptight when Otash spotted him sitting at a table in the back room with some other guy who got up and went to the bar as he approached.

"Hello, prick," Luft said as Otash sat down in the booth across from him.

"Cut the crap, Sid. I was retained by a lawyer to do a job. I'm an investigator. You know that. It's nothing personal. Christ, I've got to eat too, don't I?"

Luft stared back at Otash for what seemed a very long moment, until the waiter stood at the table. "Ah, fuck it," he snorted. "You want a drink or something?"

"Just coffee," Fred told the waiter, who left as quickly as he came.

"You know, Sid," Fred continued, "instead of putting me down, you should thank me."

"For what?"

"I think you'd be proud of your wife now. She's looking good, off the drugs and the juice, and getting herself in shape for that show in ten days."

"She really looks that good?"

"Damn right. But she's still uptight about you. Or she was, anyway. I haven't seen her in a week or so. She seemed to be mellowing near the end."

"So, if she's calming down, why she so uptight with me?"

Otash told Luft of the many late nights he sat vigil as his restless wife emptied her rambling mind of all the troubles haunting her past and present. In a moment of clarity near the end she confessed that, despite her anger over his extravagant spending, which included his expensive habit of buying Thoroughbred racehorses and his fits of rage, Judy relied heavily on Sid for his good judgment when it came to her career. She feared not being able to perform at her upcoming engagement without him by her side, as he had done so devotedly when their love was new during her record-breaking concert tours, and the making of *A Star is Born.*

Beyond what he was able to glean from his perpetual late-night crawls with Judy in the wee small hours, Otash did his homework before meeting up with Luft. He knew how they were introduced in a New York nightclub by a mutual friend in 1950, when both were unhappily married to other people— Sid to actress Lynn Bari and Judy to Minnelli—and how she pursued him despite his reluctance at first.

"You know, Sid, I've handled a lot of these cases, and I've got the feeling she still loves you very much," Fred continued as Luft listened intently, nodding in agreement from time to time, looking for a ray of hope. It was clear to him now that

Luft wanted nothing more than to get back with his wife. "Your problems with Judy are no better or worse than any other married couple, and it usually comes down to communication. I have no interest in seeing you and Judy get divorced. Those are damn good kids you have, and they need you people together. Now, if I see any signs that she's ready to sit down and talk things out with you, I'll call you right away."

Sincerely moved by his genuine concern to help him save his marriage, Luft reached across the table and fitfully shook Otash's hand, "I misjudged you, Fred. I apologize for that . . . and you've got yourself a deal."

About a week before Judy was to leave for her concert in New Jersey, Otash got his opportunity to put his plan into action when she called him in a panic to come to her home, where he found her nervously pacing up and down the living room floor, telling him she couldn't do the show alone, and begging him to come with her.

"No way, kitten," Fred told her. "You can't afford to keep paying me five hundred dollars a day. That would be stupid and besides, I've got a business to run."

Judy kept pacing and speaking quickly to the point that Fred knew she'd be looking for a fix if something positive didn't happen quick.

"I can't do it alone, Fred. Sid was always with me before. He took care of everything for me, made sure that I got there okay and that I was all right. He gave me confidence, you know? I've never trusted agents or business managers, Fred, and I'm afraid I can't do it on my own."

Otash got up and stood in her path, stopping her in her tracks as he placed his hands gently on her stiff shoulders, "Let me ask you a question, Judy. Do you love him?"

He caught her off guard, "What do you mean?"

"I mean, do you love Sid?"

It was like flipping a switch. Judy's whole body seemed to melt as she blushed. "Yeah. Yeah, I guess I do love him."

"And he loves you."

"How the hell do you know?"

"We had a little talk at Dino's," Otash confessed. "I had to meet with him because he threatened to kill me . . . and I wasn't going to wait around for the bullet."

"Oh, I don't believe it," Judy said laughing. "Sid can be an asshole, but he wouldn't shoot anybody."

"He was sore as hell with me and I can't say I blame him. I was an outsider in his home with the woman he loves. Sometimes my job ain't all it's cracked up to be. Hell, you hated me in the beginning too, remember?"

Judy had no memory of it. "I did?"

"You sure the hell did . . . because I wouldn't let you do your booze and pills act. But hey, I'm goddamn proud of how you've turned yourself around. But look, Judy, you're standing here telling me how much you miss the guy, and I know the kids miss him too."

Now Judy was crying. "Oh, God, they miss him so much," she said. "I feel terrible that I prevented him from seeing them."

"So, what are you saying, Judy? Let me see if I understand. You haven't had a drink for almost a month, right?"

Judy nodded quickly like a little girl, wiping away her tears.

"And you haven't taken any medicine for almost a month."

She kept nodding.

"So now you can communicate. Are you saying you love him?"

"Yes!" Judy exclaimed, sobbing. "But my goddammed agent and manager and the lawyers, all of them . . . they keep saying how bad he is for me, and my head gets all fucked-up."

"Hey, I don't want to hear that crap," Otash insisted. "I want to hear what *you've* got to say, not what they tell you. Screw those assholes! They have their own agenda. You love the guy, you miss him, and you want him back. Think it over and give me a simple answer . . . yes or no?"

"Yes," said the sober Judy Garland.

"Okay," Otash said as he started to leave.

"Okay what?!" Judy shouted. "What are you going to do?!"

"I'm not going to do anything right now. I just wanted to know where you stand, that's all."

When Otash got back to his home, he called Sid. "I want to tell you something, and if you tell Jerry Giesler or her agent, or any of those jerks who hang on to her like leeches, I'm going to be in trouble," he said. "But I'm convinced you two can work this out."

Luft lit up. "You really think so?"

"Listen, I'm taking Judy to Pasadena on Wednesday to catch the train for her concert. If you really want a reconciliation, the time is now. Why don't you make arrangements to be in San Bernardino and catch that train when it stops there. If this marriage is meant to be, it's going to resolve itself between San Bernardino and New Jersey. Like it ought to be."

And that's just what happened. Sid boarded that train as Otash instructed, and by the time they got to their destination, Judy and Sid were a team once more . . . and she brought down the house in Jersey. A few months later, Judy released her fifth studio album, an upbeat collection of classic love songs arranged by renowned composer and bandleader Nelson Riddle, aptly titled *Judy in Love*. The first track featured "Zing! Went the Strings of My Heart," the very song that so many years before had secured her the audition with Louis B. Mayer.

Judy and Sid's marriage, the longest of her life, would go on to weather the gale force winds of substance abuse and financial vicissitudes until 1965, when Judy filed for divorce for the last time and was awarded full custody of their children.

Otash later reflected with genuine melancholy: *"But for a while at least, Judy . . . poor Judy, looked like the kid who went over the rainbow."*

ELEVEN

WONDER BOY

By the late 1950s, the Golden Age of Capitalism had substantially transformed the fabric of American life from its postwar beginnings. Unprecedented economic growth, the birth of suburbia, television, rock and roll, McCarthyism, *Brown v. Board of Education*, and the launch of the space race would exemplify a seismic shift in the nation's sociopolitical and cultural landscape that inadvertently set the stage for one of the most turbulent decades in U.S. history yet to come.

Nineteen fifty-eight and 1959 would prove consequential years in the life of Fred Otash. The former LAPD cop who just three years earlier had traded in his badge for a detective license was now arguably the most successful, sought-after, and infamous private investigator in the country. Exploiting his well-earned notoriety, Otash expanded his brand of signature sleuth across a lucrative list of domestic and international law firms and corporations now seeking his unique services on a regular basis, executed with the aid of a curated team of field operatives and a treasure trove of state-of-the-art surveillance equipment worth over $50,000 (more than $500,000 in today's dollars).

The ex-Marine who had hoped to merely survive was now thriving beyond his wildest dreams, banking north of a hundred grand a year (more than $1 million today) when minimum-wage workers were barely scraping by on a buck an hour. More financially flush than some of the Hollywood players now tapping his talents, Otash was nearly just as famous thanks to a steady stream of salacious ink made possible by a handful of hard-boiled editors at downtown dailies like the *Evening Herald*, the *Daily News*, the *Examiner*, and the *Mirror*, all quick to capitalize on America's quenchless appetite for scandal when covering his high-profile cases or printing one of his many lip-smacking detective columns. Even the *National Enquirer* proclaimed "He's Hollywood's King of the Snoops."

"Freddie O" had a promising future stretched out before him, enjoying the spoils of his full-fledged celebrity to such a degree that even the venerated *Los Angeles Times* saw fit to feature the strapping playboy private eye and a stenographer girlfriend ten years his junior, smiling to the camera after a forty-two-year-old bartender slammed his jalopy into the bullet bumpers of his pride-and-joy Cadillac Eldorado Biarritz convertible at the corner of Fairfax and Melrose. Life wasn't just good, it was *exceptional*. But in the ominous words of Edward Aloysius Murphy Jr., the midcentury American aerospace engineer who coined his namesake Murphy's law: *anything that can go wrong will go wrong.*

Otash was burning the candle so brightly at both ends that it eventually took a toll on his physical health. A flight to New York for business in March 1959 would be followed by a quick jaunt down to Miami Beach for some much-needed R&R, a tropical respite from the daily grind that he hoped might relieve some of the burdens weighing down his broad but beleaguered shoulders. A few days in, however, severe chest pains abruptly brought his beachfront sojourn to a standstill. Fortunate to call himself an ambulance before it was too late, the thirty-seven-year-old had suffered a minor heart attack, an existential shot across the bow signaling that perhaps he wasn't so invincible as previously imagined. After four months' convalescence in Miami, he returned to LA just in time to take Colleen for a night out on the town to celebrate her tenth birthday at Dino's Lodge.

Located at 8524 Sunset Boulevard, the hottest destination on the Strip co-owned by Dean Martin treated Otash like Hollywood royalty, with his own back corner bird's-eye booth complete with private telephone reserved for him nightly unless he called to cancel or failed to show. After his recent brush with mortality, the twofold celebration meant more to him than ever before as he held court while prominent friends and acquaintances from all walks of A-list life stopped by his table to kibitz and pay their respects, but not before he made certain they first wished his darling little girl a very happy birthday.

One of the good friends to grace his table that night was best-selling crime novelist Mickey Spillane, who likened Otash to a real-life Mike Hammer of Hollywood; but when it came to his daughter, the loving, compassionate, and doting father was on full display. A consummate "girl dad" decades before the catchphrase became a popular hashtag, Fred always looked his dapper best for her, dressed in bespoke suits and custom-made shirts even if they were spending the day at Colleen's favorite Beverly Park, a massive children's amusement center at the corner of La Cienega and Beverly Boulevards. Opened in 1943, the park's Streamliner train ride, Motorama roadway, and Haunted Castle themed attractions would inspire a young Walt Disney to create his namesake Disneyland.

Dining out with her larger-than-life dad taught the young Colleen all she needed to know about how a gentleman should treat a lady: walking on the outside of the sidewalk, opening the car door, helping with her coat, assisting with her chair, making sure her beverage was always topped off, that the silverware was refreshed between courses, and forbidding any waiter to remove his dinner plate until the young lady had finished her meal. Not all nights on the town were created equal, however, especially when other women were involved. Begrudgingly at first, Colleen concealed her frustrations for having to share her father's attention, sequestered in the back seat to suffer through the sight of him snuggling up to his latest conquest. But it was only a matter of time before daddy's little girl devised a sophisticated plan to sabotage the competition.

Once seated and settled in at any given hotspot, Colleen would politely request her father's eager-to-please date to accompany her to the ladies' room. Moments later, as they stood side by side primping in the mirror making girl talk, a seemingly innocent Colleen would say, "Can I ask you a question?"

"Well, of course, sweetheart," the lady would say. "You can ask me anything you like."

"Do you like my dad?"

"Oh yes . . . very much so," she would invariably reply.

That was Colleen's cue to lower the boom. "Yeah, that's what all his girlfriends say."

Not surprisingly, Fred didn't get lucky that night, nor many nights thereafter. This masterful scheme would succeed without fail every time she was in tow until finally, when pressed by a baffled at-wits-end Otash, a more outspoken love interest fessed up to his daughter's powder room confession. Despite being angered at first and admonishing Colleen for her naughtiness, Otash couldn't help but laugh as he proudly boasted to his buddies that his chip off the old block, savvy little girl already knew how to play the angles.

Dating an assortment of young Hollywood ingenues wasn't the only means by which Otash blew off steam. An avid equestrian since his early days on the force, he regarded horses as the embodiment of peace and goodness in an often noisy and unpleasant world. Fred loved how they moved, how they worked with him, challenged him, and demanded his respect while providing a therapeutic reprieve from the daily stressors of a demanding life. As a young LAPD cop, he and his wife, Doris, would often spend quality time at Du Brock's Riding Academy near Griffith Park, where a then-unknown Tab Hunter worked as a stable boy on the weekends, and where Doris took pictures of her husband with a new state-of-the-art Polaroid 95 instant camera they couldn't afford as he rode atop a powerful stallion named "Red Boy"; or during weekend trips to Big Bear, where they trotted along the log cabin trails on their favorite ponies, with Doris on "Freckles" and Freddie on "Topper."

A decade hence, Otash was now a card-carrying member of the Sport of Kings, and much like Judy Garland's equally equine-obsessed husband Sid Luft, a regular patron of the

Thoroughbred racetracks found at Hollywood Park, Santa Anita, and Del Mar, where he hobnobbed with the rich and famous and occasionally won big from the hot tips he received in a professional sport fueled by pervasive corruption, greed, and a lack of regulation that exists to this day. Such gaming malfeasance wasn't new to Otash, who experienced it up close and personal while working off duty security for mobster Eddie Nealis, his then future wife's first ex-husband who owned the Caliente Racetrack in Tijuana, Mexico, where he frequently overheard him plotting with his partners about fixing races to further their ill-gotten gains.

A retired jockey named Kenny Godkins would be one of the myriad colorful acquaintances Fred encountered at the tracks. Since hanging up his silks, the diminutive ex-jockey was now known for playing the gray margins of horse betting. Aware of Otash's reputation, he reckoned the rule-bending private eye might be amenable to similar tactics when he met him in his Hollywood office to pitch a business opportunity and introduce him to Richard "The Wizard" Gach on the afternoon of February 4, 1959.

A native of the seaport town of San Pedro, Gach's well-earned moniker came from his uncanny ability to transform Thoroughbreds into winners, until some of his more dubious methods got his jockey agent and training licenses suspended. But despite his tarnished curriculum vitae, Godkins convinced Otash to hear him out.

"I think you and me should buy a racehorse at Santa Anita together," the Wizard proposed.

"Why in the world would I want to do that?" asked a baiting Otash.

"Because we could *cash a gamble* if the odds were long enough, and if we *hopped him*," he explained.

Otash knew the lingo: "cash a gamble" meant to win a bet, and "hopped him" meant doping the horse with a narcotic. The latter in and of itself should have raised a huge red flag prompting him to end the meeting then and there, even if such acts were commonplace among certain horse owners who considered themselves above the law. But he was intrigued and his reckless curiosity got the best of him . . . in more ways than one. "How good are the odds?" he asked.

"It's hit-or-miss," Godkins chimed in, "but better than getting a jockey not to ride his best race."

Otash already owned a horse. Purchasing another on the promise of an illicit financial windfall seemed a dangerous, albeit tempting gamble, but only if the returns outweighed the risks. Godkins and the Wizard kept champing at the bit to bring him on board until Otash finally cut them off, telling them he intended to bet three grand on a race at Caliente that weekend. If it delivered, he might consider their scheme.

Whether it was serendipity, a hot tip, or some combination thereof, that's exactly what happened. Otash's bet won big, providing him a bundle of discretionary dough. He was now riding high, feeling invincible. With hubris, good fortune, and a wallet full of courage now clouding his good judgment, he decided to double down and put up $3,500 toward buying a horse. While Gach worked with his network of reprobates to secure the animal, Otash brought Godkins along to visit Patsy D'Amore, his good friend who owned the Villa Capri restaurant in Hollywood. D'Amore, who had been involved in the Wrong Door Raid case, co-owned the renowned celebrity

haunt with Frank Sinatra who used it as his personal playground, where he was often found singing at the piano bar
with Nat King Cole and palling around with Sammy Davis Jr.,
Lauren Bacall, James Dean, Ava Gardner, Dean Martin, and
Marilyn Monroe, to name a few. Together with Godkins,
Otash pitched D'Amore to join in on their investment plan,
but despite his affection for Fred, the well-known restaurateur
with a sophisticated knowledge of racetrack operations
politely declined.

Meanwhile back at the ranch, Gach secured a six-year-old
Thoroughbred named Wonder Boy for the exact amount
Otash ponied up. Now all they needed to do was see how the
souped-up stallion would fare in a race, so Gach set up a test
run. He injected the animal with an amphetamine scored
from a lowlife veterinarian right before a trusted jockey
plucked from his former life worked the Thoroughbred out on
the racetrack. The results exceeded their expectations.

"I don't see how he can lose," an enthused Gach reported
back to Otash from a phone booth near the stables.

The following day, Wonder Boy was entered into a race at
Santa Anita for March 4, 1959. But just to be sure, Gach suggested they attempt to slow down the other horses in the race
to ensure victory. To accomplish that he would need phenobarbital, a barbiturate depressant known for its hypnotic
properties that was first synthesized in 1911.

There was silence on the other end of the telephone as
Otash pondered the gravity of his next step. Then he told
Gach to come by his office the next day and he'd see what he
could do. When he arrived, Otash handed him a bottle of
fluid that contained what he was told (by less-than-kosher
sources) to be enough phenobarbital to depress thirty horses.

B uilt by pioneer and horseman Elias "Lucky" Baldwin in 1907 on his two-hundred-acre tract of land set against the backdrop of the San Gabriel Mountains, the storied Santa Anita Park, once dubbed "the prettiest racetrack in America," had been abandoned for three years before it burned to the ground in 1912 after moral reformers forced politicians to pass an antigambling bill in 1909. Then in 1935, two years after California legalized pari-mutuel betting, a redesigned Santa Anita crowned by a glorious aquamarine art deco clubhouse reopened and quickly reclaimed its national prominence by paying out some of the biggest purses in the country. Hollywood luminaries such as Lana Turner, Clark Gable, Cary Grant, and Esther Williams were among the many movie stars who passed through its turnstiles, while racehorses owned by Louis B. Mayer, Spencer Tracy, Bing Crosby, and Errol Flynn all competed at the track.

It was there on a foggy night approximately thirteen hours before Wonder Boy's debut that Gach and three coconspirator cronies snuck into the stable area at midnight. With a hypodermic syringe, they injected as many horses as possible. On the day of the race, three minutes before the horses were due in the receiving barn, Gach climbed into Wonder Boy's stall as his cohorts kept a lookout. Once again, he injected the stimulant into the Thoroughbred's neck, only this time it was not a drill, it was showtime. He then walked to the fountain in front of the grandstand and gave Otash's contact the okay sign, which was then relayed by telephone back to Fred, who instructed him to place six thousand Washingtons on Wonder Boy to win when his odds were 50-to-1.

Shortly before the race, Gach's heightened spirits sank precipitously in lockstep with Wonder Boy's odds, which had plummeted 8-to-5 after too many bets were placed on him. Meanwhile, their prized meal ticket was now so jacked up that the poor steed was sweating profusely as he tried to bolt out the gate before the starter even dropped his flag. Gach's nerves danced with adrenaline as "And they're off!" bellowed across the racetrack and the grandstand exploded in a roar of excitement with Wonder Boy taking an early lead. But as the high horse furiously galloped round the first inside turn, he almost flew off the track before his jockey reined him in to avoid being disqualified, slowing the stallion down to such a degree that he couldn't regain his lead. When it was all over, Wonder Boy finished ninth in an eleven-horse field.

"A sure thing, my ass!" an irate Otash yelled at Gach as he sat behind a stack of torn tickets piled on his desk, accusing him of ordering the jockey not to go full-out due to his low closing odds. Gach emphatically denied the claim, squirming in his chair as he explained what he saw with his own two eyes. He suspected he used too much juice, presenting Wonder Boy's bloodstained bridle bit to prove it. Otash calmed down a bit, but now he was out $9,500 between his investment and his wager.

Gach then floated a possible remedy: race Wonder Boy up north, where he'll lose fair and square. Then, when the odds build him up to a long shot again, they'll hop him at the Tanforan Racetrack near San Francisco. Rather disgusted by the whole affair, Otash wondered aloud how the hell he got himself into this crap in the first place. Still, he wanted to recoup his losses. And besides, he rationalized, despite its illegal nature, doping horses had become ubiquitous at the tracks with far more wealthy, powerful, and prominent players now getting in on the game, so he reluctantly agreed.

Back at Santa Anita, however, Wonder Boy's reputation became the target of suspicion. How the hell could a bum six-year-old horse suddenly lose his perennial long shot status? And some of the competing jockeys were wondering why all their horses suddenly ran slow while Wonder Boy frothed at the starting gate. Word soon filtered back to the Los Angeles district attorney's office, to prosecutors well aware how such "coincidences" constituted the coin of the realm when it came to the racing world. But this one seemed curious, particularly when they learned that Wonder Boy's stable at Santa Anita was bankrolled by none other than Fred Otash. These same prosecutors resented Otash over the *Confidential* magazine trial and his history of brazenly stepping on their toes, which led to straitlaced District Attorney William McKibben assigning two top deputy DAs to probe further.

Hardly an Otash enthusiast for similar reasons, California attorney general Stanley Mosk offered the full weight of his office to help McKibben pursue the matter. An influential player in Democratic Party politics, Mosk had close ties to Governor Pat Brown and the Kennedy family. Later down the road, Otash would build a dossier of dirt on Mosk to have at the ready should JFK want to appoint him to his cabinet. But that never materialized so his findings remained secret. Instead, Mosk became an eminent associate justice of the California Supreme Court, where he served for thirty-seven years, the longest tenure in the court's history.

As Otash was preparing to leave for another vacation, a trusted source with his ear to the ground informed him that a grand jury had been convened to investigate chicanery at

Santa Anita. Fred tried to shrug it off, but knowing he had powerful enemies in high places, from the local level all the way up to the White House and FBI, weighed heavily on his mind. Shortly after he returned to Los Angeles, he touched base with Godkins, Gach, and their cohorts. He knew they could likely be called to testify, so he wanted to make sure they had each other's backs. Despite their vows to stick together, Otash should have known better. While his skillful testimony managed to evade prosecutor's questions, Godkins was bending over backward for the deputy DA to save his own skin. He even let him monitor his telephone calls with Otash, who, unaware he was being tapped, incriminated himself by reiterating their need to stick together.

On September 3, 1959, Otash, Gach, and five other coconspirators received indictments on four counts, including offering a bribe and administering a drug to a horse. Had it been any other schmuck with little to no renown, the case would have gone unnoticed. But this was Otash, so the same newspaper editors who had long enabled his celebrity now turned their keystrokes into major headlines that only worked against him.

Otash tapped Arthur Crowley to mount a strong defense on his behalf for his jury trial that would begin on November 11, 1959. Other than Gach and another coconspirator, the rest of Wonder Boy's crew flipped and cut deals with the DA. Like Godkins, they would testify against Otash, prompting Crowley to motion for a new trial, which the judge denied. To make matters worse, a pained Patsy D'Amore had to admit under oath that his good friend Otash offered him an opportunity to invest in a hot horse, an offer he had turned down.

Otash pled not guilty and refused to testify before the grand jury. A trusted private investigator, he wasn't about to divulge anything told in confidence, or be used as a funnel to satisfy ambitious political egos. In the end, he was willing to take the rap himself for the sake of his reputation and continuing his business. Unfortunately, that didn't impress the jury, who found him guilty on a single count of having knowledge of the event that occurred, a felony that came with a penalty of six months' jail time and five years' probation.

Presiding Judge Leroy Dawson, a crusty sixty-three-year-old magistrate known as a "hanging judge," had first met Otash during his time on the LAPD, where he had considered him an honest and straight cop. Still, Fred expected no mercy. Evident guilt notwithstanding, he hoped Dawson might dismiss his conviction since he too was well aware of the high-and-mighty players out to get him. But the case had received too much heat in the press for Dawson to just let it go. At sentencing, Dawson remarked that he believed the case would not have been brought against anyone else. He reduced the charges to a misdemeanor and gave Otash probation but no fine.

Otash strongly believed it was the combined efforts of Jack Baron, Bill Nolan, and Bob Barrish, all top FBI agents he had worked with over the years as an informant, who helped get his sentence reduced.

Otash later recalled in recordings: *"When I got indicted, they went to the judge's chambers and pleaded with him to give me a break. They intervened on my behalf to Judge LeRoy Dawson, one of the toughest hanging judges in town. And the judge did. He reduced my beat into a misdemeanor. Never filed me. Never spent a minute in jail. Put me on straight probation. They probably said to him, 'Now look it, this man has cooperated with us on a lot of investigations, and we'd like to keep him on the street. We feel this was a setup. We feel that the Kennedys set this guy up,' which is true! You had a Governor Brown, a good friend of Bobby Kennedy and good friend of Jack Kennedy. Parker was a good friend of the Kennedys. He was going to be considered at one time to be head of the FBI. Let's all fuck Otash, you know. Let's neutralize Otash. I figure they said, 'Let this guy run,' you know?"*

Regardless of the reduced charges, the conviction itself prompted the California Department of Professional and Vocational Standards to suspend Otash's detective license. So after the new year, he moved his business to New York, where he already had many clients, but it wasn't the same and he missed his little girl. Upon his return to Los Angeles later that year, his attempts to receive a new trial were rejected by the California Court of Appeal. Fortunately, his PI license was soon restored and his conviction was later expunged.

The sun had set on a most fortuitous and fateful period in the life of Fred Otash. As the sixties beckoned, he couldn't help but wonder how the next decade might fare . . . for him, for Hollywood, and America. For all concerned, it would prove to be more than anyone could have ever imagined.

TWELVE

THE KENNEDYS

Nearly one-third of the U.S. economy was driven by unionized labor in the 1950s, governed by a handful of mercenary leaders whose corruption and racketeering ran roughshod over the nation's most critical industries. In a concerted effort to address the crisis, the Senate launched the Special Committee on Improper Activities in Labor and Management on January 30, 1957. Known as the McClellan Committee (after the select committee's chairman, Senator John L. McClellan), the group of eight bipartisan lawmakers that included a then–U.S. senator John F. Kennedy was endowed with broad subpoena and investigative powers to examine the extent to which a pernicious enemy had infiltrated America's workforce: organized crime.

Sitting shotgun next to his brother during most of the televised hearings, the committee's chief counsel Robert F. Kennedy trained his sights on numerous union leaders, most notably International Brotherhood of Teamsters president

David Beck, his successor Jimmy Hoffa, and a litany of mafia kingpins and coconspirators called to testify before a national audience. As millions of viewers watched with rapt fascination, Kennedy quickly earned a ruthless reputation for his intolerant and contentious questioning of witnesses who would sooner plead the Fifth Amendment than genuflect themselves before the committee and its cameras.

Nearly three years, 253 investigations, 8,000 subpoenas, 270 days of hearings, 1,526 witnesses, and 20 convictions later, the Kennedys had forged a plethora of powerful enemies that included Hoffa, Chicago boss Sam Giancana, Hollywood mobster Mickey Cohen, New Orleans godfather Carlos Marcello, and mafia finance guru Meyer Lansky who owned the Hotel Habana Riviera resort and casino in Havana, Cuba—a collective personal animus that would prove to have serious and far-reaching consequences. When the committee's focus turned to the vending machine industry, Fred Otash was called as a government witness.

The all-cash vending machine business was a lucrative revenue stream for the mafia, whose malefic all-out war against legitimate businesses had reached a fever pitch in Southern California. Mickey Cohen was at the forefront of strong-arming restaurants, bars, nightclubs, hotels, and other establishments to install mob-owned vending machines in return for a small piece of the action. Those who refused faced physical harm, mangled machines, bombed-out businesses, and truckloads of hijacked merchandise on a regular basis. At the height of the gangland madness, Coast Vending Machine vice president Mike Carr and his attorney Arthur Crowley tapped Otash to investigate Cohen and his lieutenant, the notorious Hollywood goodfella Fred Sica, after the two goons tried to muscle their way into all the cigarette machines in Carr's territory. Otash had assigned fifteen men to tail Cohen's trucks, put a twenty-four-hour watch on his top thugs, then huddled with the beleaguered business owners to record their accounts of violence and intimidation.

Otash and Cohen's symbiotic bond harked back to his nascent days as a vice cop, tailing his gangster pal down the Sunset Strip for a friendly drive-by with a double-barrel shotgun perched out the window—just for fun. Given their personal history, Otash thought he could convince Cohen to back off during a private meeting in the gangster's apartment. But Cohen's only concession was a bribe to forget the whole thing. With Cohen's lawyer Sam Dash, a former Philadelphia district attorney who later served as chief counsel of the Senate Watergate Committee, looking on, Otash walked out the door. A subsequent meeting at the Los Angeles district office of the FBI would prove more auspicious after the authorities agreed to share Otash's evidence with the McClellan Committee. A few days later, Otash knew he was in deep when everyone received a subpoena to testify in Washington.

As newspapers across the country echoed the *Los Angeles Times'* front-page banner, "Mickey Cohen, Otash Called in Racket Quiz," Otash headed to Washington. On March 14, 1959, Otash, Crowley, and Carr arrived promptly for a prearranged sit-down with Bobby Kennedy in his Capitol office to discuss Otash's testimony. Despite being told Kennedy was eager to meet them, the dapper-dressed trio were kept waiting for almost an hour in a small, stuffy, windowless vestibule outside Kennedy's office, where his stone-faced secretary sat sentinel.

"What the hell is going on?" an impatient Crowley finally asked. "How long do we have to wait to see the McClellan Committee's counsel?"

"Mr. Kennedy is busy," she curtly replied. "You'll just have to wait."

Otash motioned his eyes toward Kennedy's door, cueing the exasperated solicitor to barge past the protesting secretary into Kennedy's office where he found the busy chief counsel leaning back in his tufted leather chair, his feet propped atop a scattered pile of papers on his desk, staring at the wall, munching on an apple. When Crowley confronted Kennedy's blatant disregard, his indignation was met with indifference.

"We have a lot of important witnesses to call," Kennedy calmly replied. "We don't know exactly when we'll get around to your clients, but I assure you they will be heard."

"Mr. Kennedy, if you do not talk to my clients here and now in advance of the hearing as you asked, we are simply going to pack and go home!" Crowley demanded.

Let the games begin, Otash thought as the two men locked horns in a vitriolic display of obscenity-laced epithets until Bobby finally threw down the gauntlet: "If they leave under federal subpoenas, I'll put out a warrant for their arrests!"

"Mr. Kennedy, you just dooo that," cooed Crowley. "You just do that and see where we go from there. I'm not totally unfamiliar with your tactics of trying to embarrass honest people while the television cameras are focused on you. But I'm not going to have that. My people are reputable businessmen who want to cooperate with their government, and they have furnished valuable information in this matter to the federal authorities in Los Angeles. Now, we've been intimidated as much as we intend to be. And if you force the issue, I will personally see that you are so embarrassed in front of millions of people on television that you'll wish you never heard of me."

At 10 a.m. the following day, Otash, Carr, and Crowley sat at the witness table in a hearing room choked with journalists and cigarette smoke. The chief counsel's first question brought Crowley to his feet, who declared it so unintelligible that he could hardly advise his client how to respond. Rather than lock horns with one of Hollywood's most potent litigators on national television, Kennedy hastily dismissed the entire group.

Back in Los Angeles, Otash and Carr testified before the grand jury, leading to numerous indictments and convictions. While Cohen escaped prosecution, he quickly backed off due to all the federal heat, leaving Carr and his territory whole.

Carlos Marcello, the New Orleans godfather who supplied his wise guys to assist Cohen's vending machine war, pled the Fifth when he testified before the McClellan Committee ten days later. Two months on, after having evaded federal agents for over a year, Chicago mob boss Sam Giancana responded in kind, giggling behind dark sunglasses as he awkwardly read his Fifth Amendment rights from a card in his hand. "I thought only little girls giggled, Mr. Giancana," Kennedy replied. But by the second week in September, Bobby had bigger plans and resigned his post to join his brother's presidential campaign.

Otash and Marcello went way back to one of Fred's many star-studded weekend sojourns at actor John Carroll's ranch house in Granada Hills, where the *Zorro* and *Flying Tigers* star gave the eager-to-please rookie cop his first taste of the good life, back when the Hollywood elite got a rise out of mingling with the mafia. After Carlos saw Otash at the McClellan hearings, he hired him to bug the New Orleans hotel suite where Jack Kennedy would be staying during the Louisiana leg of his campaign. With his girlfriend Susie Woods in tow, a sensational starlet who in time would come to bed a litany of powerful men, including the future president, Otash and his wireman Reed Wilson checked in to the Royal Orleans Hotel to set up operations.

Otash later revealed what happened in a taped interview: *"Marcello had no reason to develop a derogatory profile on the Kennedys. The hatred started when Marcello was subpoenaed to appear before the McClellan Committee, long before Jack ever came to New Orleans. When I was called to testify, I became the guy to hire because they assumed I had a hard-on for the Kennedys. There were other guys in New Orleans, ex-FBI men, some investigator named Ferry, but they didn't hire them. They wanted someone out of the city, and I was chosen. They had information Kennedy was coming to New Orleans and was going to rendezvous with a woman there. They knew her, and I had reason to believe that Marcello and the Republicans set her up. Someone that had met Kennedy somewhere. Maybe she was part of his campaign. I didn't even know her name. We wired up her place. She knew we were investigators and cooperated with us. I think she was doing it for Marcello. She evidently was being paid to get Kennedy to her apartment, which we finally succeeded in doing. She called us at the hotel, 'Look it, he's going to be here tomorrow at three o'clock.' The recorder was put in a shelf in her apartment, so when he knocked on the door, it was just a matter of throwing the switch. He entered her apartment, they did have sex, and it was all put on tape: his calling her, coming over, their having sex, talking about what a beautiful*

Above: Newlyweds Marilyn Monroe
and Joe DiMaggio in January 1954.

(Credit: Pictorial Press Ltd/Alamy Stock Photo)

Right: Marilyn Monroe in a publicity
still for *Gentlemen Prefer Blondes* (1953).

(Credit: ARCHIVIO GBB/Alamy Stock Photo)

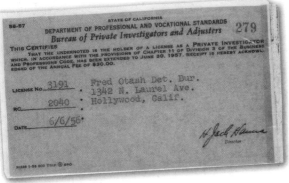

Above: Fred Otash poses with an array of his surveillance equipment at Fred Otash Detective Bureau (circa 1956).

(Credit: All images are from the Otash/Houck Archives unless otherwise noted.)

Left: Fred Otash's private investigator license in 1956.

Above: Attorney Arthur Crowley (*left*) with Fred Otash during the *Confidential* magazine trial (1957).

Right: Fred Otash's Council of International Investigators certificate (1957).

Below: Fred Otash's California Association of Private Investigators certificate (1958).

Above: Colleen with Fred and his girlfriend Jackie O'Hara during a night out on the town at Dino's Restaurant on Sunset Strip (circa 1958).

Left: Fred Otash riding in the Beverly Hills Easter Parade atop his Palomino horse (1958).

Below: Fred and daughter Colleen enjoying a ride at Beverly Park in Los Angeles (circa 1957).

Above: Robert F. Kennedy (*left*) and John F. Kennedy during the McClellan Senate hearings in May 1957. (Credit: American Photo Archive/Alamy Stock Photo)

Below left: Jimmy Hoffa testifying during the McClellan Committee's Senate racketeering trial on August 20, 1957. (Credit: Glasshouse Images/Alamy Stock Photo)

Below right: Sam Giancana testifies before Robert F. Kennedy and the McClellan Committee during the Senate racketeering hearings on June 9, 1959. (Credit: Bettmann/Getty Images)

Left: Rock Hudson and Phyllis Gates at home with their dogs in May 1957.
(Credit: Cinematic/Alamy Stock Photo)

Below: Rock Hudson on the cover of the September 1954 issue of *Photoplay* magazine.
(Credit: ARCHIVIO GBB/Alamy Stock Photo)

AMERICA'S LARGEST-SELLING MOVIE MAGAZINE

PHOTOPLAY

SEPTEMBER

HOLLYWOOD'S NEW LOOK IN SEX

ROCK HUDSON

DORIS DAY SAYS
Wake Up and Live

BILL HOLDEN'S
Exclusive Love Story

50 PRIZES
WIN A PRESENT FROM A STAR

20¢

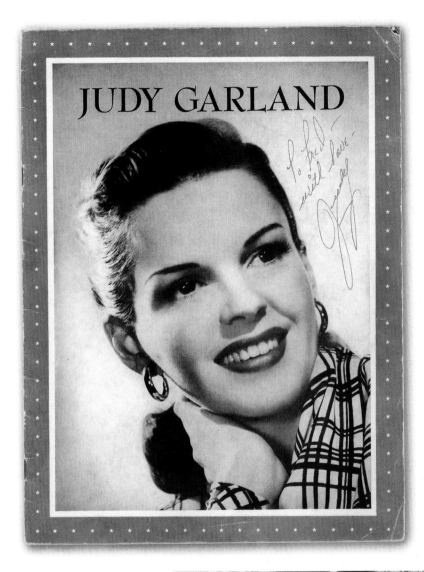

Above: Judy Garland's autographed photo to Fred Otash in 1958.

Right: Judy Garland and third husband Sid Luft with (*from L-R*) daughter Lorna Luft, daughter Liza Minnelli, and son Joseph Luft on New Year's Day 1957. (Credit: *Manchester Daily Press*/Getty Images)

Above: Star-crossed lovers Johnny Stompanato and Lana Turner
at a Hollywood nightclub in 1957. (Credit: Bettmann/Getty Images)

Above: Lana Turner (*left*), Johnny Stompanato, and fourteen-year-old Cheryl Crane arrive at Los Angeles International Airport following a two-month vacation in Acapulco, Mexico, on March 19, 1958.
(Credit: ullstein bild Dtl./Getty Images)

Right: Johnny Stompanato lies dead on the floor of Lana Turner's all-pink bedroom as police inspect the homicide on Good Friday, April 4, 1958.
(Credit: ullstein bild Dtl./Getty Images)

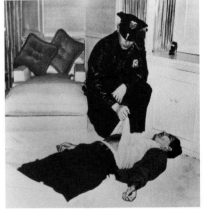

Below: Lana Turner testifies at the inquest into the death of boyfriend Johnny Stompanato on April 11, 1958. (Credit: Bettmann/Getty Images)

Above: Fred Otash holds a wristwatch microphone at his desk at Fred Otash Detective Bureau (circa 1960).

Left: Fred Otash Detective Bureau brochure (1961).

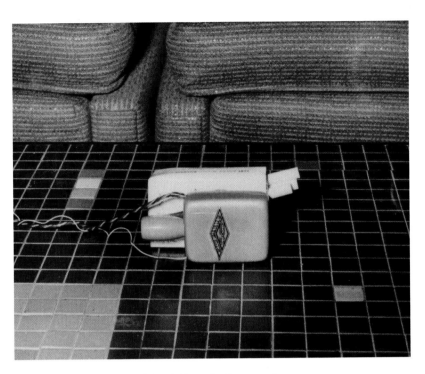

Above: Fred Otash Detective Bureau wiretap transmitter unit next to pack of cigarettes (1960).

Below: Fred Otash Detective Bureau operative with reel-to-reel tape recorder and receiver (circa 1960).

Above: The exterior of the Fred Otash Detective Bureau surveillance truck (1961).

Below: Interior of Fred Otash Detective Bureau surveillance truck (1961).

Above: (left to right) Author Mickey Spillane, comedian Marty Allen, Sherry Spillane, and Fred Otash (circa 1962).

Left: (left to right) Peter Lawford, Dean Martin, Sammy Davis Jr., and Frank Sinatra in the hit 1960 Warner Bros. feature film *Ocean's Eleven* (Credit: PictureLux/The Hollywood Archive/Alamy Stock Photo)

Right: Attorney General Robert F. Kennedy *(left)*, Marilyn Monroe, and President John F. Kennedy on the occasion of President Kennedy's forty-fifth birthday celebration at Madison Square Garden in New York on May 19, 1962. (Credit: ZUMA Press, Inc./Alamy Stock Photo)

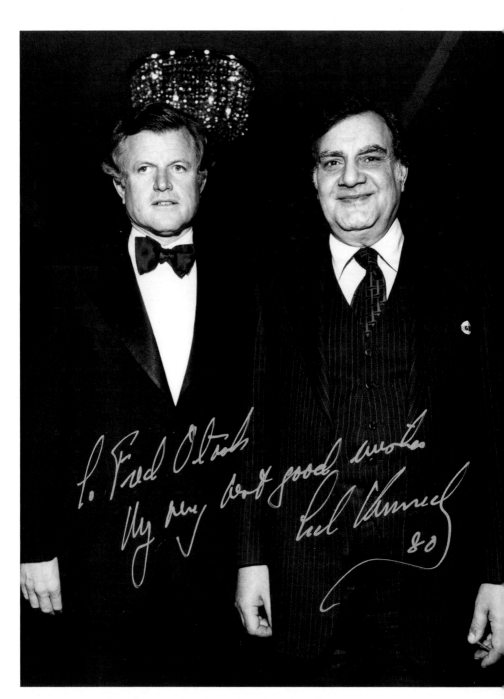

Above: Autographed photo of Fred Otash and Senator Ted Kennedy
at an "Edward Kennedy for President" fundraiser in 1980.

Above: Restaurateur Nicky Blair (*left*) and Fred Otash in Cannes, France (circa 1986).

Right: Fred Otash's business card (circa 1990).

Below: Fred Otash (*second from right*) with Tony Bennett (*far left*) and friends at the Jockey Club in Miami Beach (circa 1988).

JOCKEY CLUB OF MIAMI
11111 BISCAYNE BLVD.
MIAMI, FLORIDA 33161
(305) 893-3344

FRED OTASH

PARK WELLINGTON
1131 ALTA LOMA ROAD
HOLLYWOOD, CA 90069
(213) 659-5325

GRAND HOTEL RES.
46 LA CROISETTE
06400 CANNES FRANCE
(93) 38 65 90

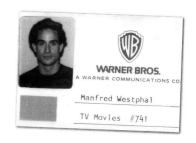

Above: Manfred Westphal's Warner Bros. Studios ID card in 1990, the year he met Fred Otash. (Courtesy: Manfred Westphal)

Left: Fred Otash's kitchen/dining room at the Park Wellington in West Hollywood, California (circa 1990).

CITY OF LOS ANGELES

IN TRIBUTE

THE LOS ANGELES CITY COUNCIL EXTENDS ITS
DEEPEST SYMPATHY TO YOU IN THE PASSING OF
YOUR LOVED ONE

FRED OTASH

IN WHOSE MEMORY
ALL MEMBERS STOOD IN TRIBUTE AND REVERENCE
AS THE COUNCIL ADJOURNED ITS MEETING OF
OCTOBER 6, 1992.

SINCERELY,

ELIAS MARTINEZ, CITY CLERK

Presented by

COUNCILMAN JOHN FERRARO

Above: City of Los Angeles Tribute to Fred Otash presented to his daughter Colleen Otash by longtime City Council member John Ferraro (1992).

girl she was, how interesting she was, how he enjoyed being with her and hoped to see her again soon, he'd be in touch. 'Here's my private number,' he said. 'I really feel good about my campaign. I think I'm gonna make it. I wish I was happily married but unfortunately I'm not, because if I was, I wouldn't be here,' blah blah blah. The pressure of the campaign, the pressure of this, and the pressure of that. 'It's nice to be able to relax and enjoy being with someone.'"

The wiretaps in his hotel suite also revealed that Kennedy had enjoyed the company of several different women during his stay in the Big Easy, which purportedly included a tryst with renowned burlesque dancer extraordinaire Blaze Starr. But while Marcello was jubilant with the results of Fred's handiwork, he kept the tapes to himself for protection, blackmail, or both, should push ever come to shove . . . and Marcello liked to shove. In a handful of years he would be frequently implicated in Kennedy's assassination.

Around this time, Jack and Bobby's movie star brother-in-law Peter Lawford visited Otash at his apartment on Laurel Avenue to ask for a favor.

Otash and Lawford went way back to his early days working on the Vice Squad, where it was common knowledge that the MGM star of *Son of Lassie*, *Easter Parade*, and *Little Women* liked cavorting with two hookers at a time, smoking grass, experimenting with heroin, and taking doctor-prescribed amphetamines and barbiturates as needed like many of his self-destructive pill-popping contemporaries. But he never got busted, thanks to the LAPD's studio protection program that shielded big stars like Peter from most legal or public embarrassment. After he married Patricia Kennedy, he was virtually untouchable due to his father-in-law's strong personal ties with law enforcement. But Lawford's voracious appetite for call girls meant his name kept appearing in the trick books of numerous Hollywood madams like the notorious Brenda Allen, whose scandalous arrest in 1948 led to much-needed reform at the LAPD and the ascent of Chief William H. Parker, who was credited with cleaning it up.

From Otash's later recordings: *"I knew Brenda Allen. I knew a lot of her girls when I worked undercover vice. I knew all about her—shit, a week after I started work. She had gals that were pursuing modeling or acting careers who needed money, and it was common knowledge that she had the greatest stable of women out here. She'd call her girls and say, 'Go meet Jack Kennedy at the Beverly Hills Hotel.' She did have a house, but it was limited. VIPs only. Up in the hills somewhere. There was some woman living there, her special pet. But she had apartments all over the place and telephone exchanges and stuff. A lot of the girls would just go to the Beverly Hills Hotel, the Knickerbocker Hotel, the Plaza Hotel or Beverly Wilshire. They were 'call' girls. You go to their place, or they come to yours. They were high-class. They weren't druggies. They lived at the Studio Club. Two or three girls would live together. They needed money to supplement their income. In those days, they'd make fifty bucks a trick. Not for all night, a trick. Like an hour, hour and a half. An exceptional girl would be in demand. You'd call up there and if she wasn't available, they'd say she's out of town. Maybe she went to Honolulu with some guy for $500 or $1,000 a day. The take was 60/40. The girls got 40 percent.*

"Whenever Lawford was getting himself in trouble, I'd go to him and say, 'Look, asshole, knock it off, okay? Every time I bust a fucking whore, your name is in the book. They got you down for fifty bucks. You're a fifty-dollar trick. Be careful! Don't get set up!' All the guys' names were in the trick book. Whenever you busted a whore, you grabbed the trick book. Being able to tell him what he paid made my comments credible. Eventually Peter came to trust me, because I was always straight with him and never hassled him unnecessarily."

But now Lawford had a much bigger ask. "Fred, have you got some means for me to make personal recordings?" he asked.

Otash barely blinked despite the surreal irony of Lawford's request. "Yeah, probably," he said. "What kind of recordings?"

"You know . . . just some recordings," Lawford managed.

Otash knew that he had to be careful. Making himself a party to this act could land him in hot water with Lawford's brother-in-law, the attorney general. He knew how to protect himself against Federal Communications Commission (FCC) rules with his own wires, and he was never responsible when the feds or law enforcement borrowed his surveillance truck or recording devices, but Lawford was a different animal altogether. A wild card who lived life on the edge, he barely paid attention as Otash carefully explained the FCC regulations. But he sure lit up when Otash showed him how to use his Magnet-a-phone and instructed how to hide the recorder, microphone, automatic relay box, and recording wire in the headboard of the bed or tape it under the box springs so it wouldn't be discovered if someone flipped the mattress.

Otash didn't know who or what Peter wanted to record, but he did know from Lawford that he and his wife were having marital troubles and planning to divorce after the election. So, he assumed it was a case of Peter wanting to tap his wife's telephone, a theory soon debunked when Otash learned that Lawford was actually serving as Jack Kennedy's sexual archivist.

John F. Kennedy's congressional record may have been indistinguishable enough, but his soaring speeches electrified voters as he presented himself as America's future, while characterizing the incumbent vice president Richard Nixon as its past. As Kennedy's mystique grew more palpable by the day, a handful of powerful GOP backers would resort to political espionage in an effort to hobble what they feared was an existential threat.

The Democrats were already planning the 1960 national convention in Los Angeles when the Republicans approached Otash to gather intel on the strategy sessions and Hollywood-laced soirées taking place at Lawford's Santa Monica beach house. The Lawfords, along with the Kennedy brothers and their friends, would inevitably become the targets of surveillance by Otash and various other political opponents, including rogue operator Howard Hughes, who unbeknownst to anyone had already wired the residence. Hughes practically owned Nixon. As America's richest citizen, he had been putting his financial might behind Nixon as far back as 1946 when the Yorba Linda native born to a poor Quaker family was encouraged by a group of small-town businessmen to run for Congress in California. Otash never spoke to Nixon directly but in hindsight, after the Watergate fiasco went down, it was his strong opinion that the then vice president was indeed the client or at the very least, well aware that his highest-level benefactors, including Hughes, had put the operation in motion and financed it.

Otash would later elucidate the situation on a taped recording: *"It was a fucking Watergate! They wanted to know the strategy of what was coming down. Now Lawford's house was the West Coast headquarters for Jack Kennedy's campaign. So those were the conversations that were going on. That's where Sinatra was. That's where the Rat Pack met. That's where organized crime guys met, Mickey Cohen and everybody else. So the purpose of wiring up that house was to establish what was going on."*

It was never about money or political partisanship for Otash; he didn't have a preferred candidate at the time. At this juncture in his career, it was about placing himself in a critical station at the highest levels of national politics, where he felt his expertise could make a meaningful impact. Had the Kennedy camp approached him first to spy on Nixon, he likely would've agreed. Fatefully, that wasn't the case, as he was never approached by the Kennedys or the Democratic operatives to spy on Nixon.

Using his specially equipped sound truck disguised as a twenty-four-hour TV repair van, Otash scoped out Lawford's palatial beach house at 625 Palisades Beach Road in Santa Monica, which was now subbing for Jack Kennedy's de facto West Coast office, crash pad, and Hollywood hospitality center. When he scanned the FM frequencies, Otash picked up several wireless transmissions from bugs already planted inside the residence, not by him, but by an unknown source that he assumed was an associate of Howard Hughes working on behalf of Nixon. This made Otash's task of bugging the Lawford house that much easier. He hired surveillance guru Bernie Spindel to use the existing equipment so that they did not have to enter the house and plant a new bug. Now all they had to do was park nearby, turn on the scanner, pick up the frequency, and start recording.

Otash noted in a recorded interview years later how he happened on the signal: *"I had a very sophisticated sound truck that could even pick up the FBI frequency. And I could go out there, when we found out the place was wired, park the fuckin' truck and started sweeping up the bands that had the fuckin' bugs. We didn't have to make an entry. It had already been done. So we, meaning me, I had nothing to do with wiring up the Lawford house. Nothing. But when I found out about it, we came in on the same frequency. So we used their equipment. We got in free."*

Marilyn Monroe was certainly the most famous movie star ever recorded having sex with Kennedy, but she wasn't the first. That dubious honor went to fellow bottle blonde actress Jayne Mansfield. A close friend of Lawford, *The Girl Can't Help It* star was considered by some to be Monroe's competition at 20th Century Fox. After listening to Mansfield romping with Kennedy, Otash dutifully placed the recording inside his dossier for the Republican Party. At that time, the Democratic Party's political strategies remained the primary focus, but everything changed once Fred's associate John Danoff recorded Kennedy having sexual congress with Marilyn.

In his recordings, Otash noted: *"Then Monroe became the central figure. The original electronics surveillance had nothing to do with her. But now, when it was established that Monroe was fucking Jack Kennedy, she became the one, the main figure, because she was the best known."*

Marilyn had first met John F. Kennedy four years earlier in 1955 at a party held at the home of Charles Feldman, producer of her latest blockbuster, *The Seven Year Itch*. The first of her two outings with Oscar-winning filmmaker Billy Wilder, the romantic comedy based on George Axelrod's Broadway play centered on a middle-aged husband in New York who fantasizes about committing adultery with a young actress living in the apartment above him while his wife and young son are summering in Maine. A critical and commercial success, the film also produced one of the most iconic scenes in cinematic history: Marilyn, in her prime and wearing a white halter-top dress, stands with legs spread and knees locked over a subway grate as a sudden updraft sends her pleated skirt billowing in the breeze. She would later describe the resulting publicity photo exposing her legs, thighs, and crotch as "the last straw" in her marriage to Joe DiMaggio, whom she divorced later that year, on October 31, 1955.

DiMaggio had no desire to attend the party that night, nor did he want his wife there. But Marilyn, who had already set her sights on playwright Arthur Miller, defiantly went solo. While his exquisite wife of two years, Jacqueline, was back home in Boston, Jack Kennedy was in Los Angeles to visit his sister and brother-in-law, network with political allies, and "go hunting" (his euphemism for bedding Hollywood starlets). While Kennedy showered Marilyn with attention that night, their friendship would remain platonic until one night after a party at Lawford's beach house two years later.

———————————

O tash would be the first to admit that a private detective, much like a politician, required a certain ethical elasticity. But he also believed that a person seeking the highest office in the land should be held to a higher standard, especially if their infidelities posed the potential threat of blackmail . . . and the Nixon camp wanted more.

Otash would later clarify: *"My job was to develop a file that would show Jack Kennedy to have serious moral failings. In other words, they wanted audiotapes of the guy fucking anyone other than his wife. I could make a file of any other sins I might discover, but adultery was enough to knock him out of the race."*

Unlike today, if a presidential candidate was caught having an adulterous in flagrante delicto affair with a movie star in 1960, their political aspirations would be dead on arrival. Otash assumed the unknown source behind the original bugs that he detected in Lawford's house was also privy to the same bombshell intelligence; they had to be. Regardless, he was morally conflicted, as a scandal of this magnitude had the potential to wreak havoc on Marilyn's personal and professional life if it ever saw the light of day.

The night before he would deliver the recording, Fred spent the evening dismantling his many memories of Marilyn over a bottle of scotch and too many cigarettes. He was grappling with remorse for what he knew in his heart was unavoidable: the first time he met the young Norma Jean at John Carroll's ranch; the day he gave her an impromptu tour of his security detail at the Hollywood Ranch Market; the countless afternoons they spent together with Sid Skolsky at Schwab's drugstore, where she invariably tried to elucidate the dizzying revolving door of men coming in and out of her life; his unrelenting solicitude for her since his early days on the LAPD, where he often fantasized what it may have been like to date Marilyn since, after all, her first husband was a police officer. Something had to give and Fred had a choice to make: either surrender to his conscience or do what was expected of him. Despite serious misgivings, the same stoic professionalism that had enabled Otash to circumnavigate the minacious depths of Hollywood's shark-infested waters ultimately prevailed. By the time he gave the tape to his powerful Republican clients, Fred had compartmentalized his personal feelings, because that's what the job required. Whatever they chose to do with the tapes was up to them, and if they came back to hurt Marilyn in some way, well, that was just part of the crazy mess that she had gotten herself wrapped up in.

THIRTEEN

SOMEONE WAS ALWAYS LISTENING

The nefarious interception of private communications was hardly a novel concept when Otash first honed his nascent skills on the LAPD. Fourteen years before the advent of the telephone, an untamed, gun-slinging California would outlaw wiretapping in 1862 after the first telegraph line reached a West Coast booming with mass migration and economic growth sparked by the greatest gold rush in U.S. history. By the time the Eighteenth Amendment plunged the nation into the dark, dry depths of Prohibition at the stroke of midnight on January 17, 1920, electronic surveillance had become a ubiquitous tool used by law enforcement to hunt down bootleggers, most notably by J. Edgar Hoover, a twenty-four-year-old rising star at the FBI who was smitten with the new technology. As head of the General Intelligence Division, he routinely employed its capabilities to monitor a mélange of suspected socialists, anarchists, and leftist labor activists in the aftermath of World War I, better known as the First Red Scare.

In 1948, as the nation struggled with widespread xenophobia, racial violence, and political repression, the American Civil Liberties Union successfully challenged the FBI's efforts to invoke a federal statute expanding the government's wiretapping authority by citing the Fourth Amendment's protections from "unreasonable searches and seizures." A fleeting victory, it was overruled in 1950 after Hoover's obdurate campaign prevailed upon President Truman. When Eisenhower took office three years later, those powers were broadened even further to manage the threat of communism at the height of McCarthyism.

Otash knew full well that most, if not all, of his recordings were illegal. Even when the LAPD ordered him to wire up mobster Mickey Cohen's dream house in the late 1940s, his superiors made it quite clear that should he or his wireman ever get caught, they would deny having given them permission. A decade later, the same advancements in stereophonic sound that gave rise to the "hi-fi" home audio revolution enabled Otash to become a master at the art of wiretapping, a cornerstone of his thriving detective bureau despite the fact that most of his equipment came with a penalty of five years in prison. Criminality notwithstanding, electronic eavesdropping was now rampant in the U.S. even if law enforcement agencies were the only institutions allowed to use it. Ironically, since they often lacked money and resources, Fred would frequently loan or rent them his own equipment, a quid pro quo gesture of goodwill that ensured a modicum of protection should he ever get caught in a Wild West of wiretapping where everyone was tuning in.

Throughout the spring of 1960, John F. Kennedy gained enough primary victories to land him the Democratic nomination. Otash kept his eyes peeled and ears to the ground for any headlines or Hollywood gossip that could rock the nation with news of Monroe and Kennedy's assignations. But it was crickets. Either everyone was clueless or, more likely, those in the know were keeping their mouths shut. Without disclosing any intel, he meandered from one topic to another during a lunch with Sid Skolsky at Schwab's, discursively probing the Hollywood gossip columnist and longtime Monroe confidant for what he might know of her relationship with Kennedy. Thankfully, the only thing Skolsky knew was that the last time he saw Marilyn she was lamenting about her pending divorce from playwright Arthur Miller.

When the Democratic National Convention took Los Angeles by storm on July 11, 1960, the Republican operatives who had hired Otash to bug Lawford's beach house no longer needed him since Kennedy was not staying there. Shortly thereafter, a man came to see Fred in his office. Secretive at first, he kept checking to discern if anyone was eavesdropping. Otash assured him that his staff snooped on others, not his own office. Satisfied, the man confessed, "I'm not who I represented myself to be on the telephone."

Otash wasn't surprised. It wouldn't be the first time a new client used a fictitious name. "Then who the hell are you?" he asked.

A business card identified him as an executive with *Life* magazine. "You've been referred to me as the hottest investigator in town by some of our mutual newspaper friends," the man said. "I've followed your career. I know the history of the *Confidential* magazine trial and all the other cases you've worked on." Then he deferentially held up his hands and added, "Your reputation is deserving."

Otash liked a compliment as much as the next guy, but he had little patience for obsequious behavior. "Look, mister, I know a big executive like you has more important things to do than sit here and tell me how great I am," he said. "What's the point?"

"We understand you probably have more information on politicians and celebrities than anybody in the country," the man continued.

"Probably," Otash agreed. "But why do you care? Is *Life* going in for the *Confidential* format?"

"What we have in mind is examining political figures," the man pressed.

"Well, at least we're getting somewhere," Fred quipped.

"We recall reading in the *Confidential* magazine era the story about Jack Kennedy consorting with women," he said, trying to lead Otash into disclosing information. "And we also read the stories in *Confidential* concerning Bobby Kennedy and women."

Otash surmised that the man's boss was Henry Luce, founder of the Time & Life publishing empire, considered one of the most influential citizens in America, and an avid supporter of Nixon's campaign (though he never found out for certain).

"So, we'd like to know if we could develop some derogatory information on these two politically ambitious men," he continued. "We feel that Jack and Bobby Kennedy are dangerous and it would be a disaster if either one of them ever becomes president of the United States."

Otash leaned in. "What makes you think I have anything that would be beneficial to you?"

"You once had a case in California when the songwriter husband of a famous blonde movie star hired you to investigate his wife's activities . . . do you remember?"

This guy has done his homework, Otash thought. The songwriter had information that his wife was seeing one of the Kennedy brothers behind his back and wanted him to verify it. "I remember the case," he conceded.

"And it's a fact you found out his wife was shacking up with Jack Kennedy."

Fred suddenly felt like his ass was in the hot seat. "Is it?"

"Don't misunderstand me, Mr. Otash," the man said, leaning in to the conversation. "I just want you to know I didn't come to you off the streets. You have information that would be very valuable to my magazine. I know that the matter came up for hearing before Judge Edward Brand in Santa Monica Superior Court, but it was such a hot potato that it was held in secret chambers. I also know that a lot of people in high places tried to get you to clean up your reports in order to save everybody embarrassment."

Despite being offered an astronomical fee and a substantial self-serving spread in one of their national publications, Otash said that he was turning him down.

"Well, Mr. Otash, I'd like you to think it over," he replied, adding: "It would assure your future."

Otash sat poker-faced as the cryptic comment raised a troubling red flag. It wasn't something a magazine executive would say. Perhaps that bullshit business card wasn't worth the paper it was printed on. *Who is this cocksucker?* he thought. More importantly, *Who the hell sent him? The FBI? CIA? Howard Hughes? The mafia? The Kennedys themselves?* It would have been pointless to confront him, so instead, Otash took the opportunity to clarify his position.

"Look . . . I've been approached by politicians many times from Washington, California, and New York," he told the stranger. "They all want me to investigate Jack Kennedy since he got the Democratic nomination. So let me tell you what I told them. It's the FBI's job to investigate a presidential candidate, not mine. I'm not going to sit as judge and jury on any presidential candidate. You know, there's a lot of scandal around about Nixon too. What if they've hired investigators to come up with some crap about him? What would you have? A Mexican standoff, that's all. And for all I know that could be the case. Maybe someone's been checking his private affairs. I certainly know there's been business deals between Nixon and Howard Hughes. I'm sure that any kind of investigator can go out and establish some derogatory information about anyone."

"Come on," the man quipped, "Nixon's the man."

"Not to me," Otash shot back. "If he becomes president, he should be above reproach. He represents two hundred million people. Now if he's screwed up, he's putting a stigma on all of us. He owes us more than that."

The meeting was over.

———————

The Kennedy-Nixon race for the White House captivated the American public like none other in modern history. It wasn't the first time Hollywood and Washington became partisan bedfellows, but never before had such a large-scale entourage of stellar entertainment titans assembled behind one presidential candidate. In addition to the Rat Pack, Tony Curtis, Janet Leigh, Judy Garland, Ella Fitzgerald, Milton Berle, Henry Fonda, Shirley MacLaine, and Angie Dickinson, among a long list of celebrities, were stepping out all over the place for their political boy wonder by lending their celebrity presence to campaign rallies, fundraisers, radio and television ads, or attending the Democratic National Convention. Sinatra even recorded a modified version of "High Hopes," his popular Oscar-winning song from his star turn in director Frank Capra's 1959 film *A Hole in the Head*, with "elect Jack Kennedy" lyrics that permeated the national consciousness and became his official campaign song.

But despite Hollywood's best efforts, the Gallup poll gave Nixon a slightly favorable margin leading into the first televised debate in U.S. history, one that would fundamentally change the way Americans voted for their political candidates. As cameras rolled, a record-breaking audience watched live as Kennedy's confident, telegenic style easily eclipsed a seemingly uncomfortable and haggard-looking Nixon, who had refused to wear makeup and couldn't stop sweating under the hot studio lights. Despite attempts to rescue his performance in three subsequent debates, the die was cast. Kennedy was now the front-runner, especially after his powerful speech before the Greater Houston Ministerial Association in Texas, where he declared before the large Protestant audience that he believed in an America where the separation of church and state was absolute, assuaging fears held by many voters that his devout Catholic faith could influence the First Amendment provision.

As election day returns came in on Tuesday, November 8, 1960, Kennedy saw substantial early gains in both the popular and electoral vote. Many news organizations made premature declarations of victory in select states, only to dial them back once Nixon began to catch up, prompting a "too close to call" slog that lasted into the night. Illinois, with its twenty-seven electoral votes, was seen as a critical state. And while Nixon took most of its 103 counties, Chicago's densely populated Cook County went to Kennedy after Sinatra and Papa Joe Kennedy purportedly tapped Chicago mob boss Sam Giancana and longtime Kennedy ally and Chicago mayor Richard Daley for "assistance." Like most Americans, a riveted Otash watched into the early morning hours until news broke that Kennedy had won a narrow victory.

Nixon appeared just after 3 a.m. eastern time, his wife, Pat, by his side, in front of a large chalkboard on which the results were tallied at their campaign headquarters nestled inside an Ambassador Hotel ballroom in Los Angeles. With rictus smiles and forced laughter scarcely masking his pained disappointment, Nixon addressed his election team and a raucous gathering of supporters with a televised speech that only hinted at a possible Kennedy victory "if" the voting trend continued. Before the Republican National Committee would anxiously attempt to contest his loss in the coming weeks with various reports of alleged voter fraud scenarios in Illinois and Texas, Nixon officially conceded the following day in the form of a telegram sent directly to Kennedy at 9:47 a.m. Pacific time.

Meanwhile, back in Hollywood, an elated Sinatra, who was filming the MGM dramatic thriller *The Devil at 4 O'Clock*, happily cashed in on a friendly election bet he had made with director Mervyn LeRoy, purportedly by having the Republican filmmaker lead him around the lot as he proudly rode atop a donkey. The promising and seemingly idyllic presidential administration, which in time would be analogized as the mythical kingdom of Camelot, had officially begun. In the real world, however, the private detective who knew too much worried what an already compromised Kennedy might do to pay back an underworld benefactor to whom he was now beholden—namely Sam Giancana, whose work helped Kennedy win Chicago.

———————

O tash had tapped into a love triangle that threatened national security. It all started when Sinatra had introduced Kennedy to his former girlfriend Judy Campbell, a young, dark-haired beauty who bore a faint resemblance to his own wife, Jackie, on February 7, 1960, at one of many cocktail parties in Dean Martin's suite at the Sands Hotel during their Las Vegas residency.

According to Otash, Jack called her as often as twice a day and met up with her in New York, Palm Beach, Chicago, Los Angeles, and Washington, D.C. She was even a frequent visitor at the White House when Jackie was away during their two-year affair. She was twenty-five, beautiful, a really nice girl, but Otash never understood what fascinated Kennedy about her, and why she wasn't dumped like the rest of his mistresses.

Then, after playing matchmaker for Kennedy and Campbell, Sinatra inadvertently created one of the most scandalous and compromising love triangles of the modern age when he introduced Judy to Sam Giancana, who wasted no time seducing her after their first dinner at Miami's Fontainebleau Hotel. For

Giancana, the best way to recon a man was through the woman, or women, closest to him. Soon he would be dating Judy in tandem with Jack, and he made certain Jack knew about it.

After Kennedy was elected president, Otash learned that Campbell was purportedly being used as a mule to transport confidential documents between her diametrically opposed bedfellows, which included plans to assassinate Cuban president Fidel Castro, as well as Hoover's organized crime briefings.

In early 1961, Giancana wanted to know Jack Kennedy's actions twenty-four hours a day. Naturally, he went to Bernie Spindel, and Spindel turned to former CIA man Bob Maheu, John Danoff, and Otash. Later that year, in December, Spindel brokered Hoffa's hiring of Otash during an AFL-CIO convention in Florida that Kennedy attended at the Americana Hotel at Bal Harbour Shops, which is where Fred first met the Teamster leader in his apartment at 9102 West Bay Harbor Drive. Ever the capitalist, Spindel assumed correctly that Hoover, a master at political calculus, would gladly dip into the bureau's funds for whatever Otash unearthed, if only to ensure his job security. A three-ring circus of surveillance ensued with Spindel serving as ringmaster as Otash performed his death-defying high-wire acts.

Otash laid the situation bare in those later recordings: *"It's Hoffa, it's Giancana, it's the CIA, it's the FBI! They all wanted something on the Kennedys. So, who's the guy who knows how to get them? Spindel and I were on the inside knowing who. He's fucking Angie Dickinson. He's fucking Marilyn Monroe. He's fucking Judy Campbell. He's fucking Anita*

Ekberg. He's fucking Susie Woods. I mean, we're the guys who are drawing up the derogatory profile, to use as a bargaining chip. A group of power-hungry men were each trying to get something on the others. Jimmy Hoffa wanted to know every move the Kennedys were making so that he could stay out of jail. J. Edgar Hoover wanted to know about both Kennedys because he hated them. Organized crime wanted to know what was happening with the Kennedys and Jimmy Hoffa. Hoffa wanted to know what was happening with Marilyn Monroe since her home was visited by the Kennedys. Marilyn wanted to know about the Kennedys because she didn't trust them. And Bernie Spindel was in the midst of everyone, wiretapping, hiring me to wiretap, and selling all the information to as many clients as possible."

It was during one of their many coffee klatch trios at Schwab's drugstore when Marilyn seized the opportunity to ask Otash if she could borrow some recording equipment, after their mutual pal Sid Skolsky euphemistically excused himself to the toilet "to see a man about a horse." Marilyn wanted something simple to record her telephone calls, nothing too intricate as the device Otash had loaned Lawford . . . not yet anyway. She was looking for a mini phone listening device. In those days a wire ran for four hours, so she could hide it in her bra. The microphone was a wristwatch or a tie clasp, and you could also put a suction cup on the phone to eliminate the need for a larger recorder. Otash surmised that Marilyn was beginning to lose trust in the Kennedys and wanted to tape her calls with them in the event that she might need the recordings later on as leverage.

Shortly after Monroe purchased the house on Helena Drive in February 1962, she asked Otash to kick it up a notch, an opportune situation for the equal opportunity detective.

Otash later revealed the extent of the wiretapping in Monroe's house: *"She wanted a sophisticated system and that was put in her house. There's a picture of me standing up with that equipment on my desk. We even wired up her phone because it started looking stupid with a suction cup on the goddamn thing. Kennedy, the night that she died, was running around trying to find where the listening devices were. Why? Because she was calling him from the phone booth. He'd say, 'Why are you calling me from the phone booth?'*

"'Well, I think my place is wired.'

"Fuck sure it was wired! She had a wire, and so did we. The funny part about it was, since she had it wired, all we had to do was tune into that frequency. Like the Peter Lawford house. I assumed that she wanted to record the Kennedys, but she was involved with so many powerful men, ranging from producers to mob leaders to politicians, that she could have had any number of reasons in mind. Whatever the case, it was as though there were sections of Los Angeles where everybody seemed to be recording each other."

———————

By the time she arrived on set in the Nevada desert in 1960 to shoot *The Misfits*, director John Huston's neo-western drama costarring Clark Gable and Montgomery Clift, Marilyn's physical and mental state had been severely compromised by a steady diet of drugs, alcohol, and despair. The film was scripted to showcase her acting ability by her soon-to-be ex-husband Arthur Miller. On the first day of shooting, Marilyn arrived with a bottle of five hundred pills in her bag, and when it soon became apparent that something was seriously off, a concerned Huston tactfully took her aside to confront her demons. While he let her believe she had convinced him she was tapering off, they both knew that was bullshit, especially when production had to be shut down for two weeks so Marilyn could be hospitalized for depression and drug dependency. In an interview two decades after her death, the venerated filmmaker admitted he felt "absolutely certain she was doomed."

What little remained of Mr. and Mrs. Miller would buckle under pressure. They planned to divorce during the shoot, but cooler heads prevailed and it was agreed they would wait until the film's release. Twelve days after completion of principal photography, the iconic movie star Marilyn had idolized throughout her youth died of cardiac arrest. Clark Gable was only fifty-nine but looked much older, a victim of his own many years of hard living. Like its polysemantic title, *The Misfits* was a complicated mixed bag from the start, both critical darling and box-office disaster after it premiered three months later. Marilyn, however, would receive rave reviews and in March 1962 win her third Golden Globe Award for "World Film Favorite." It would be her last film.

FOURTEEN

THE HOUSE ON FIFTH HELENA DRIVE

A ll endings give rise to new beginnings. This was certainly true when Monroe left the resplendent midtown Manhattan penthouse she shared with Miller at 444 East Fifty-Seventh Street after they divorced and returned to California, where she soon purchased a house in a tony Los Angeles suburb. They say every home is a reflection of its owner and this one was special, just like Marilyn. The one-story Spanish Colonial built in 1929 was tucked behind white stucco walls and a gated entry, just far enough away from the madding crowd at the end of a quiet cul-de-sac in the Helenas, a charming collection of tree-lined streets in the heart of Brentwood. Sitting on more than a half-acre, the quaint two-bedroom featured beautifully landscaped grounds, a guesthouse in need of some TLC, and a freeform swimming pool with curvaceous lines reminiscent of her own famous figure. A relatively modest sanctuary for a movie star of such magnitude, it was hers, one she casually described as "a fortress where I can feel safe from the world."

Unlike the other forty-three (!) previous residences through-out her life, 12305 Fifth Helena Drive would be the first and only home she ever owned, purchased in early 1962 after her psychiatrist, Dr. Ralph Greenson, who lived less than a mile away, suggested she "put down some roots." Four blue and white tiles embedded within the front stoop by a previous, pre-sumably Scottish, owner depicted the twelfth-century family crest of the historic Hunter Clan, who, as legend has it, accom-panied William the Conqueror's wife, Queen Matilda, from Normandy to England in her quest to take the kingdom by force. Inscribed beneath the crest read the enigmatic Latin pro-nouncement *Cursum Perficio*: "I've completed my journey."

It wasn't long after Marilyn settled into her small fortress that Bobby Kennedy, at the behest of his brother, paid a per-sonal visit to inform Marilyn that her relationship with the president was over. But what began as an attempt to gently break the bad news to the fragile movie star turned into a pas-sionate love affair that far eclipsed anything she had ever known with Jack.

It was only in hindsight that Otash realized Marilyn was on the verge of an existential crisis by the spring of 1962; he had been too busy with too many cases to be anything other than hyperfocused on satisfying his clients. And with all he was seeing and hearing on a daily basis, it was impossible to be shocked by anything. By the time she and Bobby became an item, Otash had acquired a trove of derogatory informa-tion on her two commanding officers. He had secured a drawer filled with tape recordings, photographs, surveillance reports, and other information. "Jimmy Hoffa was an oddly moral man about all of what I had," Otash told a friend. "He never released it because he thought it was obscene. It would only be used, if ever, for behind-the-scenes power broking. According to Spindel, Hoffa said he 'wouldn't embarrass their wives and children with this shit.'"

Fate leads the willing, and Otash wasn't surprised to see Lawford and Monroe becoming closer friends and talking often on the phone as their relationship now became rooted in melancholy and disillusionment with Jack and Bobby Kennedy. Both had flown too close to the sun, had been abused by the Kennedys, and now suffered from a post-traumatic stress only they could understand. Neither had the desire nor the strength to quit them, so they numbed their pain by drowning in each other's sorrows.

Otash first heard the complaining from Lawford when the actor dropped by his place to gripe about his in-laws and the way he was treated by the Rat Pack.

"I feel like a goat," Lawford told Fred one night over drinks. "Bobby treats me like shit, and Sinatra won't speak to me. That's very unfair. Unfair to me, and unfair to Frank."

Lawford was trying to appease Sinatra and get in good with the president by coordinating the details of a presidential visit to Sinatra's California golf course estate in Rancho Mirage, outside Palm Springs. Sinatra was over the moon. He convinced himself that his desert retreat would come to be known as the President's Western White House and spared no expense to retrofit the sprawling midcentury-modern home into a castle fit for Camelot as massive construction commenced posthaste.

The extensive buildout entailed cottages for all the Secret Service agents, a state-of-the-art communications center with multiple telephone lines, a massive concrete slab that would serve as a heliport for Marine One to come and go with ease, and a cherry-on-the-cake flagpole to showcase the presidential seal whenever Kennedy was in residence—just like the one he had seen at the family's Hyannis Port compound on Cape Cod. But it was all based on conversations he had with Lawford, causing Sinatra to act out on his own accord rather than any official request from the White House.

As the date drew closer, several of Bobby Kennedy's loyal staffers finally questioned why his brother would stay at the home of a man so close to the mob that Bobby was trying to bring down, and so began the deluge. After Bobby had his say, Lawford was told by his wife that the president had called her and said that he could not sleep in the same bed that had been occupied by Sam Giancana, a previous Sinatra guest. Lawford phoned the president, who told him to blame it on Secret Service security concerns so Frank wouldn't take it personally. Lawford was now left with the daunting task of breaking the news to Sinatra. To make matters worse, the president made arrangements to stay at the nearby home of Sinatra's longtime rival, Bing Crosby, a staunch Republican. Tales of what happened next are legend.

Sinatra, who had a penchant for breaking things when he got angry, went ballistic. He immediately had his valet get the White House on the phone, but the president wouldn't take his call. Next, he trashed various areas of his home that had been specially curated for the president. Then he telephoned Bobby and called him every name in the book after the attorney general informed him in no uncertain terms that his associates— meaning the mafia—made the president look bad, a somewhat hypocritical point since many of the Kennedy "associates" were just as bad or worse than Sinatra's. Finally, Sinatra called Peter back and reamed him a new one for lying to him.

Sinatra then fell silent. He rose and exited the door to his pool area and walked over to the newly poured helipad. He grabbed a sledgehammer and began pounding the concrete in a maddening attempt to turn it into a pile of rubble as his distressed valet looked on in dismay.

When the president arrived at Crosby's home, he called Frank to calm things down and asked him not to blame Lawford, for it wasn't his decision. But it was too late. Sinatra couldn't stay angry with the president, so he threw Lawford off the Rat Pack bus, cutting him from the call sheet of their next two films, *4 for Texas* and *Robin and the 7 Hoods*. To twist the knife even further, he eventually gave Lawford's role in the final film to none other than Bing Crosby.

With all the security resources he had at his disposal, Bobby executed his affair with Marilyn using a simple form of optical deception. He would first appear somewhere public and highly visible, then discreetly slip away undetected. Once he finished his business, he simply returned via the same circuitous route to the same high-profile location as if he never left. The press was none the wiser, but Otash was certain Hoover knew about the affair. Bobby was his fourteenth attorney general and knowing his every move was practically in his job description. But the Kennedys had their own shit file on Hoover, a fact that came up during a recorded conversation Otash heard between the two lovers:

"How come that prick is still there as head of the FBI? How come he's still there? How could that prick J. Edgar Hoover still be there?"

"Well, we have a Mexican standoff, okay? We've got a file on him and he's got a file on us."

"What does that mean?"

"We've got a file on him and his homosexual activities, dressed in women's clothing, and he's got a file on us. So we have a Mexican standoff. We can't fire him and he can't do anything to us."

Otash didn't know if Marilyn loved Bobby. What did seem obvious to him from listening to the recordings was that Bobby had planned all along to seduce her by taking advantage of Marilyn's need for sympathy, for a shoulder to cry on, that gradually led to bed. He eventually heard Bobby tell Marilyn that he loved her, that he would leave his wife and marry her. It was exactly what she wanted to hear, and he gave it to her. Otash believed that when Jack grew weary of Marilyn's pressuring him, Bobby assumed the role to keep her under control.

At the time, Otash was knee-deep in another messy high-profile divorce case when he received an unexpected drunk dial from a manic Marilyn.

"You've got some nerve bugging my house, Otash!" she yelled into the receiver.

"Whoa! Slow down . . ." Otash shot back.

Yes, Fred had bugs in her chandelier, in her walls, under her carpets, and anywhere else he could hide them—some she had asked for and some he had placed for Hoffa, who wanted taped evidence of her trysts with the Kennedys. But he was certain she hadn't found them, and there was no

active surveillance at the time. That would only be insti-
gated when Fred was alerted by his contacts that either Jack
or Bobby were in Los Angeles either secretly or on official
business. Then all the taps and hidden mics at Lawford and
Monroe's homes, or any other location wired to monitor the
brothers, would be activated. But neither situation had taken
place.

"Fuck you!" Marilyn screamed. "If you ever come near
my house again, I'll— "

"Marilyn, hold it! What the hell are you talking about?"

"I'm talking about you and that . . . that gun microphone.
You know what I mean."

"Shotgun mic?"

"The same."

"What's a shotgun mic got to do with me?"

Of course he had one. It could be aimed like a rifle and
pick up as much as a whisper at three hundred yards. But
what puzzled Otash was the fact that someone was using a
shotgun mic on a home whose every room was already wired.

"You own one, don't you?"

"That's no national secret, Marilyn. So what?"

"Well, I saw you outside my house, and you were listening
to me . . . while I was on the phone with a very important person."

Otash was both annoyed and concerned. This was the
second time she had falsely accused him of something. But
the fact remained she could be in trouble.

"I don't know what the fuck you're talking about, lady. I
could care less who you talk to," he lied. "Are you drunk?"

"No, I am not!" Marilyn shot back. "And you could get
into a lot of trouble. A whole lot of trouble. I have a very

intimate friend in Washington, D.C., and he knows how to take care of spies."

"Look, Marilyn," Otash said firmly. "I've never been near your house with a shotgun mic. Either one of your millions of fans is snooping on you, or you are mistaken."

"Well, just don't think I'm dumb or something . . . 'cause I'm not! Besides, I got my own tape recordings. Nobody is going to touch me. If they do, some heads are going to get chopped off. Plop! Plop! Just like that."

Then she hung up, leaving Otash in a state of unease. He knew there was a very good chance she wasn't being paranoid, and that whoever was eavesdropping might be inclined to sign her death warrant. Otash knew that anybody listening to her would know that he was possibly a player for one of the Kennedy enemies—and if *she* had reason to suspect him, whoever was listening to her had at least as much reason for suspicion.

Otash was no stranger to institutional authorities. Their inherent privileges and immunities had hounded him for most of his professional life, which is why he immediately made backup copies of everything he had and hid them in a secure location. It came as no surprise when, shortly after he had protected himself, two Secret Service agents showed up at his office unannounced with a warrant to confiscate every file he had on the president of the United States and the attorney general.

The handful of years that had passed since Otash first laid eyes on Norma Jean at John Carroll's ranch in the late 1940s now seemed like an eternity. Like all Hollywood fantasists seduced by the illusion of fame and fortune, their lives had been forever transformed by a rapacious city that fed on a steady supply of youth, innocence, and ambition. And while their capricious relationship had endured numerous vicissitudes, Otash knew that Marilyn trusted him because Sid Skolsky did, which is why he was allowed to be present during their more personal conversations at Schwab's.

It was for this reason that Monroe came to confide in Otash about her relationship with "a very intimate friend in Washington, D.C." who she believed was going to marry her.

After listening to her intimacies with the Kennedys for months, Fred knew all too well she wasn't joking, so he played along. But when he told her to be careful without naming names, she knew he suspected who it was.

"That's not a subject you should discuss so openly, Marilyn," he warned. "You could cause some serious problems for some powerful people who might, in turn, lay some heavy grief on your head."

"Oh, you men are all alike," she said dismissively. "He'll marry me. He said he would."

Otash saw a somewhat delusional but also defenseless woman, a woman who had never meant anyone any harm in her life now playing with something that could kill her when all she wanted was to be loved. And so there was nothing about the tapes that gave Otash any pleasure.

Shortly after her Golden Globe win for *The Misfits*, Marilyn began work on director George Cukor's 20th Century Fox feature *Something's Got to Give*, costarring Dean Martin.

Written by Nunally Johnson and Walter Bernstein, the remake of the 1940 screwball comedy *My Favorite Wife*, which starred Irene Dunne and Cary Grant, would be abandoned after her death.

At thirty-five years old, she was in the physical prime of her life, but not by a Hollywood standard that cast off most actresses by the time they hit forty, while their "seasoned" male counterparts received even greater opportunities. And yet it seemed she was defying this archaic and ageist paradigm. Twenty-five pounds thinner since her gallbladder surgery the previous year, Marilyn was more svelte than at any other time in her career. And despite all her adversity, she still emanated most of the same preternatural allure that made her Hollywood's greatest movie star. Before shooting began, she informed producer Henry Weinstein she'd been asked to perform at Madison Square Garden for President Kennedy's forty-fifth gala birthday celebration on May 19, 1962. Weinstein didn't foresee any issues at the time so he cleared her. But the production seemed doomed from the start.

On the first day of shooting, Marilyn called in sick with sinusitis. Cukor, who still had a bad taste in his mouth after directing her in his 1960 musical comedy, *Let's Make Love*, didn't respect her lack of professionalism. A studio physician dispatched to examine Marilyn at home determined her sickness could delay production for up to a month, but Cukor was having none of that—nor was 20th Century Fox, which was already $20 million (some $200 million today) in the red from the previous year's losses and currently burning skiffs full of cash on a daily basis at Pinewood Studios due to cost overruns on Elizabeth Taylor's sword-and-sandal epic, *Cleopatra*. They feverishly shot around Marilyn, who only showed up for twelve of the first thirty-five days of production. But unlike her brush with heroin during the filming of *Bus Stop*, this time Otash didn't have to go looking for her. Everyone knew where she was.

The film fell ten days behind schedule and Cukor made numerous last-minute alterations to the script, changes that made it difficult for Marilyn to nail down the character let alone remember her lines. She was convinced he was trying to destroy her, and as the president's birthday gala approached, Cukor and the studio protested her request for time off. Marilyn simply called in sick again, citing what she described as an extremely difficult menstrual cycle with excessive bleeding, then secretly flew to New York as planned.

Monroe's reputation for being late to work had become well-known by now. So when she suddenly became struck with a substance-induced case of severe stage fright in her dressing room, Peter Lawford used it as a running gag as he emceed the event before a fifteen-thousand-strong audience that had paid anywhere from ten to a thousand clams to celebrate the president's celebrity birthday bash cum Democratic Party fundraiser that included appearances by comedian Jack Benny and opera diva Maria Callas, among others. But Marilyn was the big attraction everyone was waiting for, especially after Lawford's two previous introductions came up empty. Finally, in the middle of his third and most illustrious overture for the world's most beloved screen siren, Marilyn shimmied onstage swathed in a sumptuous white mink wrap that, once disrobed, revealed a breathtaking Jean Louis masterpiece that made her Barbie doll figure seem like it had been swathed in a skintight sheath of cascading diamonds. Lawford's final words of introduction would inadvertently herald the tragedy that was to come.

"Mr. President, the late Marilyn Monroe!"

Standing there radiant under the bright spotlights and countless adoring eyes, all Marilyn had to do was exhale to send the audience swooning. Then, she sang the most seductive version of "Happy Birthday" in recorded history.

FIFTEEN

THE OTHER SIDE
OF MIDNIGHT

S leek, sexy, space-age lines accentuated the fire-breathing
V-8 heart of Peter Lawford's 1961 Ghia L6.4, a bespoke
luxury sport coupe tailor-made for a movie star. Hand-
crafted by Italy's Carrozzeria Ghia factory in Turin, it became
the Rat Pack's unofficial ride after the historied coach builder
gifted one to each member of the swinging coterie of
booze-swilling superstars. Peter's little rocket was one of only
twenty-six in the world, customized by legendary Hollywood
auto savant George Barris of Batmobile fame—and it was
about to give him the ride of his life.

Blasting out the gates of 12305 Fifth Helena Drive shortly
after midnight on Sunday, August 5, 1962, the Ghia barreled
out of the quiet cul-de-sac and roared far too fast onto Sunset
Boulevard. Its driver was wild-eyed and frantic, as if fleeing
the scene of a crime, careening down streets he knew like the
back of his freshly manicured, suntanned hands—left on San

Vicente, left on Wilshire, right on Santa Monica, right on Fountain, left on Laurel.

The palm-lined thoroughfares under a waxing crescent moon were practically deserted at this hour, the start of another sunny Sunday in a city whose somber beauty now juxtaposed the horror he had just witnessed: the world's most famous movie star dying, or already dead, in her bed. His brother-in-law, the attorney general of the United States—the brother of the fucking president—having just left her side hours before, leaving behind ephemera that could turn into evidence, questions that could turn into allegations, an ungodly scene that could blossom into a scandal capable of bringing down the whole bloody country in a cataclysm of shame the likes of which the world had never known.

Lawford's screaming brain screeched to a halt in front of a stunning art deco apartment complex whose residents, save for one, were fast asleep in the still Kodachrome bosom of 1962 Hollywood. He leapt from the car, sprinting up the white curvilinear staircase to pound on the door of Dreamland's ultimate fixer, a man whose services most prayed they would never require, but whom Lawford now fervidly believed the future of the country depended on, full stop. Which is why he had called Fred Otash in a blind and blathering panic less than half an hour before, waking the premier private detective from a restless sleep.

———————

A faulty air conditioner failed to comfort Otash, who had been tossing and turning all night, compliments of a temperate coastal climate turned searing hell of raging heat and humidity that made his sweaty skin stick to the sheets while his head overheated in a pounding delusional haze. And now the fucking hotline was ringing, an unlisted private line often abused by close friends and important clients who found themselves compromised at inconvenient hours.

He snatched the receiver from its cradle in the darkness, barking, "The office is closed. Talk to my secretary tomorrow."

"No! No!" yelped a gasping British brogue on the other end. "Don't hang up, Fred! It's me, Peter. Peter Lawford."

Now Otash was irate that he was calling *after ten o'clock at night*! But Lawford was scared, in "big trouble," and needed to speak with him *now*. Peter's penchant for twisting a minor problem into a fantasized "crisis" was nothing new to Otash, especially when his drama queen tendencies had been amplified by a late-night bender of too many drinks, drugs, and prostitutes.

"Call me in the morning, Peter," Otash repeated. But Lawford wasn't taking no for an answer. He needed to see the detective "immediately!" Otash was about to tell him off when Lawford hung up, jumped into his car, and commenced his bat-out-of-hell drive.

Bitterly rising from his bed, Otash yanked on his bathrobe, unleashed a string of expletives, and thought to himself, *this better be good*. Then he put a fire under a pot of day-old coffee whose burnt, pungent aroma filled his apartment by the time Lawford arrived looking like hell—drunk, stoned, an emotional wreck, trembling like a junkie who'd just seen a ghost. Otash knew the look; he'd picked up hundreds of similar losers off the streets of Los Angeles during his days as a beat cop. It wasn't befitting a movie star, much less the president and attorney general's brother-in-law, but Lawford insisted he was stone cold sober.

"Oh, Jesus God, Fred," he stammered as Otash shut and locked the door behind him. "I think Marilyn is dead!"

Marilyn . . . Otash had known her as a client, a friend, a confidante, and most recently, a person of interest. He had busted her, worked for her, counseled her, spied on her, been berated by her, and, through it all, admired her. He immediately compartmentalized the gravity of Lawford's shocking pronouncement, knowing full well he would soon learn the truth behind whatever he was babbling about. So for now, he milked the manic movie star for intel.

"What do you mean, 'think'?" Otash cross-examined. If what Peter was saying was true, news of her passing would have been on every lip, thought, news bulletin, and newspaper headline in the world. But Otash had neither seen nor heard a word of it from his vast network of sources.

"I mean she is . . . I mean . . . she was . . ." Lawford struggled, then began sobbing. "Oh, God, what'll we do?" he stammered through tears as Otash felt his blood pressure rising.

"What are you talking about, Peter?" he asked. "Was there an accident?"

"Oh, God, I don't know," Lawford answered. "I need a drink."

Otash poured two stiff ones and handed him a highball.

"She was going to get even," Lawford gasped between gulps. "That's what she said. 'Get even.' She told Bobby she was going to get even. Believe me, Fred, I begged her not to talk that way. She wasn't listening to me. But I really didn't take her seriously. She was drunk. Now I know I should have. She might not be dead."

This riled Otash even more. "You just told me you didn't know if she was dead! Is she, or isn't she?"

"I guess she is," said Lawford. "Her housekeeper is there with her." He continued sobbing. "It's all my fault . . ."

This was getting crazier by the minute. But instead of pointless anger, the levelheaded Otash cast the despondent actor some bait to lure whatever information he could out of him.

"You can't blame yourself, Peter," he said, reassuringly.

Lawford began babbling. "But she was always threatening suicide. I never took it seriously, you know, she was just blowing off emotional steam, I was used to that. I'll bet there hasn't been a week all summer that she hasn't called me or wrote that she was about to take her life. 'Tired of living,' she said."

"Are you telling me you think she committed suicide?"

"No—I mean . . . I don't know. I wasn't there when it happened. How the hell am I supposed to know?"

Otash was starting to add up the pieces. He knew that Robert Kennedy had come into the city that Saturday. He had been alerted, which is why he'd activated all the wires and recording devices, both in Lawford's beach house in Santa Monica, and in Monroe's abode in Brentwood. But he had not yet heard the tapes, so he had yet to learn about the events of the haunted day and night that had so spooked Peter Lawford. That would come later.

But something didn't make any sense. If Marilyn Monroe were truly in a mood to shoot off her mouth, why would Bobby Kennedy dare to be within a thousand miles of her? And knowing Marilyn as well as he did, whatever happened, no one usually took any of the threats she made seriously.

Otash pressed for more information before deciding what to do. "Peter, I know you're upset," he said. "Did you leave before the police arrived?"

Lawford shot him a look. "What police?"

Otash rose from his chair, towered over him, and let him have it. "What police? What do you mean *what police*? You tell me a woman is dying, and I'm assuming the cops are crawling all over the place. What do you mean, 'What police?!'"

Then, it hit him: Lawford *hadn't* called the police. *Maybe Lawford hadn't done anything for Marilyn.* Had Lawford come to his home after midnight to try to convince him to help him cover his own ass?

"Jesus, Fred, I couldn't call the police!" he said in a panic. "I came right over here. You've got to get to the house *before* the police are called!"

"Who else is in the house?" he asked.

"Just Mrs. Murray, the housekeeper."

Eunice Murray was Marilyn's bespectacled live-in house-keeper of less than one year, whose story of what happened that night would change in puzzling ways over the years.

"Didn't *she* call the police, for chrissakes?" Otash asked, his mind reeling. He'd later tell friends that he always knew Lawford was weak, but to do nothing to help a so-called dear friend that might still be alive was beyond imagination.

Lawford hedged his answers. "Maybe . . . I don't think so . . . I don't know. She said to leave Marilyn alone. Let her sleep."

Then he switched back to ass-saving mode.

"But you've got to get over there *right now*! We've got to get all of that shit out of there. They can't find shit that implicates the president or the attorney general! You've got to help me!"

We're talking about a *presidential scandal!* You're an ex-Marine, for chrissakes. You want to dishonor your president?"

"I can't go, Peter," Otash said. "Who the fuck doesn't know me?!" Then, he softened. "But for your sake, I'll arrange for someone to go out there, and we'll try to sanitize the place and find out if there's something you left behind. That, I'll be happy to do, but you're going to have to go with my guy."

It took all of five minutes to get Reed Wilson in his apartment. The discreet, dependable associate who, unbeknownst to Otash, was also working undercover for the CIA cut a deal with Lawford before they left together to commence a secret sweep of Marilyn Monroe's home.

When Wilson arrived, there were cars everywhere. He pulled a phony LAPD badge and breezed in. He looked around, saw the place was in pretty good shape. He noticed a filing cabinet in Marilyn's bedroom that looked like it had been forcefully opened.

Otash later said in a taped interview: *"I don't know who broke into the file cabinet. We didn't pick that up. Anytime. I don't know. I was not there. I don't know if someone broke into the file cabinet. What had transpired only God knows."*

Wilson saw a lot of empty pill bottles lying around, but none of the detectives were dusting them for fingerprints.

Otash: *"And there was a glass. There was a glass and they say there was no water. That's bullshit. There was a glass next to her bed on the floor. Whatever was in the house was removed and turned over to Lawford for delivery, supposedly to his brother-in-law."*

Of the later reports of a "missing" red diary, which purportedly revealed the secrets of Marilyn's life and death, Otash confirmed it did exist, though it did not contain any personal stories or rumored secrets: *"They keep talking about Monroe's red diary. You don't have to be a mental giant to know that a fucking diary only lasts for twelve months. The diary that everybody's talking about with Monroe was a fucking address book, a phone book. I got twenty-five diaries. Every year is a different diary. I got one on my desk right now. So if Monroe had a diary, she must have had twenty. So why are we always talking about one fucking diary? She had a red address book. That is a fact. That was a gift given to her. She had a red address book with all the phone numbers there and everything else in it. I had seen it and the ones used in preceding years many times. If Peter Lawford took it that night, it was only because it contained private lines for both the Justice Department and the White House. But there was no book containing a daily record of her sexual relations with Jack or Bobby Kennedy."*

At that moment, that information existed only in the possession of one individual: Fred Otash. So after Peter Lawford left his home in those early hours of August 5, 1962, and the world converged on Monroe's home a few hours later, the detective left his apartment and drove out to the car whose trunk contained the secrets for which everyone was searching. It was still before dawn when he retrieved the tape recorder and prepared to listen. Soon Otash would know *everything*, both the angels and demons who had taken part in the seismic event that would ensnare the world's imagination for decades to come. He pressed play. The old reel-to-reel tape recorder began rolling and famous voices filled his ears in a series of gasps and groans, plans and protestations, and, through it all, the death of a superstar.

Monroe had been feeling depressed that day, despondent and desperate to reach Bobby Kennedy. What she did not know but Lawford did was that Kennedy was visiting friends in the San Francisco area.

Otash: *"I listened to her trying to reach Bobby Kennedy in Hyannis Port. I listened to her trying to reach him at the Department of Justice in Washington, D.C."*

And when she couldn't reach Kennedy, she called Lawford, the one person in the world with whom she could voice her anger and frustration for the manner in which she— they—had been treated by his in-laws. Otash had heard rumors she had gotten pregnant, presumably by either Bobby or Jack. He had also been tipped off by a police officer contact that she had recently traveled to Tijuana with a skilled American doctor in tow in order to have a safe abortion. Since it was performed in a country where the procedure was legal, the doctor would avoid any stateside prosecution, as abortion would remain a criminal offense in California until 1969.

In one of his earlier conversations with Bobby that day, Peter had alerted him to Marilyn's state of mind. He asked Peter to calm her down so she wouldn't embarrass him, to "get her away from the house to your place, to keep her quiet." So Lawford went to work, asking Marilyn to join him and their mutual friends at an impromptu gathering at his mansion on the beach.

"I'm having a party this evening, Marilyn," he told her. "Come on down. It'll do you good to get out of the house. You won't have to drive. I'll pick you up." At that point Marilyn inquired about the guest list.

"Who will be there?" she asked.

"People you know."

"What people?"

"Bobby . . . isn't that what you want to hear?" Peter teased.

"Who else?" she probed further.

The additional names included a bevy of young starlets, women who reminded her of a previous life before she met the Kennedys and experienced their sexual indifference, triggering her current state of anger.

"Go to hell," she told Lawford, then hung up the phone.

Peter and Marilyn would speak numerous times that day. She kept trying to reach Bobby on the phone, and when that didn't work, she'd ring Lawford again.

"For chrissakes, Marilyn, he's out and about," Lawford told her.

But as much as he tried, Marilyn refused to attend Peter's party. She just kept insisting she had to reach Bobby. Lawford then convinced the attorney general that the situation was critical, so they made arrangements for Bobby to fly down from San Francisco and go straight to Monroe's home. When he arrived the first time, alone, Marilyn was very upset, but he managed to quiet her down. Her maid, Eunice Murray, wasn't there.

Otash: *"He fucked her around eleven o'clock that morning, and then he left."*

When Bobby arrived the second time with Lawford, a hysterical Marilyn went after the attorney general like there was no tomorrow, confronting him about his treatment of her, how he had promised everything and delivered nothing, insisting to know why he wasn't going to marry her.

Otash: *"On the recording that Reed Wilson and I heard was uh . . . a serious problem. She had made some threatening statements to him that he had made a lot of commitments and promises to her."*

"Where were you when I had to get an abortion of your kid, you no-good bastard!" Marilyn screamed as Lawford and Bobby tried to quiet her down.

"Come on, we'll discuss it tonight after dinner," Bobby said. "Peter is going to have Chinese food brought in. You're coming."

But it didn't work. Marilyn's screams and protests got louder until she was completely out of control.

Otash: *"Either Peter or Bobby grabbed a pillow, okay, and they had her on the bed, and they had the pillow to quiet her down. And she finally, what it appeared is that they finally got to quiet her down. There was no more screaming going on."*

During an interview with KABC-Los Angeles some twenty years later in 1982, Los Angeles County Chief Coroner Thomas Noguchi would admit he had found bruises on Monroe's arms and back when he performed the autopsy. This rather important detail that he had kept to himself for two decades was consistent with the violence Otash listened to when they manhandled Marilyn onto the bed.

"We'll talk about it later," Bobby said. "We'll have dinner, then I'll come back with you tonight." Then he said: "Marilyn, you know you're hysterical, you're having problems, you've been drinking, something's going on with you. You know, I came here at great risk to sit here and try to give you some understanding. I heard you're having some problems. I'm here to do what I can to give you the comfort you need."

Marilyn started up again, and soon everyone was screaming at each other. She returned to her previous arguments about the way they had treated her, passed her back and forth. She felt that her strong relationship with Frank Sinatra had been partially destroyed after what they had done to him, a grievance Otash heard once before during a previous phone call when Bobby was staying at Peter's house.

Otash: *"And then she railed, 'You dirty bastard, what's this shit you're pulling on Sinatra? What's your story? Why do you want his ass? After all he did for you and your brother, getting the Rat Pack out together to raise millions of dollars, running around the Sports Arena trying to get delegates to vote for your brother. And then you guys shun him when he was supposed to come down to celebrate your brother and the Secret Service. And you, Bobby, are the one that convinced him that he should not stay there because you're going to sleep in the same bed that Giancana slept in. And not only that, you cause a breach between your brother and Sinatra, and you forbid him to have any further contact with him.'*

"She got pissed-off that her best friend and former lover, Sinatra—and they stayed friends until the day she died—was fucked over by the Kennedy administration. She really, really . . . all the information that came to us through whatever sources or means we had, she really loved him very much. I knew she was dating Frank Sinatra when she was living at 828 North Doheny Drive, where he was also living. At one time, I'm quite sure, that she would have been very happy to have been married to him, but he went out and married somebody else. But she only had the kindest things to say about him. She depended on him continuously with Jack Kennedy and Bob Kennedy, and this came off the recordings."

"Do me a favor . . . do me a favor," Bobby implored. "Let me get you a glass of water, okay? And why don't you take something to help you sleep for a while, then come out and have dinner with us later, okay? And we'll continue the conversation, I'll drive you back, and we'll continue the conversation at that time. In the meantime, cool down. Relax."

Otash: *"And he wasn't saying it in a kind way. He was sort of saying it in an antagonistic way, you know? And when she refused, he became emphatic."*

"Jesus Christ, take some fucking pills and go to sleep," Bobby told her. "We'll call you later, come have dinner with us. Christ, stop screaming. It's not the end of the fucking world."

Otash: *"We had two tapes. One that we had in the morning, which would cover the afternoon. Then there was another tape made in the afternoon, it wasn't one tape all day long. But on one of the tapes was Bobby running around trying to find out if the place was wired. Somehow, some information had been developed that it might have been bugged. Now he's looking to get out of there* [Los Angeles]. *The mayor saw him there that day, neighbors saw him there, helicopter pilots. And . . . I don't know, I don't know . . . and Reed doesn't know, if maybe he gave her something. Or Peter gave her something. Because Peter had told me he could have saved her life, okay? Peter's the one who said that. I didn't say that. Peter said that to me when he came to my house that night. In fact, he had that guilt complex until the day he died."*

Bobby Kennedy hadn't the slightest intention of having dinner with Marilyn that night or returning to her home. He wasn't going to risk being seen with her, so Peter spirited him back to the area where the helicopter was waiting for him. He would be nowhere near Los Angeles when the news of her death broke.

Otash: *"He was so pissed. Bobby came in and said, 'You know, I want to get the fuck out of here. If she comes out to this party, man, it's going to be a fucking scene. I'm getting my ass out of here.' So they arranged to get him out. Bobby Kennedy left the second time around five thirty p.m. I can't pinpoint the time. I didn't have a clock on the recording device so I can only try to place the time. I can repeat what was said, but I can only place the time. Bobby Kennedy could have saved her life, as far as I'm concerned."*

Otash had kept the bugs activated because Peter and Bobby said they were going to call her later about coming out to dinner.

"Are you coming out, are you coming out?" Peter asked.

"No, I'm too tired," Marilyn replied. "I don't feel good. I'm not up to it. I want to go to sleep. It's been a bad couple of days for me."

Otash: *"She called Lawford twice. She tried to find Jack. He never took her call. She called him in Hyannis Port. Then she calls Lawford and it's common knowledge of what she said, you know, 'Say goodbye to Pat. Say goodbye to the president and say goodbye to yourself because you're a nice guy.' She never even mentioned Bobby."*

Then she didn't respond, as if she had dropped the phone. When Lawford called back and got a busy signal, he got very concerned, enough to get up and drive out to Marilyn's home, ringing the doorbell until Miss Murray finally answered.

Otash: *"He went out there around eleven o'clock and he had access to her bedroom. That shit about the door being locked was just bullshit. It might have been locked later, but I don't know how the hell it was locked. And he went in there and he just looked at her and he knew she was dead. There was no question in his mind. Then he started rummaging around, trying to pick up—he's half fucking drunk—trying to pick up all the shit he could that would implicate anyone. Earlier that day, Bobby Kennedy was looking around for any listening devices, the bugs and wires, because he had become extremely suspicious when she started talking about possibly going public.*

"Where is it? Where the fuck is it?" Bobby implored. "We have to know. It's important to the family. We can make any arrangements you want, but we must find it."

O tash couldn't sleep for two days after listening to the final tape. The celebrated Superman of sleuths, able to squash the tallest Hollywood scandal, now found himself grimly overwhelmed by a haunting salvo of kryptonite whose sheer possession could ruin him forever. He was tormented by the events and circumstances surrounding his friend, the world's greatest screen siren, dying on his watch. Sure, she had a history of overdose. Just three weeks before she had downed too many sleeping pills while visiting Sinatra at the Cal-Neva Lodge & Casino in Lake Tahoe, her unconscious body discovered in Chalet 52 by housekeeping staff before it was too late—a convenient truth for those who would later seek to discredit foul play in her death. But Otash only knew one thing for certain now: he had to put the tape in the hands of someone in law enforcement he could trust, and there was only one man he *could* trust: Thad Brown, the former deputy chief of detectives at the LAPD who was Fred's old boss, best friend, and confidant on the police force.

Brown had been at Marilyn's home the night that she died, along with another friend of his who used to be a federal prosecutor.

Otash: *"I lived with that for a week. And I finally called him to tell him I had to talk to him . . . and there was something I had to tell him. I didn't mention every word, just told him I had something to talk about. And I told him about Peter Lawford, having come by that night. And I gave him the tape. The only thing I said to Thad Brown was, that under no circumstances was he to tell Chief Parker that I gave him this fucking tape. Under no circumstances!"*

Otash didn't know what Brown did with the tape after that, whether he kept it or gave it to Parker.

Otash: *"I never knew for sure what Thad Brown did with the tape. I don't know why he would give it to Parker. When Thad Brown died in 1970, they shook down his garage and found Marilyn's records in there and a whole bunch of shit on Marilyn, when the LAPD couldn't find anything. He was obsessed with her. I'm so shook up now talking about this shit. Brown felt she was murdered."*

But what Otash did know was that Chief Parker, or someone, was scheduled to take a trip to Washington with the Monroe information for Bobby Kennedy following her death. He also heard rumors that J. Edgar Hoover's job may have been in question at the time and that Parker wanted to replace him.

Otash: *"You have to understand something: Parker was being considered to head the FBI. Parker was a lawyer. He got a degree out of Chicago. I was in his office enough to see his fucking degree on the wall. Parker was a very honest guy, okay? Don't misunderstand me. But knowing Parker, who was an opportunist, he's sitting there saying to himself, Jesus Christ, I can make points, you know, with them. Now, when people make a statement that J. Edgar Hoover covered up the relationship*

*about Bobby and Jack Kennedy, I gathered, for that reason,
that had to be true. There's all kinds of FBI reports of the relationship. If Thad Brown gave him that tape, it had to wind up in
Bobby Kennedy's hands in Washington . . . unless they found it
in Thad Brown's garage, which I don't think they did. It was
never destroyed. But it is gone."*

At the time, Otash had no idea of all the people Bernie
Spindel had been dealing with. He had sent him anywhere
from sixteen to eighteen tapes during the course of his investigation, and it was only later that he came to qualify the list:
Sam Giancana, Jimmy Hoffa, the CIA, and J. Edgar Hoover.

In 1966, four years after Marilyn's death, investigators
armed with a search warrant from New York district attorney
Frank Hogan's office raided Spindel's home and seized all his
tapes, evidence, and information on Marilyn Monroe. His
lawyers sued for recovery, citing that the information included
"tapes and evidence concerning circumstances surrounding
and causes of death of Marilyn Monroe, which strongly sug-
gest that the official reported circumstances of her death are
erroneous." Spindel would tell *Life* magazine reporter John
Neary: "Hogan really did Kennedy a favor by pulling the
raid. They stole my tapes on Marilyn Monroe and my complete file."

Spindel's lawsuit would fail, as well as another attempt
after his death by his widow, Barbara Spindel. In a letter to
Otash dated October 17, 1973, she would reminisce: "Many
times he told me about recording Bobby Kennedy, of tapping
Kennedy's telephone and knowing when and how he was
planning to meet his various girlfriends. Bernie also told me
stories of wearing a belt transmitter when he went in to see
Bobby Kennedy and of Kennedy searching Bernie—while

their conversation was being transmitted to a recorder in Bernie's car."

Otash: *"Why would the feds go and confiscate everything in his house? Why? Who the fuck knew about it? How come they didn't confiscate stuff from my place? That's the reason I never kept anything around there, no diary or any report that would involve me."*

SIXTEEN

HINDSIGHT IS 20/20

Forget it, Freddie O . . . it's Hollywood.

For years, he heard that phrase intermittently echoing in his thoughts. But no matter how many times the calendar pages turned as the years flowed by, he couldn't forget. The events of the night of Marilyn's death were a haunting chapter in his life, and he knew the time would come when he would have to decide to tell the full story, if only for his own peace of mind.

That day came on August 15, 1985.

Otash, now sixty-three and retired, was sitting on his sun-drenched terrace, enjoying the magnificent view of the Mediterranean Sea from his pied-à-terre above the bustling Promenade de la Croisette in Cannes, when the telephone rang. The caller identified herself as Ene Riisna, a producer for ABC's *20/20*, the network's flagship newsmagazine co-anchored by Hugh Downs and Barbara Walters. After a brief exchange of pleasantries, Riisna cut to the chase. She asked Fred if he would be interviewed on camera for a special episode devoted to the life, the love affairs, and the controversial death of Marilyn Monroe.

Since her death at age thirty-six on August 4, 1962, Marilyn's legacy had steadily skyrocketed. Dozens of books were written about her, including one by Norman Mailer with the salacious claim that she had been murdered by the CIA and FBI. Andy Warhol's silkscreen paintings of her became iconic works of modern art, and her image became a valuable and influential commodity on Madison Avenue.

Endless conspiracies about what had really happened to her continued to swirl in the collective consciousness. Was it murder? An overdose? Suicide? Suffocation? Speculation persisted about who was with her in those final hours. Was it her housekeeper, who was doing laundry when the police arrived that fateful night? Her psychiatrist, who visited her daily to wean her off her habit of taking too many sleeping pills? Her physician, who made regular house calls to service her with vitamin B_{12} injections? Her movie star friend and confidant, Peter Lawford? U.S. attorney general Robert F. Kennedy?

Otash had quite a bit to add to the story. He heard what happened that fateful night because he had wired her Los Angeles house on Fifth Helena Drive. This had been done, he would explain, through channels, at the behest of CIA counterintelligence leader James Jesus Angleton, who was concerned what President John F. Kennedy might disclose over pillow talk with the actress, and on behalf of Teamsters chieftain Jimmy Hoffa, who hired Fred to get the goods on Attorney General Bobby Kennedy, who was investigating Hoffa.

Otash's initial reluctance to come forward stemmed from his sense of patriotism, having served in the Marine Corps in

World War II and for a decade on the LAPD. Yes, he had gathered morally incriminating evidence about President Kennedy, and he felt that some of this information could have serious repercussions if made public. But he believed that whoever was occupying the White House should be accorded honor and respect and not be torn down by personal issues. The Camelot mystique may have been overly romanticized in the aftermath of Kennedy's assassination in Dallas on November 22, 1963, but no one could deny that JFK had inspired a nation to help effectuate a better world during a pivotal time in U.S. history. Bobby's presidential run, cut short by his own tragic death on June 6, 1968, had imbued a similar enduring influence on the American psyche. Both men had devoted their lives to public service, inspired an entire generation to follow in their footsteps, and now their family was continuing that selfless tradition, led in large part by their younger brother Ted Kennedy, one of the most respected U.S. senators.

Otash had been a study in contradictions when it came to the Kennedys. He spent years chronicling their reckless sexual exploits for Hoffa and powerful Republicans while privately praising to his friends John F. Kennedy's vision, leadership, and tireless efforts to transcend the status quo with game-changing initiatives like the establishment of the Peace Corps, laying the groundwork for landmark civil rights, voting rights, and fair housing legislation that would become law after his death, and landing a man on the moon before the end of the decade. He also applauded Jack and Bobby's strategic diplomacy in averting nuclear war after hawkish military advisors urged them to attack the Soviet Union during the Cuban Missile Crisis in 1962.

With the willful blindness of a patriotic ex-Marine, he
believed such thoughts and actions could be mutually exclusive, and if his years of private detective work had taught him
anything, it was that no man, or woman, was a paragon of
virtue. Whatever their personal frailties, Otash recognized
that the Kennedy brothers were skilled politicians who loved
their country and put its best interests first. It was this strong
reverence that initially discouraged him from airing their
dirty laundry in the public square, but after both men had
been separately gunned down by assassins, he put to rest any
remaining thought of telling his story out of respect for their
grieving widows and families.

Mostly, Otash had refused to talk about that night as an
act of self-preservation. On the rare occasion that he did, his
words and disclosures were strategically measured. The detective who had wired the homes of both Marilyn Monroe and
Peter Lawford and had critical evidence that he had not
reported to the police at the time had always wondered: Could
he be guilty of withholding evidence in a felony? Could he
face serious jail time? Such basic questions always led him to
the same conclusion: better to lay low and keep quiet.

It was only when others began lying about their experi-
ences, attempting to gain fame for incidents that never happened, that he began to consider coming forward. When men
who had worked for him, who had heard some of the tapes,
began talking with reporters, often inaccurately, he felt that
Marilyn was being further disrespected.

And so that sunny afternoon, Fred Otash decided the
time had come to unburden himself of the terrible memories
of that night. It was time that the truth be known, or at least

the part of the truth that only he could contribute. The Kennedy brothers, Hoover, Hoffa, and the wiretappers Bernie Spindel, former CIA man Bob Maheu, and John Danoff were all long gone. Lawford, who suffered from kidney and liver failure after years of alcohol and substance abuse, had passed the previous Christmas Eve. This left Otash as one of the last people with firsthand knowledge of what transpired the night Marilyn Monroe took her last breath.

Yes, Fred told the ABC News producer, he would appear on the *20/20* special. As he hung up the phone, he calculated that it had been twenty-three years and eleven days since Marilyn's death. But somehow to him it felt like yesterday.

An ABC News attorney soon followed up to confirm the details. The network would provide him with a first-class airline ticket from Nice to Los Angeles to New York and back to Nice, along with accommodations and $250 a day for twelve days as reimbursement for other expenses. In exchange, Fred agreed to be available in New York for an on-camera interview. But he would not be paid for the interview—nor did he ask to be paid, as he didn't want what he had to say to be tainted.

———————

Early one morning ten days later, he found himself in New York, his stomping grounds for a time after his California detective license was revoked in 1965. He believed losing it stemmed from his and Marilyn's final conversation when she accused him of bugging her house. Her specific allegation was off the mark, but still had merit, so much so that Otash's gut told him to stash the files in case Marilyn said something about it to Bobby Kennedy.

The Kennedy ties had continued to shadow him during that period when he had his PI agency in New York. One high-profile client who paid handsomely for his sleuthing services was a powerful billionaire who hired him to investigate the sex life of a widow he was thinking of marrying. Otash researched it and came back with a report that met with his client's standards. As a result, Greek shipping magnate Aristotle Onassis married the former Jacqueline Kennedy.

Otash's career also took an unexpected detour in his New York days when he signed on as the head of security for Hazel Bishop, one of the largest cosmetic companies in the world. He eventually parlayed that into owning his own cosmetic salon in Bal Harbour, Florida. The tropical weather down there suited him perfectly, as did being out of the gumshoe game. Now he had the freedom to travel the world whenever he wished, instead of being on call every hour of every day. He was also liberated from the emotional toll private investigating took on him, not the least of which was his experience with Marilyn's last day on earth—and so he had come to New York to try to let go of that haunting memory.

That afternoon, he arrived at the headquarters of ABC News in New York, where his interview would be conducted over two consecutive days by *20/20* correspondent Sylvia Chase. *TV Guide* had consistently dubbed Chase, a venerated and award-winning investigative reporter, "the most trusted woman on TV" during her tenure at the newsmagazine, which began upon its inception in the summer of 1978 after a seven-year stint at CBS News, where she championed women's rights and empowerment while rising to prominence during the era of Walter Cronkite.

Otash was pensive, anxious, but at long last ready to claim his role in the life and death of Marilyn Monroe, to unburden his soul of secrets kept buried for decades, and to debunk or corroborate the myriad conspiracy theories that had obfuscated her legacy and hijacked history. His recollections would be used in whole or in part for an in-depth exposé on the troubled actress that Chase, her coproducer and life partner Stanhope Gould, and Riisna had spent three months and $150,000 (nearly $450,000 today) in network resources investigating. Given a running time of twenty-six minutes, twice the normal length of a *20/20* segment, the story had been earmarked as the blockbuster lead of their new fall season premiere on September 26, 1985.

Chase and her team had also relied heavily on the imminent publication of author Anthony Summers's book *Goddess: The Secret Lives of Marilyn Monroe*, an extensively researched biography that delved into the screen siren's private life like never before, including staggering assertions that President Kennedy had shared state secrets—and his brother Bobby—with Monroe leading up to her tragic death, which Summers alleged the Kennedys had a hand in covering up. Otash was well aware of the book. While he refused the author's request for an interview, he had helped him locate certain elusive documents and sources.

The *20/20* interview proved an unsettling experience for Otash, but he managed to maintain his composure for the cameras as he confronted the ghosts of Hollywood past. He was ambushed, unaware of the information that the producers had dug up, such as records of Marilyn's calls to Bobby at the Justice Department, or that they had located and interviewed Reed Wilson, the rogue detective Otash procured for a desperate Peter Lawford in the early morning hours of Marilyn's death when he needed help sweeping her home of any evidence connecting her with the Kennedys before the police arrived. Wilson had told the *20/20* producers that there was a tape that Otash had destroyed, which wasn't the case, as that was the tape Otash gave to Thad Brown.

After Otash concluded the second day of the interview, worrisome thoughts arrived. What if his public statements weren't universally believable to the viewing audience? America was so mired in conspiracy theories; they might suspect him of whitewashing the cause of Marilyn's death. Or what if an ambitious law enforcement officer in California, looking to make a name for himself, doubted her death was accidental? What if RFK and Lawford were deemed to have preyed upon Marilyn's emotional state by telling her to take or by giving her sleeping pills? That could be involuntary manslaughter or second-degree murder and make them criminally liable. And with Otash not coming forward after hearing the audiotapes, he himself may have committed a felony by withholding evidence. Prosecuting a deceased person posthumously is legal, though rarely pursued. But being the only living person who had pertinent information at the time could leave Otash in a vulnerable position.

So instead of heading to Miami and watching the ABC show from there as planned, he decided to fly to France and lie low in Cannes when the show aired to avoid a possible grand jury subpoena, because if one came and he were forced to testify, he didn't want to find out what might happen to him.

Two weeks after Otash's interview, ABC News chief Roone Arledge, one of the most accomplished, powerful, and respected network programming executives in the industry, the man who created *Monday Night Football, ABC World News Tonight, Nightline,* and *20/20*, sat in the executive screening room to watch the first cut with his senior vice president and former Columbia University classmate, Richard C. Wald. Arledge had concerns that more definitive proof was required. He sent his producers back to the drawing board and delayed the broadcast to supposedly make room for a special report on a massive earthquake that had rattled Mexico City earlier that month.

The Marilyn segment was edited down to eighteen minutes, then sixteen after two more days of internal meetings, and then again to thirteen as producers tried to appease their boss, who by then felt it was nothing more than "just a gossip story" that neither proved or disproved the Kennedy-Monroe affairs and failed to address the larger context as to whether or not the president and attorney general had made themselves vulnerable to blackmail by organized crime. Finally, on October 3, 1985, Arledge pulled the plug entirely, citing that all that remained in the segment were the assertions of a private investigator hired by Jimmy Hoffa who claimed to have tape-recorded evidence that Monroe had separate affairs with the Kennedy brothers. It was death by a thousand cuts for Chase and her producers.

When news got out that the segment had been spiked, Arledge went into full damage control mode, desperately trying to appear conscientious as he circumnavigated a tidal wave of criticism and candid outrage within his own ranks stemming from his refusal to air the story. During a series of curated interviews with key press outlets, he told the *Los Angeles Times* that the segment needed a larger context than simply whether the Kennedy brothers engaged in illicit affairs with the world's most famous movie star. He also denied reports that his longtime close friend Ethel Kennedy, the widow of Robert F. Kennedy, had played a role in his decision to deep-six the controversial segment. It turned out that Arledge wasn't the only employee at ABC News with personal ties to the Kennedy clan. His thirty-three-year-old assistant Jeff Ruhe was married to Courtney Kennedy (the fifth of Bobby and Ethel's eleven children), and ABC News vice president David Burke's former job as an aide to Ted Kennedy only deepened suspicions that a major conflict of interest was afoot.

Neither *20/20* co-anchor Barbara Walters nor the show's executive producer, Av Westin, would comment for the *Los Angeles Times* story, though they would later claim through a spokesperson that they felt "the piece should have been aired." Prior to Arledge seeing the segment, Westin had commented: "I don't anticipate not putting it on the air. The journalism is solid. Everything in there has two sources. We are documenting that there was a relationship between Bobby and Marilyn, and Jack and Marilyn. A variety of eyewitnesses attest to that on camera."

For their part, other key ABC staff members would attest that the segment included eyewitness accounts of wiretapping of Marilyn's home by Jimmy Hoffa that revealed meetings between her and the Kennedy brothers, accounts of a visit to Marilyn by Robert Kennedy on the day of her death, and accounts made by Otash that were corroborated by three other wiretappers. Another staffer commented, "Sylvia Chase was in the studio getting her hair and makeup done when it was canceled."

But co-anchor Hugh Downs would be the most vocal of his peers, publicly stating that he was "disturbed" by the decision.

"I have no quarrel with the network's policy of controlling what goes on their airwaves," said Downs, who felt the story had "air-tight documentation" and was displeased by the reasons Arledge was quoted as having given for canceling the story. But what annoyed Downs the most was an item in Liz Smith's popular New York *Daily News* column that quoted Arledge calling the segment "a sleazy piece of journalism" that was "just not good enough for us," a comment that Downs felt unduly criticized the "great team" that had painstakingly worked on the story.

"I don't work with sleazy programs and sleazy people," he said, adding: "I will not be involved in a cover-up for the company." Furthermore, Downs disagreed with Arledge's assertion that the segment's allegations had not been adequately substantiated, stating that the segment was "more thoroughly documented than the network's coverage of Watergate at its height."

Downs, Walters, and *20/20* reporter and correspondent Geraldo Rivera—who according to Sylvia Chase had "double-checked the segment"—even stood together linking arms on the news set in protest of the network's decision to kill the story.

Otash later recalled on a taped recording: *"One of the producers told me: 'Off the record—and if you say I said it, I'll*

deny it—Roone Arledge and the powers that be at ABC screened
the segment for [matriarch] Rose Kennedy and Teddy Kennedy.
And they were completely paranoid. What bothered them the
most is that they didn't want to show that organized crime had
infiltrated the White House.'

"That was the main thrust of their feeling, number one.
Number two, they got a commitment from Teddy Kennedy, that
if you run for president we must now screen the show. We have
no choice. But so long as you're going to be quiet, we can handle
it. But if you're going to go out there and start running for pres-
ident, then I don't know who's going to come in and take over
this operation."

A few weeks following the controversy, on October 24, the
Emmy Award–winning Rivera announced his resignation,
saying he was leaving the network after fifteen years and telling the Associated Press that he already considered himself
"a square peg trying to fit in a round hole of network news,"
and that the decision to kill the Monroe story had accelerated
his decision to leave. When Geraldo read Arledge's comments
in Liz Smith's column, he was quoted as saying, "I'm appalled.
I think that story was a solid piece of TV reporting. They are
not going to get away with this. It's going to be a major controversy," and that "the decision smacks of cronyism, though
I can't prove that."

A month later, Sylvia Chase resigned from ABC News to
become an anchor and host documentaries for KRON-TV,
the NBC affiliate in San Francisco. She admitted she was disappointed when Arledge shelved the story, that she felt he
made the wrong decision, but denied that her leaving was
related to the event. Five years later, she would return to *20/20*

as a correspondent, but her Kennedy-Monroe report would never see the light of day.

It had all been a surreal twist of fate for Otash, who had struggled for more than two decades after the fact before finding the courage to tell *his* truth. But when he finally broke his silence, it was buried once more—only this time by a handful of powerful individuals bent on quelling what could have given rise to one of the biggest scandals of the twentieth century.

THE REMAINS OF THE DAY

Monday, October 5, 1992.

It's 7 a.m. in paradise—Beverly Hills adjacent. Five, two-story glass pavilions crown the palatial porte cochere of a resort-style condominium just off Sunset Boulevard. Inside, down a long colonial corridor, past the double-door threshold of Unit 302, a seventy-year-old man lies prostrate, motionless, his half-naked body wedged beneath his kitchen table. Tousled garments spill haphazardly from two open suitcases in the bedroom, signaling a rapid retreat from something—or someone gone awry. It's a macabre tableau, worthy of a Raymond Chandler novel. Only this is real, not fiction. And the lifeless corpse face-planted on the ceramic tile in his pajama bottoms is no less than the most notorious private detective who ever lived: "The Man Who Bugged Marilyn Monroe"!

Ten hours earlier, Fred Otash had sat in my parents, Fred and Orietta Westphal's, condo at the Park Wellington, bathing in the afterglow of a Friars Club dinner in his honor celebrating the completion of his manuscript. Now the doorman was calling their residence with concern, explaining that Mr. Otash had buzzed the front desk at 5 a.m. for a taxi to take him to Los Angeles International Airport at 6:30 a.m., a request he would confirm forty-five minutes later. When the cab arrived at 6:15 a.m., multiple attempts to alert Mr. Otash by phone, intercom, and knocks on his door were unsuccessful, so the doorman told the driver to go around the block while he continued searching for his missing resident, a scenario that would repeat itself three times until just past 7 a.m. when he dismissed the taxi and telephoned my parents, knowing they had a key to Fred's unit.

My father was in the shower, so my mother was the first to venture out to check on Fred. Often considered the clairvoyant in the family, she later recounted a mounting sense of dread as she walked down the long corridor, more visceral with each step, before she rang the bell and then knocked on his door. Receiving no answer, she inserted the key, unbolted the lock, cracked the door open, and called out: "Freddie? Yoo-hoo! Freddie? It's Orietta. Did you call a taxi?"

My mother entered and saw that the lights in the foyer, kitchen, and bedroom were on despite the morning sun now bathing the interior of the unit through floor-to-ceiling plantation shutters. She took a few steps in before stopping in her tracks at the sight of Fred's bare feet protruding from beneath his kitchen table. Frightened beyond measure, she swiftly departed, closing the door behind her and running to fetch my father.

When they returned moments later, my father entered Fred's unit alone while my shaken mother waited outside. He would later tell me that the first thing that caught the corner of his eye were two open suitcases in the bedroom that looked "as if he had been packing in haste." A second later he was struck by the same shocking visual of Fred's pajama-clad lower torso sticking out from beneath the kitchen table. *How in the hell did he get like that?* he thought, before kneeling down to feel his ankle for a pulse, though certain there was none.

My mother was crying when he reappeared in the corridor; she knew before he told her. Back in their condo, my father located the business card of Fred's lawyer, the one Fred included when he first gave them a set of keys to his unit, which was to be used if anything should happen when he was out of town. He then placed an urgent call to that infamous pit bull attorney Arthur Crowley, who he would soon learn was also the executor of Fred's estate.

Crowley, who often bragged to colleagues he "had dental work done without Novocain," then quickly orchestrated a cleanup operation worthy of his reputation. First, he arranged for the coroner's office to speedily retrieve Fred's body. Without autopsy or investigation, it would be swiftly "determined" that Fred had taken his last breath shortly after 6:35 a.m., a sudden death that was ruled a heart attack by the West Hollywood division of the Los Angeles County Sheriff's Department—a neat and tidy end to a man whose life was rarely neat or tidy.

When the Los Angeles City Council adjourned on October 6, 1992, its renowned president John Ferraro, the former USC Trojans football star and successful businessman whose historic tenure on the City Council from 1966 until his death in 2001 established him as the longest-serving civic leader in Los Angeles history, stood alongside his fellow council members in silent tribute and reverence to honor the memory of Fred Otash. That same day, Crowley had a padlock shackled to the front door of Fred's condo through which no one could enter.

But while his corpse may have been rendered mute, Fred had left behind volumes: tape recordings, surveillance reports, interview transcripts, his unpublished manuscript, copious case files, and a secret box of photographs he often joked kept him alive—evidence that could be used to tell his story, a story that some, apparently, wished not be told because now, under Crowley's directive, Fred Otash began to systematically disappear. Out went his red filing cabinet that contained his "hot files." Out went all of his earthly possessions, including letters, personal effects, and the two immense scrapbooks containing his clippings and other memorabilia chronicling his extraordinary life and scandalous cases. Out, presumably, went the story of Fred Otash, dispatched to a storage facility of Crowley's choosing, never to be seen again.

It would be three weeks after Fred's funeral when I called Colleen as I had promised during her father's wake. My mother and I met her for dinner shortly thereafter, where sincere condolences led to fond memories. Colleen would learn how I had been working with Fred for the past two years to tell his life story, how I wished to continue my efforts to help her keep his legacy alive by seeing that his manuscript be published posthumously. She gave me her blessing. We soon began working together toward these goals, and Colleen arranged to have her father's remaining eleven boxes of files delivered to my office at Warner Bros. Studios, including a copy of his unpublished manuscript.

As interacting with the subsidiary rights departments at major New York publishing houses was part of my daily routine at Warner Bros. Television, it was a simple task to navigate my way to the desk of Fred's editor. After identifying myself, my affiliation with the studio, and informing the woman that I was reaching out on behalf of Fred's daughter, I asked if they still planned to publish his book. My query would be met with a palpable silence at first, after which I was informed that since Fred was, essentially, "unavailable" to promote his book, it had been decided internally that the memoir would not be published. Unwilling to accept her logic, I passionately questioned their reasoning. Our opposing arguments lobbed back and forth during an increasingly heated conversation.

"It's a book that will practically promote itself!" I finally exclaimed. "I mean, have you read the title?!"

Well, that did it.

"Mr. Westphal," she snapped, "we will not be publishing this book. Good day, sir."

And then she hung up the phone.

———————————

Over the next two years, I would pitch Fred's story to every high-level development executive, production company, and producer at every major studio who would listen. There were many, and they know who they are. I began with my bosses at Warners, who practically laughed me out the door for pitching an "expensive period piece." While most everyone I spoke to would find my project fascinating, all ultimately passed, citing its controversial subject matter. Some were simply afraid, while others, I would later discover, were either friends or, in some cases, even former classmates with one or more members of the Kennedy clan, relationships and connections they would dare not compromise.

"I love this, Mannie," said one powerful producer friend when she called me back from her brownstone offices in New York City, high above the streets of Tribeca. "But I can't do this... I'm friends with Caroline Kennedy."

At the end of the day, I was naïve in thinking that any Hollywood producer or studio executive would be willing to risk pursuing such explosive material. As one power agent friend joked over dinner as I lamented my inability to set up the project, "You can't give this away with a set of dishes." He was right. So I packed all of Fred's file boxes in my car, drove to the San Fernando Valley, and deposited everything in a climate-controlled secure-storage facility for safe keeping until such a time when the cultural zeitgeist was ready to hear Fred's truth. That day, I promised myself, would come.

With this book, it finally has.

––––––––––

In many ways, the Hollywood life and death of Fred Otash was as nuanced and enigmatic as what happened to Marilyn Monroe. We will never know the truth. We will never know the full story. Not until decades after he passed would I myself begin to finally understand the intricacies that comprised the totality of the man behind the façade, and to attempt to fully appreciate his humanity. It is a far cry from the person I thought I knew the day after his death, when I snuck down to the garage at the Park Wellington and secretly removed the rear personalized OTASH license plate from his classic Eldorado Cadillac Biarritz, just hours before Arthur Crowley had it towed away. I was desperate for a keepsake, for a piece of him, for *something* physical that could remind me in years to come that our time together really happened, and of those halcyon afternoons when the private detective to the stars chauffeured me with guided tours through the dreamland that was his fabled city, for at the moment, I thought there was nothing left. Thankfully, I was wrong.

As of the writing of this book, more than sixty-one years have passed since the mysterious death of Marilyn Monroe on August 4, 1962, a woman whose talent, radiance, timeless beauty, and worldwide acclaim are more relevant today than at the height of her mortal stardom. Fred Otash, one of a handful of individuals to have known what really happened that fateful night, saved the first full account for his own book, one he finally found the courage to write thirty-one years later. He would hold back nothing, including the emotions that, by the end of the recording, overwhelmed the hard-boiled detective.

It would be the most accurate—and only—true account of Marilyn's last night ever produced. But shortly after telling his story on tape, and before his book revealing the secrets could be published, Otash died. So he never lived to confront the liars, the con artists, and the self-aggrandizing opportunists who have attempted to and have indeed capitalized on Marilyn's life and death. Instead, much of the truth seemed to die on his kitchen floor at 6:35 a.m. on October 5, 1992, when the gale force known as Fred Otash took his last breath. But by then, he had already sat in front of the tape recorder and, in fits and starts, the seventy-year-old detective finally revealed the most controversial case that had come to consume his life and define his storied Hollywood career.

The words he recorded represented witness to what happened in the rooms where Marilyn spent her last moments. Because he had wiretapped her home so carefully and completely, it was as if he had been present during Marilyn's last, torturous hours. Then he told the heartbreaking details of all that he had heard, before, during, and after Marilyn Monroe's death, and, at long last, one of the most monumental untold mysteries of our age was revealed, as much as it can be.

He began: *"I listened to Marilyn Monroe die . . ."*

AFTERWORD

had just returned from a whirlwind tour of Europe and the Middle East. The lengthy flight back to California left me so severely jet-lagged that I thought I was still dreaming when I woke up to find two policemen knocking on my front door on Monday, October 5, 1992. As I stood in the foyer still half-asleep in my bathrobe, they kindly relayed a message that I was to call my father's home immediately. No other details were given, and then they left.

I was anxious and didn't know what to think when Arthur Crowley answered the phone. A permanent fixture in my father's life, the powerful Hollywood attorney who had been his longtime lawyer and close friend for as long as I could remember gently delivered the devastating news: my dad had been found dead earlier that morning, and Arthur needed me to come to his home at the Park Wellington as soon as possible to identify his body. My father was all I had left of my immediate family, and like any person who has suffered the loss of a loved one, I was heartbroken and inconsolable when I looked at him for the last time, knowing that my world would never be the same. Never again would I be able to embrace

A uniformed Fred Otash with his daughter Colleen on
the steps of her grandmother's house (March 1951).

him, to hear his commanding voice, to ask his advice and
seek his wisdom as he listened intently with his strong, loving
hand cupped over mine.

It seemed like only yesterday he was carrying me on his
shoulders when I was a little girl, chauffeuring me around in
his classic wing-tipped baby blue Cadillac convertible for
special nights out on the town, or shopping for new school
clothes where I'd twirl around in beautiful dresses seeking his
approving smile. I remembered our countless sunny
afternoons together by the pool, how he taught me how to
play backgammon, and the time he let me explore his amazing
detective van—having no clue what any of it meant, but just
feeling impressed and proud of my amazing dad. I thought
about all our family dinners together when my grandmother
was alive, how she waited patiently for her baby boy to come

home and brighten her day while I helped my aunt Evelyn prepare all my father's favorite Lebanese dishes just how he liked them, and how he invariably held court at the head of the table, the life of the party entertaining our family and friends with his never-ending stories.

You see . . . behind his tough-guy, private-eye exterior, the Fred Otash that I knew was a doting dad and a kind, caring, and compassionate family man who always protected and provided for the people he loved. Some of these memories are encapsulated in this book, while others I carry in my heart with gratitude for all that he did to support and take care of his family. Never one to shirk his many responsibilities, my father was a man of integrity and conviction.

After his passing, I was contacted by many people wanting to be involved with projects about my father's extraordinary life, but I knew that Manfred Westphal was the right person for the job because he had a close and personal relationship with my dad, as well as a deep respect for all he had accomplished against the odds. He has passionately spearheaded this endeavor since its inception, and together we have spent countless hours combing through my father's business and personal archives, those of my mother, Doris Houck, numerous public and genealogy records, as well as my collective family memoirs to provide as much accuracy and detail as possible.

I would personally like to thank Manfred and Josh Young for their tireless work in bringing this faithful homage to my father to fruition. They have written a very comprehensive, compelling, and fascinating story by closely researching and examining his character, career, and personal life in great detail. I hope you get a better understanding of the whole person, the real Fred Otash, in contrast to many of the misleading and inaccurate reports in the media and other works of fiction.

Thank you all for taking the time to read this memoir. It means a great deal to me to provide you with a more realistic account of my father's legacy.

—COLLEEN OTASH

ACKNOWLEDGMENTS

The authors wish to thank the following individuals for their invaluable contributions:

Colleen Otash, for her unyielding faith and trust, her precious family memories, and for providing us with unfettered access to her father's priceless archives.

Jim Gosnell and Steve Fisher at IAG for their bespoke representation and unwavering support from day one.

Lisa Dallos at High 10 Media for introducing the authors.

Janice Min, Stephen Galloway, and Shirley Halperin for their collective vision and assistance in helping kick-start this incredible journey over a decade ago in the *Hollywood Reporter*.

Julie Shapiro for her profound friendship and expert counsel over the years.

Alan Mandel for his work on the project.

Timothy Shaner and Christopher Measom at Night & Day Design for their creative and editorial prowess.

Our amazing team at Grand Central Publishing for sticking with this book through fits and starts: our terrifically talented editor Suzanne O'Neill for her thoughtful and steady-handed guidance, our wonderfully efficient associate editor Jacqueline Young, publicist Roxanne Jones, marketer Alana Spendley, audiobook producer Elece Green, cover designer Phil Pascuzzo, and of course the C-suite, nonfiction editorial director Colin Dickerman and publisher Ben Sevier.

NOTES

PROLOGUE: FREDDIE O

2 **"The Man Who Bugged Marilyn Monroe":** Anthony Cook, "The Man Who Bugged Marilyn Monroe," *GQ*, October 1990.

6 **prowled Hollywood by night:** Myrna Oliver, "Fred Otash: The Colorful Private Eye and Author," *Los Angeles Times,* October 8, 1992.

10 **his revelations were brilliant:** Fred Otash Archives, File: "Ellroy," Personal Correspondence (1989–90).

11 **"The Man Who Kept Marilyn's Secrets":** James Spada, "The Man Who Kept Marilyn's Secrets," *Vanity Fair*, May 1991.

12 **Housed in a windowless building:** Daniel Miller, "Friars Club in Beverly Hills Being Razed," Reuters, January 28, 2011; John Kobler, "The (Million Dollar) Sting at the Friars Club," *New York*, July 21, 1975.

13 **an exact replica of its historical counterpart:** Forest Lawn, Facebook, January 16, 2020; www.facebook.com/ForestLawn/posts/old-north -church-at-forest-lawn-hollywood-hills-was-dedicated-on-october -10th-19/2812892715454260/; FO Archives.

14 **Larry introduced her as:** *Larry King Live*, August 5, 2003, transcript, "Panel Discusses Marilyn Monroe," www.cnn.com /TRANSCRIPTS/0308/05/lkl.00.html.

CHAPTER ONE: THE CITY OF ANGELS

20 **Selma Hotel:** Fred Otash, *Investigation Hollywood* (Chicago: Regnery Books, 1976).

20 **"LAPD NEEDS YOU!":** FO Transcripts, "The Early Years 1," 1.

21 **Marion and Habib Otash:** FO Archives, FO biography.

21 **He joined the Civilian Conservation Corps:** FO Archives, FO biography; National Park Service archives, www.nps.gov.

22 **the day after seeing the LAPD billboard:** FO Archives, "The Early Years," 1, 2.

26 **The strike had started seven months earlier:** FO Transcripts, "The Early Years 1," 2; FO Archives; Scott Harrison, "Hollywood's Bloody Friday," *Los Angeles Times*, October 3, 2019.

29 **merged their respective production banners:** Peter Hay, *MGM: When the Lion Roars* (New York: Turner, 1991).

CHAPTER TWO: THE OTASH TOUCH

31 **was assigned the beat:** FO Transcripts, "The Early Years 2," 19, 20.

34 **picked up some extra cash working:** FO Transcripts, "The Early Years 1," 4.

36 **when Cohen was building his house on Moreno:** FO Transcripts, "The Early Years 2," 26; FO Archives.

37 **He partnered with a policewoman:** FO Transcripts, "Gangsters & Working Undercover," 54.

38 **Paramount had:** FO Transcripts, "Hollywood 101," 37, 38; FO Archives.

39 **prostitutes who operated through popular hotels:** FO Transcripts, "The Early Years 1," 2; FO Archives.

42 **MGM production of *The Bride Goes Wild*:** FO Transcripts, "Gangsters & Working Undercover," 54; FO Archives; Otash, *Investigation Hollywood*, 3, 4.

44 **Otash also cultivated bartenders:** FO Transcripts, "Gangsters & Working Undercover," 52.

46 **Liberace:** FO Archives.

46 **Will Mastin Trio:** FO Transcripts, "The Early Years 1," 16.

46 **"I had bodygards on Sammy for years":** FO Transcripts, "Gangsters, Partners & Monroe," 70.

46 **When he married the white Swedish-born actress May Britt:** FO Transcripts, "The Early Years 1," 20.

47 **It happened when Otash acted on a tip:** FO Transcripts, "Gangsters & Working Undercover," 52, 53; FO Archives.

48 **Another night Otash and his vice squad partner:** FO Transcripts, "The Early Years 2," 26; FO Transcripts, "Monroe: Life & Death," 107.

CHAPTER THREE: THE STARLET

51 **The Broadway department store:** Broadway Hollywood Building Historical Information, City of Los Angeles, Mayor's Office of Economic Development.

52 **The answer to his dilemma came:** FO Transcripts, "Gangsters & Working Undercover," 50, 51; FO Transcripts, "Hollywood 101," 38; FO Archives; Colleen Otash Archives.

55 **One Sunday morning after church:** FO Transcripts, "The Early Years 1," 12; FO Archives.

59 **the conversation turned to the Red Scare:** Albert Fried, *McCarthyism, the Great American Red Scare: A Documentary History* (Oxford: Oxford University Press, 1997).

61 **During one Saturday barbecue:** FO Transcripts, "The Early Years," 13, 14; "Gangsters & Working Undercover," 55.

63 **she persuaded writer-director John Huston:** Mary Rourke, "Lucille Ryman Carroll, 96; MGM Talent Manager Mentored Actors," *Los Angeles Times*, November 2, 2002.

64 **when he brought home a guard dog:** FO Archives, interview with Colleen Otash, "Memories of My Father."

65 **Nealis, who still hated Otash:** FO Archives; FO Transcripts, "Gangsters & Working Undercover," 50, 51; "Husband Sues to Establish Claim to Paternity of His Wife's Child," *Los Angeles Times*, August 21, 1950; "Actress Finally Makes Choice Between Mates," *Los Angeles Times*, March 22, 1951; "Doris Houck Wins Divorce," *Los Angeles Mirror*, June 19, 1952.

CHAPTER FOUR: RENEGADE COP

69 **He had left the force during World War II:** John Buntin, *L. A. Noir: The Struggle for the Soul of America's Most Seductive City* (New York: Harmony Books, 2009), 104–10.

70 **"Bloody Christmas":** Edward Escobar, "Bloody Christmas and the Irony of Police Professionalism: The Los Angeles Police Department, Mexican Americans, and Police Reform in the 1950s," *Pacific Historical Review* (2003): 171–99; "The Bum Blockade, Zoot Suit Riot and Bloody Christmas," *LA Weekly*, September 4, 2002.

70 **His anticorruption stance:** Buntin, *L. A. Noir*.

70 **Otash's animosity toward Parker:** Otash, *Investigation Hollywood*, 8; FO Transcripts, "The Early Years," 9; "Monroe Death & Rock Hudson," 121.

71　**Located at the corner of Fountain:** FO Transcripts, "New in Hollywood," 15.

71　**radio star and actor Rudy Vallée:** Otash, *Investigation Hollywood*, 9.

71　**a struggling hopeful named James Dean:** Otash, *Investigation Hollywood*, 9; FO Transcripts, "New in Hollywood," 15.

72　**Many young actresses who lived:** Bill Davidson, "The Dick," *Los Angeles*, May 1991; FO Transcripts, "Shakedown on Sunset," 45; FO Transcripts, "The Early Years 2," 29.

75　**To drive home his alpha-dog status:** FO Transcripts, "The Early Years 1," 8; "The Early Years 2," 22; Otash, *Investigation Hollywood*, 2–21.

76　**Not long after the exchange:** Otash, *Investigation Hollywood*, 13–21.

80　**Otash's policing merry-go-round continued:** FO Archives: LAPD Investigative Officer's Final Reports & Undercover Officer's Memorandums, 1947–55.

81　**blue telephone call from Paul Coates:** Otash, *Investigation Hollywood*, 10, 11, 17.

84　**name-checked on the hit series *Dragnet*:** Thad Brown, *Dragnet*, "The Big Fraud," Episode 1954, Walter Sande as Thad Brown, IMdB. com.

84　**So Parker called Otash's bluff:** Otash, *Investigation Hollywood*, 13–21; FO Transcripts, "Death of Monroe 1," 121.

87　**The war with Parker was taking its toll:** Otash, *Investigation Hollywood*, 13–21.

CHAPTER FIVE: IT'S CONFIDENTIAL

89　**Otash formed Otash Investigations:** FO Archives: Otash Biography; Cook, "The Man Who Bugged Marilyn Monroe"; Davidson, "The Dick."

89　**At considerable expense he retrofitted:** FO Transcripts, "Dino & Wiretapping," 77; Cook, "The Man Who Bugged Marilyn Monroe"; Davidson, "The Dick."

90　**Otash's go-to gadget:** FO Archives; Hi-Fi Haven, "All Things Stephens Tru-Sonic," Leben, April 27, 2022; Cook, "The Man Who Bugged Marilyn Monroe."

91　**Otash and *Confidential* were meant:** FO Archives & Biography; FO Transcripts, "Hollywood 101," 31, 34; Neal Gabler, "The Scandalmonger: *Confidential*'s Reign of Terror," *Vanity Fair*, April 2003.

92   **"The lid is off!":** "Purveyor of the Public Life," in Tom Wolfe, *The Purple Decades: A Reader* (New York: Farrar, Straus & Giroux, 1982), 81; FO Archives.

92   **But the August 1953 issue:** "Why Joe DiMaggio Is Striking Out with Marilyn Monroe," *Confidential*, August 1953; Gabler, "The Scandalmonger."

93   **the highest-paid professional American:** Roscoe McGowen, "Yankees to Offer Another $100,000 Contract to DiMaggio for 1951 Season," *New York Times*, January 6, 1951.

94   **As Humphrey Bogart put it:** Henry E. Scott, *Shocking True Story: The Rise and Fall of Confidential Magazine, America's Most Scandalous Scandal Magazine* (New York: Pantheon, 2010).

94   **run by Harrison's niece Marjorie Meade:** Gabler, "The Scandalmonger," 200.

96   **"The Wife That Clark Gable Forgot":** "The Wife That Clark Gable Forgot," *Confidential*, 1955; Katherine Yamada, "Verdugo Views: Clark Gable's first wife helped launch his career," *Glendale News-Press*, September 6, 2018; Scott, *Shocking True Story*.

97   **Seven years after Robert Mitchum's drug bust:** David Thomson, "Chinatown," *New Republic*, January 10, 2010; Seth Abramovitch, "Hollywood Flashback: In 1957, the 'Confidential' Trial Scandalized Hollywood," *Hollywood Reporter*, April 4, 2022.

98   **Under a plan hatched by his lawyer:** Lee Server, *Robert Mitchum: "Baby, I Don't Care"* (New York: St. Martin's Press, 2001), 290.

99   **everyone gave tips to Hollywood Research:** FO Transcripts, "Gangsters & Working Undercover," 52.

99   **Cohn's mobster pal Johnny Roselli:** FO Archives; FO Transcripts, "Monroe, Mob, Kennedy and Dino," 96–100.

101 **"coldness and indifference":** Aline Mosby, "Weeping Marilyn gets divorce after telling judge Joe was 'cold,' 'indifferent' to her," UPI, October 27, 1954.

101 **But DiMaggio couldn't get over her:** Otash, *Investigation Hollywood*, 73–84; Scott, *Shocking True Story*; FO Transcripts, "Shakedown on Sunset," 43; "Gangsters & Working Undercover," 52; "Gangsters, Partners & Monroe," 68; "Kennedy, Sinatra and Hoffa," 84, 85; "Monroe: Life & Death," 113.

CHAPTER SIX: THE WEE SMALL HOURS

105 **Wheaties, the popular breakfast cereal:** Scott, *Shocking True Story*, 157.

106 **Doris Duke, the high-profile socialite:** FO Transcripts, "Kennedy, Sinatra and Hoffa," 87; Stephanie Mansfield, *The Richest Girl in the World: The Extravagant Life and Fast Times of Doris Duke* (New York: Pinnacle, 1999), 221, 281; "The Press: Sewer Trouble," *Time*, August 1, 1955.

106 **The July 1957 issue outed Liberace:** Horton Streete, "Why Liberace's Theme Song Should Be 'Mad About the Boy,'" *Confidential*, July 1957, 16–21, 59–60.

107 **he sued the magazine for $20 million:** FO Archives; Streete, "Why Liberace's Theme Song"; Darden Asbury Pyron, *Liberace: An American Boy* (Chicago: University of Chicago Press, 2001), 216, 223.

107 **O'Hara, red-haired and radiant:** FO Archives; "It Was the Hottest Show in Town When Maureen O'Hara Cuddled in Row 35," *Confidential*, March 1957, 10–11, 46.

108 **Crowley explained to Otash:** Otash, *Investigation Hollywood*, 73–84.

112 **Hollywood that rivaled Moses leaving Egypt:** FO Archives: "The Trial of Confidential Magazine"; Daniel Miller, "The Hollywood Superlawyer Whose Death Went Unnoticed," *Hollywood Reporter*, March 28, 2011.

113 **Wallace first questioned Otash about money:** FO Archives, LP record copy of sound recording of *The Mike Wallace Interview*; "The Mike Wallace Interview," August 25, 1957, video and transcripts, Harry Ransom Center, University of Texas at Austin; "TV's Mike Wallace in the Hot Seat"/Special TV-Radio Report," *Newsweek*, September 16, 1957.

115 **Clark Gable's former jilted lover:** FO Transcripts, "Gangsters & Working Undercover," 62.

116 **Chalky Wright:** "Chalky Wright Found Dead In Bathtub," *New York Age*, August 17, 1957.

116 **Otash made headlines:** FO Archives, "The Trial of Confidential Magazine"; Scott, *Shocking True Story*.

117 **Marjorie's friend Jackie O'Hara:** FO Archives, "The Trial of Confidential Magazine"; Scott, *Shocking True Story*.

117 **In its heyday, *Confidential* netted:** J. Howard Rutledge, "The Rise of the Expose Magazines," *Kansas City Times*, August 10, 1955.

CHAPTER SEVEN: A MARILYN MONROE PRODUCTION

119 **Jewish deli on North Beverly Drive:** "Seeing Stars: The Ultimate Guide to Celebrities & Hollywood," seeing-stars.com, February

2022; Matt Donnelly, "Players Assemble to Save Iconic Deli Nate n' Als," *Variety*, January 30, 2019.

119 **His old buddy Sid Skolsky:** FO Transcripts, "Monroe: Life & Death," 108.

120 **under her new Marilyn Monroe Productions banner:** Donald Spoto, *Marilyn Monroe: The Biography* (New York: Cooper Square Press, 2001), 352–57.

120 **But what really turned heads:** Aubrey Solomon, *Twentieth Century–Fox: A Corporate and Financial History* (Lanham, MD: Rowman & Littlefield, 2002), 120.

120 **directed by revered Broadway:** "Joshua Logan, Stage and Screen Director, Dies at 79," *New York Times*, January 13, 1988.

121 **Marilyn secured a new contract:** Maureen Lee Renker, "How Marilyn Monroe Founded Her Own Production Company," *Entertainment Weekly*, September 28, 2022; Spoto, *Marilyn Monroe*, 271.

121 **Monroe would comment on the impetus:** Edward R. Murrow's *Person to Person* TV Show, April 8, 1955.

122 **Adler explained they were now:** FO Archives: File "Monroe."

123 **Otash then hired Barney Ruditsky:** FO Archives: File "Monroe"; FO Transcripts, "Monroe: Life & Death," 113; FO Transcripts, "Monroe, Mob, Kennedy and Dino," 100.

124 **Otash ran point from his office:** FO Archives, File "Monroe."

125 **When *Bus Stop* was released:** Bosley Crowther, "The Screen: Marilyn Monroe Arrives; Glitters as Floozie in 'Bus Stop' at Roxy; Stork Over Britain Tasteless Melodrama," *New York Times*, September 1, 1956.

CHAPTER EIGHT: FOR THE LOVE OF LANA

127 **Crane would've met Fred at the Luau:** Besha Rodell, "From the Los Angeles Public Library Menu Collection: The Luau, a 1950s Tiki Bar in Beverly Hills," *LA Weekly*, October 12, 2012; FO Archives.

128 **Crane's youthful attempts to forge:** "'Just a Lark' He Says," *Times News*, August 25, 1967.

128 **Crane still received ample notoriety:** Cheryl Crane, *Detour: A Hollywood Story* (New York: Arbor House, 1988), 323.

128 **Crane at the Mocambo nightclub:** Lana Turner, *Lana: The Lady, the Legend, the Truth* (Boston: G. K. Hall, 1982), 82.

128 **when the tabloids trumpeted the shocking:** Jeanine Basinger, *Lana* (New York: Pyramid, 1976), 141–42.

128 **ill-fated lovers remarried:** Lou Valentino, *The Films of Lana Turner* (Secaucus, NJ: Citadel Press, 1976), 28.

128 **their beloved screen goddess was expecting:** Turner, *Lana*, 70.

129 **Crane's incessant gambling and unemployment:** Turner, 77.

129 **Crane would again become engaged:** Crane, *Detour*, 323; "Mitchum Busted at 'Reefer Resort,'" *Los Angeles Times*, September 1, 1948; FO Transcripts, "Gangsters & Working Undercover," 53.

129 **twenty-eight-year-old actress Martine:** Crane, *Detour*, 323; "Martine Carol Dies," *Canberra Times*, February 7, 1967, 1.

130 **Crane still kept in touch with Lana:** FO Archives.

131 **Being the daughter of a living legend:** "Cheryl Turned Over to Police," *Los Angeles Times*, April 6, 1958.

132 **The son of Italian immigrants:** FO Archives, File: "Lana Turner/ Steve Crane"; Otash, *Investigation Hollywood*, 184–86; FO Transcripts, "Dino & Wire Tapping," 76; FO Transcripts, "Monroe: Life & Death," 121; "3 Cohen Mobsters Arrested," Associated Press, August 31, 1949; "Board Lists Chief Cohen Gang Members," Associated Press, February 14, 1950.

133 **That afternoon, an anxious Crane:** FO Archives; Stephen Galloway, "Rock Hudson's Wife Secretly Recorded His Gay Confession," *Hollywood Reporter*, June 6, 2013.

135 **Lana had four marriages:** *Lana Turner . . . A Daughter's Memoir*, documentary (Turner Classic Movies), 39:40, 56:23; Greg Archer, "The Kid Stays in the Picture," *Advocate*, January 26, 2008.

136 **The minute Stompanato heard the rumors:** George Simpson, "Sean Connery beat up Lana Turner's gangster boyfriend for threatening him with a gun," *Daily Express*, February 7, 2021; Steve Powell, "Johnny Stompanato and James Bond," Venetian Vase, January 8, 2013; Goran Blazeski, "Lana Turner's gangster boyfriend pulled a gun on Sean Connery. It didn't go well," Vintage News, July 7, 2017.

137 **Crane didn't mince words:** FO Archives; FO Transcripts, "Dino & Wire Tapping," 74.

138 **In February 1958, when Lana:** Turner, *Lana*, 180–87; FO Archives; Hadley Hall Meares, "Two Survivors: The Scandalous Saga of Lana Turner and Cheryl Crane," *Vanity Fair*, June 8, 2023.

140 **There are three sides to every story:** Robert Evans, *The Kid Stays in the Picture: A Notorious Life* (New York: It Books, 2013).

140 **Cheryl had retired to her bedroom:** *48 Hours,* "The Goddess & the Gangster," CBS News Archive; Nicholas Yapp, *True Crime* (Bath, UK: Paragon, 2006), 278; Gordon Morris Bakken and Brenda Farrington, *Women Who Kill Men: California Courts, Gender, and the Press* (Lincoln: University of Nebraska Press, 2009), 163, 170, 180; "Police Satisfied with Story of Stompanato Stabbing," Associated Press, April 10, 1958; Tim Adler, *Hollywood and the Mob* (London: Bloomsbury, 2007), 137; Joe Morella and Edward Z. Epstein, *Lana: The Public & Private Life of Miss Turner* (New York: Citadel, 1971), 191; "Lana Says Boyfriend Tried to Kill Her," Associated Press, April 11, 1958; "Girl Justified in Killing Stompanato, Jury Rules," *Philadelphia Inquirer,* April 12, 1958, 9; FO Archives; FO Transcripts, "Dino & Wire Tapping," 74–76.

147 **Years later:** Patricia Bosworth, "The Gangster and the Goddess," *Vanity Fair,* 2012; Eric Root, *The Private Diary of My Life with Lana* (Beverly Hills, CA: Dove Books, 1996).

CHAPTER NINE: BETWEEN A ROCK AND A HARD PLACE

149 **The Golden State would emerge:** W. Bradford Wilcox, "The Evolution of Divorce," *National Affairs,* Fall 2009.

149 **marriage to movie star Jane Wyman:** Claudia Luther, "Jane Wyman, 90; Oscar Winner, First Wife of Reagan," *Los Angeles Times,* September 11, 2007.

150 **Married couples seeking a divorce:** Wilcox, "The Evolution of Divorce."

150 **Into this most propitious milieu:** FO Archives: File: "Bette Davis"; File: "Luft vs. Luft"; File: "Gabor"; Otash, *Investigation Hollywood;* FO Transcripts, "Monroe: Life & Death," 113.

151 **Otash had a history with Hudson:** FO Archives: File: "Hudson vs. Hudson"; FO Transcripts, "Monroe Death & Rock Hudson," 116.

151 **Otash clarified what was known:** FO Archives; "Personalities" (excerpt: Janet Zappalla interview Fred Otash [Fox] Summer 1991).

152 **Crowley sought out Otash's expertise:** FO Archives: File: "Hudson vs. Hudson"; FO Transcripts, "Monroe Death & Rock Hudson," 116; Otash, *Investigation Hollywood,* 31.

152 **"The Fairy Godfather of Hollywood":** Robert Hofler, *The Man Who Invented Rock Hudson: The Pretty Boys and Dirty Deals of Henry Willson* (New York: Carroll & Graf, 2005), 112; Richard Barrios, *Screened Out: Playing Gay in Hollywood from Edison to Stonewall* (New York: Routledge, 2002); *Tab Hunter Confidential,*

documentary (dir. Jeffrey Schwarz), 2015; "Rhonda Fleming Interview" (Warner Archive Podcast/Warner Bros. Entertainment).

154 **Inspired by the young man's force:** "Rock Hudson," *Britannica*.

154 **Modern Screen named Rock Hudson:** Camille McCutcheon, "From Shooting Star to Falling Star: The Trajectory of Rock Hudson's Career in Film and Television," University of Nevada, Las Vegas, Track 3, Session 1: Identity and Independence.

155 **In what he no doubt believed:** Hofler, *The Man Who Invented Rock Hudson*; John Rechy, "Agent Provocateur," *Los Angeles Times*, November 6, 2005.

155 **All seemed to go according to plan:** Gabler, "Confidential's Reign of Terror."

156 **Phyllis would happily oblige:** Phyllis Gates with Bob Thomas, *My Husband, Rock Hudson* (Garden City, NY: Doubleday, 1987).

158 **Fabrizio Mioni and Franco Rossellini:** FO Archives, File "Hudson vs. Hudson," Recorded Surveillance Transcripts (January 21, 1958); FO Archives, File "Hudson vs. Hudson," Affidavit of William V. Lowe; FO Archives, File "Hudson vs. Hudson," Jim Terry recorded transcripts with Fabrizio Mioni; FO Archives, Franco Rossellini letter to Rock Hudson (1958).

164 **A few days later, Giesler informed:** Dennis McClellan, "Phyllis Gates, 80; Former Talent Agency Secretary Was Briefly Married to Rock Hudson in '50s," *Los Angeles Times*, January 12, 2006; FO Archives: "Hudson vs. Hudson."

166 **Otash sent his best electronics man:** FO Archives, File "Hudson vs. Hudson," Affidavit of William V. Lowe.

166 **She didn't want to admit:** FO Transcripts, "Marilyn Death & Rock Hudson," 116.

166 **What follows are the extraordinary:** FO Archives, File "Hudson vs. Hudson," Recorded Surveillance Transcripts (January 21, 1958).

174 **Otash and Crowley met with Greg Bautzer:** FO Transcripts, "Marilyn Death & Rock Hudson," 116.

175 **Hudson ended up giving Gates:** FO Archives, File "Hudson vs. Hudson."

CHAPTER TEN: JUDY IN LOVE

177 **It was an auspicious Friday the thirteenth:** Lorna Luft, *Me and My Shadows: A Family Memoir* (New York: Gallery Books, 1999); judygarlandnews.com (Reference: September 13, 1935).

178 **Garland's personal hardships read:** Anne Edwards, *Judy Garland: A Biography* (New York: Simon & Schuster, 1975), 108; Gerold Frank, *Judy* (New York: Da Capo, 1999), 75.

178 **Replaced by Ginger Rogers:** David Shipman, *Judy Garland: The Secret Life of an American Legend* (New York: Hyperion, 1992).

178 **just a decade earlier:** Irene Lacher, "A Big Battle Over Garland's Mini Award," *Los Angeles Times*, March 22, 2002.

178 **But the seeds of her misfortunes:** "Judy Garland Was Put on a Strict Diet and Encouraged to Take 'Pep Pills' While Filming 'The Wizard of Oz'—The studio took extreme measures to make sure the actress was big screen ready. A move that eventually resulted in her early death." Biography, October 10, 2020.

179 **Garland wed second husband:** Gerald Clarke, *Get Happy: The Life of Judy Garland* (New York: Random House, 2001), 223; Hedda Hopper, "No More Tears for Judy," *Women's Home Companion*, September 1954.

179 **Despite her demoralizing exit:** "Judy Garland, MGM Studio Call It Quits," *San Bernardino County Sun*, September 30, 1950; Frank, *Judy*, 284–85; Ronald Randano, *Music and the Racial Imagination* (Chicago: University of Chicago Press, 2000), 135; "British Give Judy Garland Big Ovation," Associated Press, April 10, 1951; "Garland in Comeback with Palladium Contract," UPI, April 10, 1951.

179 **Garland wed tour manager and producer:** Jack Garver, "Judy Garland Married with Simple Ceremony," UPI, June 12, 1952.

180 **Two years later:** Clarke, *Get Happy*, 308.

180 **Garland filed for divorce once again:** Otash, *Investigation Hollywood*, 159.

180 **Needed a trusted keeper:** Otash, 159–70.

CHAPTER ELEVEN: WONDER BOY

195 **the Golden Age of Capitalism:** Stephen A. Marglin, *The Golden Age of Capitalism: Reinterpreting the Postwar Experience* (Oxford: Oxford University Press, 1992).

196 **He's Hollywood's King of the Snoops:** Leo Gould, "He's Hollywood's King of the Snoops," *National Enquirer*, 1959.

196 **Freddie O had a promising future:** "Private Eye Otash Hurt in Car Crash," *Los Angeles Times*, February 1958.

197 **Otash was burning the candle:** FO Archives; "Private eye, Fred Otash, who worked on the Confidential magazine case, is

recovering from a heart attack," Sarasota, Florida, *Herald Tribune*, April 2, 1959.

197 **One of the good friends to grace:** FO Archives, Colleen Otash Archives, "Memories of My Father."

200 **A retired jockey named Kenny Godkins:** The People, Respondents, v. FRED OTASH, Appellant; Court of Appeal of California, Second District, Division One (November 4, 1960).

203 **Built by pioneer and horseman:** "Last of 'Lucky' Baldwin's Great Barony Subdivided," Daily Racing Form, University of Kentucky Archives, June 27, 1942; "California Racing Gets Fatal Blow," *New York Times*, February 5, 2009; Braven Dyer, "The Story of Santa Anita," *Sport*, 1947, archived from original March 11, 2014.

206 **Otash, Gach, and five other:** The People, Respondents, v. FRED OTASH, Appellant; Court of Appeal of California, Second District, Division One (November 4, 1960).

207 **"When I got indicted, they went":** FO Transcripts, "Monroe Life & Death," 103.

CHAPTER TWELVE: THE KENNEDYS

209 **Nearly one-third of the U.S.:** Laura Feiveson, "Labor Unions and the U.S. Economy," U.S. Department of the Treasury, August 28, 2023.

209 **In a concerted effort to address:** Arthur M. Schlesinger, *Robert Kennedy and His Times* (New York: Ballantine Books, 1978); Judie Mills, *Robert Kennedy: His Life* (Brookfield, CT: Twenty-First Century Books, 1998); "New Senate Unit to Widen Inquiry in Labor Rackets," *New York Times*, January 24, 1957; "Senate Votes Inquiry on Labor Rackets," *New York Times*, January 31, 1957; James Hilty, *Robert Kennedy: Brother Protector* (Philadelphia: Temple University Press, 2000).

210 **The all-cash vending machine:** Otash, *Investigation Hollywood*, 179; Waldron Lamar, *The Hidden History of the JFK Assasination* (Berkeley, CA: Counterpoint, 2013); Hilty, *Robert Kennedy*; Robert Kennedy to Sam Giancana, "I Thought Only Little Girls Giggled," *Chicago Tribune*, June 10, 1959.

214 **Marcello had no reason:** FO Transcripts, "The Early Years 2," 32, 33, 34, 41, 42; Lamar, *The Hidden History*.

216 **I knew Brenda Allen:** FO Transcripts, "The Early Years 2," 36, 37.

217 **But now Lawford had a much bigger ask:** FO Archives.

218 **The Democrats were already planning:** FO Transcripts, "Monroe: Life & Death," 115.

219 **It was a fucking Watergate:** FO Transcripts, "Dino & Wiretapping," 76.

220 **"I had a very sophisticated sound truck":** FO Transcripts, "Dino & Wiretapping," 77; Cook, "The Man Who Bugged Marilyn Monroe."

220 **That dubious honor went to:** FO Transcripts, "Gangsters, Partners & Monroe," 74.

220 **Then Monroe became the central:** FO Transcripts, "Dino & Wiretapping," 76.

221 **She would later describe the resulting:** Colin Bertram, "Inside Marilyn Monroe and Joe DiMaggio's Roller Coaster Romance," Biography, November 17, 2020.

223 **may have been like to date Marilyn:** FO Transcripts, "Monroe: Life & Death," 107.

CHAPTER THIRTEEN: SOMEONE WAS ALWAYS LISTENING

225 **nefarious interception of private:** April White, "A Brief History of Surveillance in America," *Smithsonian*, April 2018.

225 **As head of the General Intelligence Division:** Tim Weiner, *Enemies: A History of the FBI* (New York: Random House, 2012); Robert K. Murray, *Red Scare: A Study in National Hysteria, 1919–1920* (Minneapolis: University of Minnesota Press, 1955).

226 **as the nation struggled with:** "ACLU History: Wiretapping: A New Kind of 'Search and Seizure,'" ACLU, September 1, 2010.

226 **since they often lacked money and resources:** FO Archives.

227 **Throughout the spring of 1960:** FO Archives, "The Kennedys"; FO Transcripts, "Kennedy, Sinatra and Hoffa," 90.

227 **a man came to see Fred:** Otash, *Investigation Hollywood*, 239.

228 **the man's boss was Henry Luce:** Robert Edwin Herzstein, *Henry R. Luce, Time, and the American Crusade in Asia* (Cambridge: Cambridge University Press, 2005); "Henry R. Luce: End of a Pilgrimage," *Time*, March 10, 1967; Cook, "The Man Who Bugged Marilyn Monroe."

230 **The Kennedy-Nixon race for the White House:** Byung Joon Lee, "Attacking the Airwaves: How Television Changed the American Presidential Campaign," *New England Journal of History*, September 2016; Tim Ott, "Inside John F. Kennedy and Frank Sinatra's Powerful Friendship," Biography, May 19, 2020.

231 **As cameras rolled:** "The Kennedy-Nixon Presidential Debates 1960," Museum of Broadcast Communications; James Reston, "Sen. Kennedy More Effective in TV Debate," *Los Angeles Times,* May 6, 1960.

231 **Kennedy was now the front-runner:** "Historic Speeches: Address to Greater Houston Ministerial Association," JFK Library, September 12, 1960; John Huntington, "The Kennedy Speech That Stoked the Rise of the Christian Right," *Politico,* March 8, 2020.

232 **As election day returns came in:** Michael Beschloss, "No Concession, No Sleep: Glued to the TV on Election Night 1960," *New York Times,* October 29, 2016; Peter Carlson, "Another Race to the Finish," *Washington Post,* November 17, 2000; "Remarks Conceding the Presidential Election in Los Angeles, California," American Presidency Project, March 17, 2022.

232 **Meanwhile, back in Hollywood:** Army Archerd, "1960: Sinatra on Politics," *Variety,* November 10, 1960.

233 **Otash had tapped into a love triangle:** Jeff Leen, "A.K.A. Frank Sinatra," *Washington Post,* March 7, 1999; FO Transcripts, "Kennedy, Sinatra and Hoffa," 84; Kitty Kelley, "The Dark Side of Camelot," *People,* February 29, 1988, 106.

234 **Spindel brokered Hoffa's hiring:** FO Transcripts, "Kennedy, Sinatra and Hoffa," 87.

234 **"It's Hoffa, it's Giancana, it's the FBI, it's the CIA":** FO Transcripts, "Death of Monroe," 119.

236 **She wanted a sophisticated system:** FO Transcripts, "Monroe: Life & Death," 115; FO Transcripts, "Shakedown on Sunset" (Page 47); Cook, "The Man Who Bugged Marilyn Monroe"; Spada, "The Man Who Kept Marilyn's Secrets."

237 **absolutely certain she was doomed:** Peter S. Greenberg, "Saints and Stinkers," *Rolling Stone,* interview with John Huston, February 9, 1981, 25.

237 **Twelve days after completion of principal:** Phil Hardy, *The Encyclopedia of Western Movies* (London: Octopus, 1983), 279.

CHAPTER FOURTEEN: THE HOUSE ON FIFTH HELENA DRIVE

239 **The one-story Spanish Colonial:** Gary Vitacco-Robles, "Cursum Perficio: Marilyn Monroe's Brentwood Hacienda: The Story of Her Final Months," iUniverse, August 1, 2000; Remy Tumin, "The Battle to Save Marilyn Monroe's Home," *New York Times,* September 13, 2023.

240 **It was only in hindsight:** FO Transcripts, "Monroe: Life & Death," 103, 104.

241 **Lawford was trying to appease Sinatra:** Spada, *Peter Lawford*; George Jacobs and William Stadiem, *Mr. S: My Life with Frank Sinatra* (New York: It Books, 2004); Alice Vincent, "Sinatra, snow storms, and a smashed-up helipad: The story behind John F. Kennedy's star-studded inauguration," *Telegraph*, January 19, 2017.

243 **"How come that prick":** FO Transcripts, "Death of Monroe 1," 119.

244 **"You've got some nerve":** FO Archives.

247 **Otash knew that Marilyn trusted:** FO Archives; FO Transcripts, "New in Hollywood," 14; "The Early Years," 29; "Kennedy, Sinatra & Hoffa," 81; "Monroe: Life and Death," 108.

247 **Shortly after her Golden Globe win:** Spoto, *Marilyn Monroe*, 524–25; Lois Banner, *Marilyn: The Passion and the Paradox* (London: Bloomsbury, 2012), 391–92; Carl Rollyson, *Marilyn Monroe Day by Day: A Timeline of People* (Lanham, MD: Rowman & Littlefield, 2014), 264–72.

CHAPTER FIFTEEN: THE OTHER SIDE OF MIDNIGHT

252 **Lawford's screaming brain screeched:** FO Archives; FO Transcripts, "Death of Monroe 1," 126; Spada, "The Man Who Kept Marilyn's Secrets."

257 **"I don't know who broke into the filing cabinet":** FO Transcripts, "Death of Monroe 1," 126, 127.

257 **And there was a glass:** FO Transcripts, "Death of Monroe 1," 120.

258 **"They keep talking about Monroe's red diary":** FO Transcripts, "Shakedown on Sunset," 46; FO Transcripts, "Death of Monroe 1," 120; FO Archives.

260 **"He fucked her around eleven o'clock":** FO Transcripts, "Death of Monroe 1," 117.

260 **"On the recording that Reed Wilson and I heard":** FO Transcripts, "Death of Monroe 1," 117.

261 **"Where were you when I had to get":** FO Transcripts, "Death of Monroe 1," 117.

261 **Either Peter or Bobby:** FO Transcripts, "Death of Monroe 1," 117.

261 **"We'll talk about it later":** FO Transcripts, "Death of Monroe 1," 118.

262 **"You dirty bastard":** FO Transcripts, "Kennedy, Sinatra and Hoffa," 83.

262 **"Let me get you a glass":** FO Transcripts, "Death of Monroe 1," 118.

263 **"Jesus Christ, take some fucking pills":** FO Transcripts, "Death of Monroe 1," 118.

263 **"We had two tapes":** FO Transcripts, "Death of Monroe 1," 122; "Monroe: Life & Death," 103; "Death of Monroe 1," 118.

263 **"He was so pissed":** FO Transcripts, "Monroe: Life and Death," 104.

264 **"No, I'm too tired":** FO Transcripts, "Death of Monroe 2," 125.

264 **He went out there around eleven o'clock:** FO Transcripts, "Death of Monroe 2," 126.

265 **"Where is it?":** Anthony Summers, "Marilyn Monroe's Final Hours: Nuke Fears, Mob Spies, and a Secret Kennedy Visitor," *Vanity Fair*, March 23, 2022.

266 **"I lived with that for a week":** FO Transcripts, "Death of Monroe 1," 121, 122, 124.

266 **"You have to understand":** FO Transcripts, "Death of Monroe 1," 121, 122.

267 **In 1966, four years after:** Spada, "The Man Who Kept Marilyn's Secrets"; John Neary, "The Big Snoop: Electronic Snooping— Insidious Invasions of Privacy," *Life*, May 20, 1966.

267 **Spindel's lawsuit would fail:** FO Archives, File "Spindel."

268 **"Why would the feds go":** FO Transcripts, "Death of Monroe 1," 123.

CHAPTER SIXTEEN: HINDSIGHT IS *20/20*

269 **The caller identified herself:** FO Archives, File "20/20" (Telex from Ene Riisna/ABC, August 13, 1985.

273 **An ABC News attorney:** FO Archives, File "20/20" (ABC Deal Memo to Otash dated August 15, 1985).

274 **The Kennedy ties had continued:** FO Archives.

274 **Otash's career also took:** FO Archives, Otash Personal Biography.

274 *TV Guide* **had consistently:** John King, "Sylvia Chase, former KRON news anchor and award-winning TV Journalist, dies," *San Francisco Chronicle*, January 5, 2019.

275 **Otash was pensive, anxious:** FO Archives; William Plummer, "The Monroe Report," *People*, October 21, 1985; Jay Sharbutt, "'20/20' Probe: ABC Reviews Kennedy-Monroe Story," *Los Angeles Herald Examiner*, October 7, 1985; Peter Brennan, "New Marilyn Monroe Scandal: The Story that TV Censored," *Star*, October 22, 1985;

Gregg Kilday, "Hi-Ho, Geraldo," *Los Angeles Herald Examiner*, October 23, 1985; Jay Sharbutt, "Emmy-Winner Rivera to Resign as ABC Investigative Reporter," *Los Angeles Times*, October 23, 1985.

279 **One of the producers told me:** FO Transcripts, "Shakedown on Sunset," 47.

280 **A few weeks following the controversy:** Kilday, "Hi-Ho, Geraldo"; Sharbutt, "Emmy-Winner Rivera to Resign."

INDEX

Note: Page numbers in *italics* preceded by *"P-"* indicate photos from two photo inserts—the first insert contains pages *P-1* to *P-16*, and the second insert contains pages *P-17* to *P-32*.

ABOUT THE AUTHORS

JOSH YOUNG has written five *New York Times* bestsellers, four additional *Los Angeles Times* bestsellers, five books that were made into feature documentaries, nineteen books that have been ranked No. 1 in their category on Amazon, and two novels. For more information, please visit joshyoungauthor.com.

MANFRED WESTPHAL is a former corporate communications and public relations executive who has spent the last twenty-five years spearheading story-driven media campaigns for some of the most recognized entertainment brands in the world. He began his career working in development at Walt Disney Studios, 20th Century Fox, and Warner Bros. Television, where in 1990 he began collaborating with legendary Hollywood private detective Fred Otash to tell his extraordinary life story before Otash's untimely death in 1992.